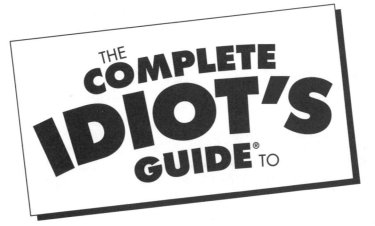

**THE**

# COMPLETE IDIOT'S GUIDE® TO

# Decorating Basics

## *Illustrated*

### *by Mary Ann Young*

**ALPHA**

A member of Penguin Group (USA) Inc.

Most Alpha books are available at special quantity discounts for bulk purchases for sales promotions, premiums, fund-raising, or educational use. Special books, or book excerpts, can also be created to fit specific needs.

For details, write: Special Markets, Alpha Books, 375 Hudson Street, New York, NY 10014.

**Publisher:** *Marie Butler-Knight*
**Product Manager:** *Phil Kitchel*
**Senior Managing Editor:** *Jennifer Chisholm*
**Senior Acquisitions Editor:** *Randy Ladenheim-Gil*
**Development Editor:** *Lynn Northrup*
**Senior Production Editor:** *Christy Wagner*
**Copy Editor:** *Keith Cline*
**Illustrator:** *Chris Eliopoulos*
**Cover/Book Designer:** *Trina Wurst*
**Indexer:** *Tonya Heard*
**Layout/Proofreading:** *Rebecca Harmon, Donna Martin*
**Graphics:** *Tammy Graham, Laura Robbins, Dennis Sheehan*

# Contents at a Glance

# Contents

# Foreword

When I was a little girl, I loved playing with my dolls not because of their clothes or how I could style their hair, but because of what I could do with the furniture in their homes. I would spend countless hours playing with these dollhouses. Many days I would rearrange the furniture, color the walls, hang clippings from my mother's magazines for artwork, or create new ideas for tomorrow's play. Later in life, when I realized there was a profession that would allow me to do this for a living with real furniture and homes, I knew I was on to something big.

Decorating a home can be so scary and overwhelming when you aren't equipped with the knowledge and know-how: What color should I paint the walls? How should I dress the windows? What artwork would look best over the fireplace? What type of flooring should I use? How on Earth should I arrange this furniture? It doesn't have to be—and shouldn't be—so overwhelming and exhausting. It should be as fun to decorate your home as it was playing with my dollhouses. This book is going to equip you with the tools you need to effortlessly answer all your decorating questions.

I have always believed that our homes and the decorations inside shape us into the people we ultimately become. When you are in a home or environment filled with antiques and finer things, you will behave very differently than you will in a room filled with beanbag chairs and vibrant colors. Our personalities, values, and beliefs are ultimately shaped because of the places in which we have lived. Our homes are also an outward expression of who we are as people and families. The decorations, fabrics, and colors help tell the story of our lives. Don't be afraid to share who you are with those you invite into your life and home.

All this brings us to this book you are about to begin reading. There is an amazingly huge amount of information in these pages to help you tackle anything and everything in your decorating projects. I do believe Ms. Young has left no stone unturned. Allow her to guide you, encourage you, and show you how you can decorate your home.

And at the end, if you are still overwhelmed and afraid to go out on your own, don't be afraid to hire a professional designer. These people have studied, trained, and worked to know the answers to your questions. At the very minimum, this book will give you the encouragement and education you need to be an informed consumer.

Now, as you begin your decorating journey, remember the wisdom and knowledge you have learned from this book. Come back from time to time and use it as a reference tool. And last, remember to always have fun and not to be afraid of your decorating decisions.


Much decorating success!

Rhonda M. Layton
Owner, MyInteriorDecorator.com

Rhonda M. Layton has been an interior designer since 1992 and owns MyInteriorDecorator.com, an online interior design firm that provides design services and advice to clients all over the country. Ms. Layton is also the author of *The Decorating Bible*, a how-to guide to decorating your home.

# Introduction

First and foremost, decorating is meant to be fun! If the interest and passion come first, the learning and confidence will follow. Take time to observe, learn, read about, and most of all *enjoy* the art of decorating. Discover and define your personal style through your use of color and texture with patterns and furnishings.

Although there is more to decorating than knowing what your favorite color is, if you go step by step and learn the basic elements of design, you are well on your way to understanding why a fabric pattern or an entire room works—or doesn't! Any art revolves around the basic principles of design—color, texture, scale, and balance. Look around you and you will notice them in everything you see—even nature!

Throughout this book you will gather ideas for every room in the house, including where to find inspiration, nifty ideas on stylish storage, flea market redos, and decorator tricks. I'll share some easy do-it-yourself project ideas as well as more advanced projects for the busiest rooms in the house.

Although there are no hard-and-fast rules, here is what I consider the most important "rules" of decorating:

◆ Let your style break the rules! Throw out conventional decorating wisdom. Don't abide by the herd mentality. Add personal touches to mass-marketed goods. Give your imagination free rein! Mix decorating styles for an eclectic look. Put furniture in the kitchen and bathrooms. Try a dark color in a small room. Combine animal prints and florals.

◆ Be flexible about your style. As your needs change, your style will change. Be a good editor, get rid of things when they don't work for you anymore or are less appealing. Change is good!

◆ Be practical about your style—be sure your choices are compatible with your living style and financial resources.

◆ Most of all, be passionate about your style! Experiment with decorating techniques that you've never tried. Be brave! Build your home around beauty and surround yourself with the things and people you love.

## How to Use This Book

Although successful decorating is full of creativity, self-expression, artistry, and fun, it doesn't always feel that way. Designing plans for decorating a room or an entire house can be a time-consuming task—and very demanding! Certain projects entail significant expense, maybe more than you can afford. You need to make decisions and make purchases that fit your lifestyle, appeal to your sense of beauty, and are within your budget. It is a constant process of discovering, learning, testing, doing, and editing.

*The Complete Idiot's Guide to Decorating Basics Illustrated* is designed to help make learning about decorating a joy. You don't want to just jump into a decorating project; you must take the time to do some reading and creative thinking. After reading this book, you will be ready to figure out where in your home you want to start, what is the first priority, and how much everything will cost.

Here's how this book is organized:

**Part 1, "Not a Born Decorator? You Can Learn!"** is for the novice decorator. This is where you need to begin to learn the basic elements of design, from which all decisions are made. You will learn about personal style, how to draw floor plans, and the best ways to arrange furniture. This part also includes resources on where to find inspiration and purchase goods.

**Part 2, "Decorating from the Floor Up,"** points out everything a decorator should know about in a home and some ideas from the author.

**Part 3, "One Room at a Time,"** shows all of the possibilities for redecorating. Each chapter has a section on flea market finds that reveal creative reuse of items.

**Part 4, "The Finishing Touches,"** is like the frosting on the cake, showing you the additional accessories and stylish storage ideas that make a room go from bland to beautiful … all from a pro.

**Part 5, "Quick-and-Easy Room Makeovers,"** gets your creative juices flowing, showing you how to make some simple and pleasing changes in your kitchen, bathroom, and bedroom.

## The Extras

Throughout this book you'll find boxes that share fun ideas or tell you how to solve a dilemma, give tips from the pros, define decorating terms, and offer other useful tidbits of information.

**Pro Workshop**
Look in these boxes for ideas that add pizzazz or solve decorating dilemmas.

**Homematters**
These boxes offer extra information of interest in the home décor world.

**Style Pointers**
Check these boxes for expert decorating advice and useful tips that you can use in every room of the house.

**Decorating 101**
Here you'll find definitions of decorating terms that will help you speak the decorating language. These terms and more are also listed in the Glossary.

## Acknowledgments

I would like to thank all of the people and companies who made this book possible: the American Lighting Association, Larry Mahurter at Couristan, Janet Partridge at Garnet Hill, Sonya Kennedy at Gear Home, M. Hackett, Brandy Shannon at the Hon Company, Laura Ashley, Kate Williams at Susan Becher Public Relations for Pierre Frey, Waterworks, Sherry Craig at Lee Industries, Sue Waters at Wolf Appliances, Florentine Jalil at Roche Bobois, Katy Muller at F. Schumacher, the Smallbone Company, and Heather Wiroll at Baker Furniture/Kohler.

A sincere thanks to my development editor, Lynn Northrup of Northrup Editorial Services, who is a real professional and team player with superb editorial guidance.

Most of all, thanks to my acquisitions editor, Randy Ladenheim-Gil, whose expert vision and consistent support were of immeasurable help!

## Trademarks

All terms mentioned in this book that are known to be or are suspected of being trademarks or service marks have been appropriately capitalized. Alpha Books and Penguin Group (USA) Inc. cannot attest to the accuracy of this information. Use of a term in this book should not be regarded as affecting the validity of any trademark or service mark.

# In This Part

# Not a Born Decorator? You Can Learn!

Feeling overwhelmed when it comes to all the decisions to be made about decorating your home? Take a deep breath and begin the process of discovering … you! Yes, you! What you like, what you need, what you think is beautiful; what your personal style is! In these chapters, you will find it enjoyable to get to know yourself and assess your lifestyle. Only then will you be able to express your individuality in your home! This will be part of the foundation of all your successful decorating.

Another skill to be gained in this part is understanding the basic elements of design—another very important part of your foundation of successful decorating—through color, texture, balance, and scale. And to get you outfitted for the challenge of drawing plans, I'll introduce you to the basic tools of the decorator's trade to keep your furnishings in scale with your rooms. And if you need inspiration or thoughts on where to purchase goods, you'll find a plethora of resources to help you out as well. It's never too late to start! Read on.

# In This Chapter

- ◆ Discovering your personal style
- ◆ Enhancing the style you've got
- ◆ Styles that match your personality
- ◆ A decorative history lesson: period styles

# Style: It's All Around You!

Style is defined as distinction, excellence, originality, and character in any form of artistic expression, a smart design. And you are surrounded by it! Whether you are aware of it or not, your home has style right now. It's you! Just like the outfit you chose to wear today, or the flip of your current hairstyle, your home is an intimate expression of your personality. Unanimated or vivacious, carefree or fastidious, humorous or serious, your character traits create a style that is evident throughout every detail in each room in which you live. You put a distinctive mark on your home—you "decorate" it automatically—just by being you, surrounding yourself with things you love, things that are appropriate for the way you live, and things that are full of beauty to you.

But for many of us, that natural process might seem downright intimidating or impossible. We've been taught that "beautiful" home style is something that only experts have—and based on spaces and possessions that most people can't afford. And the multibillion-dollar home furnishings industry is eager to convince us to try someone else's style, to be contemporary like Calvin, Martha, Ralph, or Laura. Or to be classic like some long-departed characters named Louis, George, Victoria, or Art Deco.

Don't buy it! You can learn from the styles of others and from the beauty of the past, but a home decorated to satisfy you has to be founded upon your unique sense of beauty and taste, and the manner and time in which you live. You may think this is impossible. You may think you are color-blind or geometrically impaired; you may not know chintz from a chaise, an *étagère* from an entryway; and you may insist that you have no style at all. In this chapter, you will discover that style can be cultivated by familiarizing yourself with different decorating styles. Most of all, you will learn that you already have within you the foundation of personal style—and that's your best decorating guide of all. Let it evolve!

# Where Does Personal Style Come From?

A personal style emphasizes what you love and how you live. It is that unique blend of tastes and preferences that you have acquired and shaped over your lifetime. It is inspired by the home that you grew up in, the places you have visited, the people you've met (both admired or detested), and just about everything else that you have experienced: music and museums, literature and movies, gardens and garage sales.

Think back. Discovering and asserting your likes and dislikes started very early in your life. As a baby, you may have preferred a fuzzy blanket to a smooth one; you might have adored squash but hated bananas. That's the start of personal style. Think of your own kids, if you have them. Have you ever tried to dress a three-year-old in a color that she didn't want to wear that day? Or tried to tell your teenager what color to paint his room? Personal style occurs naturally. Like every other fashion, it is never set. It can grow and deepen, shift and develop. As your life changes, your needs change, and your tastes change with them. And your evolving style will guide the new choices you make each day.

# Cultivating Your Style

Gain confidence in your personal style through reading and critiquing, exposure and observation. Start perusing home magazines and books on interiors. (See Chapter 4 and Appendix A for some of my favorites.) Note the rooms and designs that seem logical and doable for your lifestyle. Start a filing system for these new ideas. Label folders with all the names of the rooms and spaces you might want to decorate someday; for example, master bedroom, children's bath, entry and hallway, and so on. (Use a sturdy cardboard file box or wicker file basket to hold them all.) Read, evaluate, cut, and file.

These folders will form the master resource for your decorating projects. You can then make a board for each room and attach your clippings to form a viewing board to compile an emerging style. You will gradually fine-tune your vision. If you see a sofa detail that you like but the entire room isn't your style, cut out the detail and glue it on your living room board. If a wrought iron lighting fixture catches your eye, paste it on the board where you would hang the light. The accumulated pictures and brochures will become pieces of a puzzle that you are putting together to reveal a style suited to yourself and your home.

## Style Pointers

Expose yourself to as many different decorating styles as possible by visiting your local furniture and home stores. Gather brochures and swatches of fabrics and samples of wallcoverings, paint chips, and flooring. Be on the lookout for inspiration in unusual places: Perhaps a silk scarf or a bouquet of flowers has all of the right color combinations for a dining room wallcovering; there might be pictures of interesting interiors or furnishings in mail-order clothing catalogs.

To get an even clearer picture of your tastes, review your boards for each room weekly. Refine your files and select your favorite pictures, colors, and paint chips, tacking them on each board. Remove the ones that don't work anymore. Clarity comes with a clean approach; files overflowing with random bits of paper and other ephemera are hard to compose into thoughtful, cohesive ideas. Be sure this board is placed where it can be easily viewed so that your personal choices and styles can be critiqued daily until final decisions are made.

# Selecting a Style That Works for You

Although choosing a color scheme for a home can make even the most confident person wince, there are some ways to make choosing a style easier—a style that will fit your sense of beauty, your budget, and your lifestyle. Start by considering your living space. Take your cue from your home's architecture and geographical location. Is it a studio apartment in the city, a rambling farmhouse in the country, or a modern ocean-side retreat? Does the inside have "good bones" with fine architectural details? A fireplace? Carved moldings? *Vintage* light fixtures? If not, you may use an item you already own, such as a hooked rug or a wonderful sofa, as the starting point for defining your style.

If you live in a colonial home, for example, beautiful wood floors can dictate your choice for furniture style and arrangement. A modern home with many large windows allows tremendous light, creating airy spaces. In this environment, you may want to stick to a sparsely furnished room and revel in the ample breathing space. A country retreat may contain natural elements on which to focus—from stone floors to old wood ceiling beams.

### Decorating 101

**Vintage** means representative of or dating from a period long past. For example, a vintage textile from the 1950s might be the perfect pattern and color for a retro look to cover your dining seats; vintage doorknobs from the 1930s of crystal or mercury glass add striking contrast to today's new interior doors for an eclectic look.

But don't worry about decorating with only a single period or regional style. Those types of rooms tend to look like a museum or a cliché of the latest fad. Develop your own style through education. Scour the bookstores for decorating books that appeal to you. Read or subscribe to magazines that picture appropriate room settings to match your lifestyle. Critique the pictures in depth. Figure out why you love an idea or, just as important, why you *don't* like it. Go over your files again and again. Change your boards. Your style is surfacing. As your taste in styles develops through awareness and research, let your rooms benefit by allowing them to evolve as well. The best style for you is the one that is in harmony with the way you live—a constant balance of form and function. Are you formal, casual, slick, or eclectic, or a combination? A few current popular styles are discussed in the following sections. Which one appeals to you the most?

## Rustic and Refined

A well-balanced mix of simple furniture and objects showing the patina of age, perhaps in a modern room or "contemporary shell," reflects good editing (knowing what to include as well as what to leave out), a sense of humor (obvious through the juxtapositions), and confidence in selections (eliciting responses such as, "Who would have thought those things would look so good together?"). Many professional designers excel at this type of styling. They understand the formula for the rustic and refined look: furniture proportional to the space, attentive detail to what "works" in the room and what doesn't (which results in the appropriate "editing" of the room), and the fundamental concept of simplicity.

## Traditional

Traditionalists appreciate the finely polished lines of classic furniture and time-tested details. Traditional design respects the past while blending periods for today's living, pairing antiques and period reproductions with comfortable seating and livable furniture arrangements. Ornate window draperies, stuffed seating, regal colors, and botanical prints—these are all telltale signs of a more formal décor, a safe classic look that doesn't threaten. Does this sound like you? Correct proportions and serious detailing are important, but keep in mind that too much formality can be museumlike and stodgy.

Traditional design can take on a fresh interpretation, mixing unexpected modern bright fabrics in varying patterns on traditional furnishings—for instance, a bold gingham on period Queen Anne chairs within a spare backdrop (uncluttered by a lot of furniture or accessories).

The traditional style. *(Photo by Gear Home, Bettye M. Musham, Chairwoman/CEO)*

Traditional seating pairs nicely with a modern coffee table for an elegant, eclectic-styled living room. *(Photo by Lee Industries)*

## Clean and Sassy

Spare and minimal furnishings that pack a powerful punch with color and form are trademarks of a clean and sassy look. A few tongue-in-cheek touches of exaggerated forms or unexpected color show off a "not too serious" look that's fun and invigorating, like a headboard that is overscaled with curvaceous outlines in a bold black stripe. Are you a sassy type? A creative, vivacious and enthusiastic personality is revealed with this type of design.

## Eclectic

Although inspiring, pure period-decorated homes can be expensive and stiff and highly unlikely to fit a contemporary lifestyle. By taking the best lessons from the various historical and regional styles, combining your treasured pieces, and arranging them with your own personality and lifestyle, the *eclectic* approach can be the most fascinating and interesting way to decorate. It's not as easy as just throwing everything together, however. The eclectic style requires an adherence to the basic elements of design (which I'll discuss in Chapter 2)—particularly color, texture, form, and scale. An eclectically designed room may combine slick modern chairs with an old worn pie safe and a colorful Southwestern rug.

Many professionals identify themselves with eclectic design and not one type of style. It is the most difficult to pull off with flair, but is extremely clever.

**The eclectic style.** *(Photo by Roche Bobois)*

**Decorating 101**

**Eclectic** refers to a form of interior design that is composed of various periods and styles that are harmonious.

## Flea Market Style

Flea market style is actually a form of eclectic style created with objects and pieces found from garage sales, lawn sales, antique fairs, and, of course, flea markets. Decorators use clever design ideas to reinvent uses for items, such as using salvaged porch columns for bed posts, old iron gates (with added legs and a glass top) for coffee tables, and potholders for college dorm-room wall art! (But refrain from using all flea market items or your home will look like a salvage store.) A combination of the new with the old is the most interesting aspect of this style—perhaps a new, modern sofa with a suitcase used as an end table, for instance; the crisp fabric of a new sofa contrasts pleasingly with a well-worn leather suitcase.

**Pro Workshop**

A flea market find of 30 apple crates stacked just so can create a fantastic wall-size bookcase! Be sure to browse through the "Flea Market Finds" sections in Chapters 11 through 17 for other innovative ideas on how to use your found treasures in each room of your home.

# Historical Decorating Styles: Beauties with a Past

As you gain knowledge of yourself and your surroundings, your sense of style is heightened. Aside from personal style, another type establishes identities of a period of historical decoration or that of a particular region or country. For example, traditional decorating schemes suggest time-honored furniture styles and colors, whereas a country scheme emphasizes a sense of place and natural materials. And a modern approach strips itself down to the basic elements free of much decoration. You may like to experiment with items from many different styles for a very personal décor. Familiarize yourself with different decorating styles so that you can translate them into the best feeling for your home.

**Style Pointers**

To avoid creating a stiff, impersonal, museumlike atmosphere, take care not to imitate one period style. Don't be afraid to mix elements from different styles to create one that is uniquely your own—that's what makes an eclectic style!

## Neoclassical

Neoclassicism is a style with ancient beginnings in Egypt and Greece. The classic rules of scale and balance dictate every furniture line and decorative motif. The style has reemerged in several countries since the eighteenth century, each interpreting it in its own way. The federal period style of the United States was popular in the late eighteenth and early nineteenth centuries. France had its Empire style, England had its Regency style, and Austria and Germany had a neoclassical style called Biedermeier.

The common denominator of these neoclassical movements is simple furniture lines in light-colored woods and Egyptian and military motifs on wall coverings and upholstery. Sheer, light, and airy fabrics hang asymmetrically on windows, and the naturals—muted terra cottas, stone, and cream colors—are revived. (This look is very popular today.) From country to country, the colors may change to brilliant greens, yellows, and reds.

**The neoclassical style.**   *(Photo by Roche Bobois)*

## Colonial

The colonial period style is probably the most familiar because it is one style that has endured since the 1600s. The mid-eighteenth-century colonial period evokes a time of simple elegance that is widely reproduced today. Rooms are simple but rich in classically designed furniture. Only the best-quality materials of fine woods, silk and needlework fabrics, and silver metals are used. Dining chairs have a thin wood slat in the back—and surround space-saving drop-leaf tables—side tables stand on pedestals; desks open up for writing; and high chests stand tall on dainty, curved legs.

Window coverings are kept simple, and upholstery is covered in figured patterns of muted shades. At the same time, Americans were influenced by the Georgian period occurring in England. S-shaped legs and carved shell motifs decorated chairs, tables, and chests. Japanning (the art of covering furnishings with opaque varnishes, which may be decorated later with paint or gilding) and chinoiserie (an ornate style of decoration, based on Chinese motifs, of furniture, textiles, ceramics, etc., especially popular in the eighteenth century) became the rage. The late Georgian period, influenced by the English neoclassical architect Robert Adam, retired the curves and ornateness. People responded to Adam's reinterpretations of the neoclassical style of light and airy colors and effects. The fashion soon entered the mainstream of American decorating, giving way to the federal period.

## Victorian

Queen Victoria of England reigned from 1837 to 1901. During this time there was an enormous expansion of her empire, and private fortunes were amassed in England (as well as in the United States). Neoclassical styles were still appreciated and were mixed in with the new age. Excess was best, using the most ornate, carved furnishings in dark woods; marble-topped tables; large, round, pedestal dining tables; over-stuffed leather chairs; and heavy, mirrored hat stands. Fabrics made of needlepoint, velvet, silk, and damask in rich, deep colors covered everything from mantels to chaises to shelves.

Windows were stained glass or elaborately dressed in layers of lace and heavy fabrics trimmed with fringe and cording. Patterned rugs were scattered throughout the room and walls were covered in fabriclike textures similar to damask. Accessories such as botanical prints, animal trophies, Grecian busts, needlepoint pillows, and knickknacks were used extravagantly. Used with restraint, Victorian details can be adapted to a contemporary interior, mixed with new and old pieces, collections (similar objects that are grouped together, from simple beach rocks to valuable Faberge eggs), and framed pictures.

## Baltic

Northern European style, also referred to as Baltic style, covers designs from Scandinavia to Russia from the second half of the eighteenth century well into the nineteenth century. With their own take on design and regional influences, furniture makers took their cues from the tastes of England, France, Germany, and Italy and created a unique style all their own. Neoclassicism and rococo (exaggerated styling) played a big part in their designs. The colder climate inspired designers to create uplifting rooms with reds, peacock blues and golds, and hot pinks.

The Swedish influence combined with Queen Anne style, resulting in furniture with funny feet and funny legs, led to the Gustavian era, a strong influence even today. Gustavian furniture and décor possessed a clean and simple look that is very pleasing to the eye. Floors were scrubbed and laid with rag rugs, windows were dressed in loose gauze, and chairs were covered with home-made covers. Rooms were painted in light colors with mixtures of gilded, painted, and natural wood furniture covered in cotton materials, creating an unpretentious atmosphere—a breath of fresh air from the period rooms that were so richly decorated.

**Homematters**

Carl Larsson of Sweden (1853–1919), a painter, was a timeless interpreter of Swedish provincial style, where furnishings are arranged with classic formality in an atmosphere of informality.

## Arts and Crafts/Art Nouveau

The arts and crafts movement was born around the turn of the century. The cheapening of the quality of mass-produced furnishings and the extravagance of decorating during the Victorian period gave way to a new philosophy of simple style and pure function. William Morris of England and Gustav Stickley of the United States produced the arts and crafts styles of plain oak furniture that was upright, rectilinear, solid, and handcrafted. Morris used fabrics and wallcoverings inspired by the Middle Ages for his interiors, whereas Stickley borrowed themes and colors from nature. These sparsely adorned interiors were to bring about the advent of the modern age.

Art nouveau (new art) originated just before the turn from the nineteenth to the twentieth century and was popular in many European countries. Its spare but elegant style is characterized by lavish floral motifs, curvaceous lines, and light colors of lavender, pink, pale green, and white. Hand-painted wallcoverings, stenciled borders, silk fabrics, and Japanese art are common among the various interiors associated with art nouveau. The most famous art nouveau designer, Scotsman Charles Macintosh, is recognized for his elongated furniture lines reminiscent of the arts and crafts style, and color combinations hinting at the debut of the Art Deco and modern era.

## Modern

The positive acceptance of a new industrial age paved the way for artists to create with new machines and materials. A variety of modern styles occurred after World War I. Art Deco and modernism shared the decades of the 1920s and 1930s. Art Deco still engaged the past with touches of neoclassicism and Orientalism, but embraced the new use of plastics, chrome, and glass with fervor. The speed of trains, planes, and autos influenced the designers to streamline chairs and sofas, removing hard edges in favor of rounded corners. Chrome was combined with glass to form tables and with leather to create chairs. Early on, unusual color schemes were derived from modern ballet sets incorporating exotic greens and oranges, with touches of black or gold. Muted colors of mauve, gray, cream, and yellow with black as an accent were also popular. The style was characterized by round mirrors, lacquered furniture, and walls with geometric designs with stylized female, Jazz Age, and Egyptian figures.

Modernism, on the other hand, celebrated the paring-down of interior elements. "Only useful furnishings" was the mantra of modernism. Walls were painted white; windows dressed in simple blinds or plain drapes; floors had wall-to-wall commercial carpet or bare wood; tables were freeform or geometrically designed of light-colored woods, glass and chrome, or plastic laminate. Highly contrasting white upholstered sofas with black accents typified many modern interiors, whereas leather, animal skin, and earth tones contrasted nicely with cool steel and plastic. European designers of the 1920s and 1930s were Mies van der Rohe, Marcel Breuer, and Le Corbusier. The most famous American master of modernism was Charles Eames.

Many modern furnishings portray clean lines and monochromatic color schemes. *(Photo by Cassina USA)*

## Postmodernism

Postmodernism developed in response to complaints from people about industrial materials used in homes and the sterile environments created by such. Italian and American designers were at the forefront of change in the 1980s, using colors in outrageous ways to inject humor into everyday objects. As people accepted the movement, serious designs were being produced for fabrics and furniture. Designers of the postmodern approach are known as the Memphis Group. They emphasized a mix of styles from different periods with magical artistry, combining new finishes and colors all in one piece!

# Country

A country interior is a warm, less formal, eclectic, traditional style. Country style is comfortable. All of the many regional country styles include stripped pine, painted chests, and large cupboards. Windows are curtained with lace, simple wooden shutters, natural rollup blinds, or are left plain. Walls sport a rough texture with beams exposed. Floors are wide pine, ceramic tile, or stone. Accessories are the personality of country style, including worn ceramic ware, exposed collections, weathered fabrics, and wood and natural materials.

## American Country

American country is all about furnishings and objects made by our ancestors: for instance, quilts and homespun fabrics of rusty reds, pale blues, and creams; hooked rugs; duck decoys; crocks; and painted floor cloths. Other American country furnishings include the clean and simple furniture of the Shakers, Windsor-style chairs and settees, four-poster beds, and rocking chairs. The Southwest region of America's country style adheres to the same relaxed, unpretentious, comfortable, decorative style but uses materials indigenous to the American and Spanish cultures—for example, adobe walls that showcase Navajo hangings and local pottery. Furniture is large and rough-hewn. Colors are bright, and accessories are cast with Native American designs, which are very popular today.

**Homematters**

Furnishings that are American country style are referred to as Americana, referring to the furnishings, designs, and colors historically typical of America.

Comfortable and casually arranged seating, pillows, throws, and quilts add a relaxed air to this American country style living room. *(Photo by Gear Design)*

## English Country

English country style is defined by cluttered spaces—for instance, rooms filled with upholstery with worn flowered slipcovers in faded colors of green, pink, yellow, and blue. Floors are wood or stone with sisal matting or are covered with well-worn oriental rugs. Plaster walls are decorated with pictures from the country life of field sports, dogs, and horses. Old pine furniture, casual flower arrangements, and old throw blankets are also a part of this relaxed style.

The English country style. *(Photo by Smallbone)*

## French Country

French country is closer to the styles of the Mediterranean countries. It embodies the use of provincial prints in deep reds, yellows, greens, blues, and terra cottas. Fabrics are gingham checked or faded *toile de Jouy*. Furniture may be made of walnut or chestnut, plain or painted with a floral motif. Chairs have woven seats and curved legs, and armoires are fabric-lined. Floors are terra-cotta tile, brick, or bare wood with sisal matting.

The French country style. *(Photo by Roche Bobois)*

**Decorating 101**

**Toile de Jouy** (often referred to as simply "toile") is traditionally ivory-colored cotton fabric with scenic designs of pastoral life in red, navy, or black. It was originally made in a town in France called Jouy. Today toiles are also made in vibrant backgrounds with various contrasting colors such as lime green and fuchsia or mustard and red.

## The Least You Need to Know

- Your personal style forms the foundation of your home decorating.
- Exposure, observation, reading, and critiquing enhance your personal style.
- From rustic and refined to modern and minimal, there's a style to match every personality.
- A crash course in the history of period styles will heighten your awareness of the art of decoration.

# In This Chapter

- ◆ The magic of color
- ◆ How color affects mood
- ◆ The doubly sensual nature of texture
- ◆ The weight of scale and balance

# Chapter 2

# Decorating 101: Elements of Design

Feeling desperate? Struck by momentary panic? Face to face for the first time with a room in need of redecorating? Worried that you'll make some awful mistakes?

Relax. There are no Interior Design Police, and no absolute rules to decorating. There *are* general principles of design that you can easily learn and put into practice. In this chapter, you will get a grasp on how color and texture work together in decorating, and how they can work for you. You'll see how easy it is to put physical space into basic balance and pleasing scale.

## The Power of Colorful Thinking

No other design element has the quick impact or dramatic effect of color. With just a gallon of yellow paint, you can transform a room from dull-as-a-dungeon into a vibrant, energizing space. For the experienced pro or first-time home improver alike, color is the most powerful design resource there is.

Now you might think that choosing a color for your home is easy. After all, you have pre-ferred certain colors all of your life, and you make color selections every day with relative ease—for example, your clothing, flowers, and even your hair color. Yet it is precisely the lasting power of home color that makes people nervous. Even normally assured, do-it-yourself home decorators get in a dither about a color for one room, not to mention a color scheme for an entire house. Sometimes I consider this a "fear of commitment." When you are going to live with a color for a long time, you have to know what you are really getting into. The key to choosing correct and pleasing color for your home—colors you can commit to—is under-standing just what color is, how it behaves, and how you behave around it. You can learn to narrow down your preferences by testing color combinations or selecting ones already tried and tested by the pros.

## The Effect of Warm and Cool Colors

One power of color is its effect on your mood. Sunny colors like red, yellow, and orange can enliven your soul or even stir your fiery passion! On the other hand, cool blues, greens, and purples turn down the visual heat and emotional intensity. Use these effects in your living areas: You can select warmer colors to make a chilly room feel cozier. Similarly, if you have a very bright area, you could use cooler colors to create a more relaxed atmosphere.

Color also has the power to alter your perception and trick your mind. Warm and dark colors make elements of a room advance and appear closer to you. Cool colors cause elements to recede. These advancing and receding qualities can be used to alter the perception of room size and proportions. With a few simple tricks, you can use these optical illusions to make small rooms appear larger and make an oversized area cozier. Even the height of your room can be transformed with color.

**Pro Workshop**

Live in a warm climate? Paint your porch ceiling a pale blue. You'll feel cooler just looking at the color!

Try the following color tricks to change your room size without so much as picking up a hammer!

◆ Both dark colors (such as chocolate) and warm colors (such as brilliant yellow) can be used to make a room seem smaller. If you have a large room with a cold and uninviting atmosphere, paint the ceiling and walls a warm tone (any color between yellow and red on the color wheel; see the following section). This will draw in the walls and bring down the ceiling.

◆ Use cool and pastel colors to make a small room grow larger. Pastels, which contain a lot of white, reflect light, and cool colors recede. For example, a small room with ceilings, walls, and floor painted in tones of pastel blues, greens, or purples will appear bright and spacious.

◆ Raise the ceiling by painting it a lighter color than the walls. Or lower a high ceiling by painting it a tone slightly darker than the walls. If the ceiling still feels too high, you can bring it "down" further by painting a band of the dark tone around the top of the wall (where it meets the ceiling) the same dark tone as the ceiling.

◆ Shorten a lengthy room or hallway by painting the end walls a warm and dark color (such as deep reds, oranges, or yellows) so that they "advance" into the room.

Apply color tricks to furnishings and other elements, too: A sofa chosen in a hot color will be accented and appear larger, whereas a pale-colored sofa will remain subtle and inconspicuous. Highlight strengths. Outlining such elements as door and window casings, baseboards, and moldings in a darker or lighter color than the walls will draw the eye to desired details.

**Homematters**

The associations we make with different colors—based on our everyday experiences, our past, and the world we live in—can have a profound effect on our response to interior space. Pleasant or unpleasant, these often unconscious feelings can affect the way you feel about any colors in your house. For example, the combination of orange and black may always remind you of Halloween, and hence it may conjure up good or frightening associations.

You can also use color to mask weaknesses. Ugly radiators, unattractive woodwork, and poor-quality doors or bookcases can be "painted out" by making them the same color as the walls, blending them away from the viewer's attention.

We can see the component wavelengths of light—what we think of as a rainbow—when a beam of light passes through a prism and breaks up into the visible spectrum of light hues. This progression of colors through the wavelengths is often presented as a circle—"a rainbow in the round."

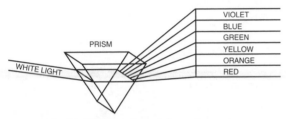

A ray of white light projected through a prism separates into the colors of the rainbow.

# Color Wheel

The color wheel, included in the color insert in the middle of this book, provides reliable and fascinating ways to explore color schemes. It's an essential tool used by designers to create successful color schemes. You can either link color families or take advantage of their contrasting qualities. A simple approach is a monochromatic color scheme that uses one hue in various tints and shades but provides enough contrast so as not to appear dull.

Using *harmonious* colors—colors that are next to each other on the color wheel—is another method, either combining like tones or different ones. A combination of blue, blue-violet, and violet illustrates a harmony of colors. You can even use the *primary* colors on the wheel for wonderful possibilities. Although the intensity of the pure hues may be too strong for you, you could subdue the yellow to gold, the red to

claret, and the blue to navy; the primaries take on a whole new feeling. Another triangle of colors—the secondaries of violet, orange, and green—might be just the combination that you are looking for.

*Complementary* colors are pairings of colors that are opposite each other on the color wheel, such as red/green, orange/blue, or yellow-green/red-violet. Sometimes the more receding color (the cooler color) is given dominance and the more advancing color is used as an accent. Think of drapery in sage green and trimmed in a muted red. The colors are modified to lessen the visual contrast.

Finally, some color schemes provide the maximum visual contrast. These are contrasts of tones such as black and white, black and yellow, or white and dark blue. This approach stresses the dark to light tones.

## Decorating 101

Harmonious colors are closely related colors that lie between two primaries on the color wheel, such as blue, blue-violet, and violet. Red, blue, and yellow are the pure or **primary** hues that all other colors are derived from. They are not mixed from any other colors. They are spaced equidistantly from one another on the color wheel. **Complementary** colors are directly opposite each other on the color wheel; for example, red and green, blue and orange, and yellow and violet.

Here are some other terms that make up the language of color:

◆ **Hue.** An identifying name for a specific color, such as apple green, sea green, or hunter green.

- **Tint.** A color's range from a pure hue to white (for example red to pink to white). These are light-colored tones.

- **Shade.** A color's range from a pure hue to black (for example, yellow to deep gold to black). These are considered dark tones.

- **Monochromatic.** Colors that use one hue in various tints and shades (for example, a red scheme with claret, burgundy, rose, and pink).

- **Secondary.** Orange, green, and violet are the three colors mixed from equal amounts of two primary colors (red + yellow = orange; yellow + blue = green; red + blue = violet).

## Color Schemes

The basic step to learning how to combine colors is observing. Noting great combinations—whether in travel, nature, or in inspiring photographs—is a sure way of adding to your bank of color knowledge. Think about how you dress yourself by putting together various pieces of clothing. Is there a particular piece of clothing with a color combination that you can translate to your home décor—possibly a scarf, blouse, or tie? Flowers in the garden may draw your attention with their harmonious arrangement, or dress patterns in fashion magazines just might get your creative juices flowing.

As always, start with something you love in a room: perhaps a piece of fabric, set of draperies, or a treasured heirloom such as a rug, needlepoint, or painting. It may contain the color combination that will guide you to a scheme for the whole room. Of course, there are the experts to turn to for completed schemes sold through large retailers (from designers such as Laura Ashley). These are schemes for the entire house with everything coordinated: paint, wallcoverings, fabrics, upholstery, and accessories. Ralph Lauren and Martha Stewart

prepackage paint colors available through home improvement and paint stores. Often these are marketed as "theme" palettes—with names like Thoroughbred, Country, and Santa Fe—that specify colors that work together.

> **Style Pointers**
>
> If you decide to use commercial designers' off-the-shelf color plans, you won't make big mistakes, but you could easily look "overcoordinated"! There is nothing less interesting than a perfect-looking interior, one that looks prepackaged. Impart your personal style by adding heirloom pieces or flea market items, such as pillows or carpets that have colors that are somewhat related but not exact matches to the packaged design.

Whatever color you choose, remember that light in an interior space has a tremendous effect on its color. Eastern-facing room? Early morning sun, colors change at night in artificial light. Western-facing room? The setting sun will make colors glow but look a little flat in the morning. Southern exposure? Hot rays can be cooled with neutral or cool colors. Northern exposure? A cool room can be warmed up with reds, yellows, or oranges. Evening light? A bluish cast changes colors like red to maroon and yellow to yellow-green. Artificial light? Warms colors with a certain softness with a yellowish cast.

## Getting a Feel for Texture

Without texture, a room would be devoid of sensual pleasure. Every material in it—whether it's a stainless steel range or an overstuffed chair in a family room—has a unique textural appeal that touches your senses. The stove feels cool and smooth; the chair beckons, soft and warm. Texture, like color, stimulates emotions, and to create a feeling of well-being, the interior of your home must use variations in textures that are warm and inviting.

With regard to decorating your home, texture provides two kinds of powerful impact: visual and tactile. Visual impact can be produced through paint finishes on everything from walls and furniture to floors and accessories. Designs printed on fabrics or various weaves create appeal (for in-stance, raw silk or burlap). Wood floors, sanded or a little rough, create different visual textures due to the differences in wood grains, like pine or cherry. I'll be giving you many suggestions for how to use texture in Part 2.

Tactile texture is that which you can feel. Your dining room chair seats may be covered in soft and smooth fabric or a rougher woven natural jute. The linens you select for your table may be fine and pressed or an old quilt with uneven dimensions. Your floor coverings also add tactile texture so that when you walk on them barefoot, you feel soft carpeting or smooth polished wood, either adding to the overall texture of the room.

Here are some other ideas for imparting texture in your home:

◆ **Windows**

Copper *Venetian blinds*—cool and smooth, reflect light.

Ornately swagged drapery—soft and warm, soften hard edges.

Sheer curtains—airy texture accentuated with light shining through porous weave.

Wood shutters—warm look with architectural feel.

◆ **Walls**

Wood paneling—warm, weighty look.

Brick/stone—rough solid feel.

Paint color and techniques—creates harmony among different textures in a room. A trompe l'oeil technique (French for "fooling the eye") can fool your eye by creative illusion of textures in three dimensions. Paint finishes such as matte, eggshell, and gloss create different moods.

Fabric—soft and textural, solid or printed, a cozy feeling.

◆ **Wallcoverings**

Painted, embossed, or woven—all add warmth to plain sheetrock.

◆ **Furnishings**

Various shapes and styles—polished wood, brass, chrome, glass are cool and smooth, whereas worn wicker, peeling paint, rusted iron, or handmade wooden pieces are warm and natural.

◆ **Flooring**

Wood—natural or painted, grainy, stained, bleached, highly polished, various patinas.

Carpet—smooth, bumpy, sculpted, or patterned.

Area rugs—splash of color and pattern, define a space.

Marble/stone/tile—hard and cool, solid feel.

Vinyl—smooth, plain or patterned, or used to simulate stone, tile, or brick.

Cork—soft and warm, porous, natural look.

### Decorating 101

**Venetian blinds** are slatted window shades named after the early Venetian traders who brought them to Europe centuries ago. But they were really invented by the Persians. In Italy they call them "Persiani blinds." They are a popular choice for windows, and come in various materials such as wood and metal.

Varied textures of exposed beams, pine cabinets, tiled floor, and walls of old brick combine naturally to give this kitchen a warm atmosphere. *(Photo by Smallbone)*

Soft bed linens are a nice contrast to an iron bed.

There was a time when protocol demanded rigid adherence to textural styles, but we are living in an era when unusual combinations are accepted; in fact they are essential to the most sophisticated eclectic interiors (see Chapter 1). Artistic pairings of rough and refined fabrics, such as denim and velvet or burlap and silk, often make for the most interesting decorating today. How does one put them together? Start with a piece that you love. If a rich velvet sofa is your focal point in the room, for example, you may want to counteract that plush look with curtains fashioned from nubby, rugged natural burlap. Each texture plays off the other divinely.

## A Matter of Scale and Balance

If color and texture can be thought of as some of the raw ingredients of design, then scale and balance may be considered the binding agents that complete the recipe for successful decorating. Scale is an ingredient of balance and involves the relationship of the size and shape of a part to its whole—for example, the size of a chair back compared to the height of the legs, a lamp shade to the size of its base, or a coffee table appropriately sized for a sofa. Balance appeals to our sense of equilibrium, a visual "weight" as opposed to an actual weight of an object.

Both balance and scale tell us how and why certain combinations and relationships of elements please us or perhaps seem slightly off-kilter. Balancing patterns, textures, colors, and emotions throughout the elements in your home creates harmony of design.

## Forms of Balance

There are three forms of balance that apply to room design:

◆ **Symmetrical balance** is achieved by arranging furniture or objects on each side of a center or dominant point like two wing chairs on either side of a fireplace or the proverbial candlesticks placed on either side of the fruit bowl. This formal type of balance is expected and requires little imagination.

The symmetrical placement of seating on either side of the fireplace is balanced by the varied accessories of artwork, fireplace tools, and flowers.

### Style Pointers

To help visualize asymmetrical balance, think of a child's teeter-totter. Two children of equal weights placed equidistant from the center of the board are balanced. Place children of unequal weights on the teeter-totter, and the balance is disturbed. If you place the heavier child closer to the center, the difference in weight is offset. Use this concept when arranging furnishings or accessories.

◆ **Asymmetrical balance** is achieved by arranging equal visual weights that are not identical, like a picture frame and a trophy placed on either side of a bureau top. Although their actual weight may not be the same, their visual weights are balanced.

Asymmetry in a room is an artistic form of furniture arrangement. The chaise is placed to the left of the window while the cocktail table and vase are placed directly in front of the window to create perfect balance of scale.

◆ **Radial balance** is a circular balancing of parts or objects around a center, often found in small items or accessories such as plates, bowls, or pillows. Radial balance can be asymmetrical like the circular flow of a spiral staircase, or symmetrical like a dining table with chairs.

The chandelier, glass-top dining table, and traditional chairs mix nicely in a radial-balanced design.

- ◆ Rough textures or busy patterns seem "heavier" than smooth or plain ones. Burlap is heavier than taffeta. A floral chintz fabric is heavier than a solid pink color.

- ◆ Warm and bright colors have greater visual weight than cool duller colors. An orange sofa would "weigh" more than a pale blue one of the same size.

- ◆ Brightly lit areas in a room have greater visual weight than dimly lit ones.

- ◆ Diagonal lines call attention more so than straight ones. A wallcovering with a diagonal pattern has more visual weight than a vertically striped one.

**Style Pointers**

Choose a focal point in each room, creating a starting point for balancing furnishings, colors, and textures. A fireplace is a natural focal point for furniture placement. Everyone loves to sit around a fire. Use it as the center of your seating. For an updated look, flank the fireplace with two loveseats or place four comfortable chairs in a half circle in front of the fireplace.

## Weight of Balance

The scale or proportions and "weight" of varying elements in a room play a significant part in establishing their impact on the total design. Earlier in the chapter you learned that strong, warm colors advance and can be used to call attention to an object. Textures that reflect light or patterned areas also tend to increase the importance of an area. Rectangular or square furniture carries less weight than freeform furniture. This applies to art, accessories, and patterns. You will notice swirling shapes more than plain shapes. In Chapter 10 you'll learn how brightly lit areas of a room are "heavier" (carry more "visual weight") than dimly lit areas.

Reviewing the weights of balance will help you become better at judging the equilibrium of objects and of entire rooms:

- ◆ Large sizes have greater visual weight than smaller sizes. A dining chair appears heavier than a small wooden chest.

- ◆ Freeform shapes have greater weight than geometric shapes. A freeform coffee table is heavier than a rectangular table of approximately the same shape.

## Creating Harmonious Balance

For every decorative decision made in each room of your home, there needs to be an equal counteraction. The harmony of a room depends on the relationship among the elements. A fuchsia sofa can be anchored by basic gray walls and carpeting. A frilly dressed bed can be balanced by a heavily distressed armoire. This creates a delicate look "weighted" by a solid, textural piece. Colorful curtains of blues, greens, and yellows can be echoed in a painting or by splashes of colorful pillows on a sofa on the other side of the room or by area rugs. Tall bookcases along a long wall can be "shortened" by filling them with small collectibles and books. Even brightly colored areas of a room can be balanced with a neutral color in another area.

## The Least You Need to Know

◆ Color is the most powerful element in room design.

◆ Color has magical effects on our emotions and mental perceptions.

◆ The sensuality of texture is an important element in creating the feel of a room through its visual and tactile qualities.

◆ Scale and balance affect each decision in home decor, color, pattern, furniture selection, lighting, and room arranging. Each room needs emotional balance as well!

# In This Chapter

- ◆ Necessary tools for the home decorator
- ◆ Budgeting: matching plans and resources
- ◆ What to ask yourself before you begin
- ◆ Prioritizing your needs and wants
- ◆ Arranging like the pros

# Chapter 3

# Decorating Essentials: What You Need to Know

Are you full of grand decorating ideas, just waiting with your hammer in hand to start knocking down walls this very minute? Or are you confused about which way to turn? Successful decorating begins with the right tools, setting a budget, and assessing what needs to be done first.

Based on how you live, your particular style, and knowledge of a few basic design elements, you can decide which room to start with and learn the art of successful arranging. By going step by step and room by room, at your own speed, you then can effectively come up with a grand plan for your entire home. This chapter shows you how to get started!

## Tools of the Trade

With careful consideration of your personal style, a review of decorating history, and knowledge of basic design elements, you're ready to start. But before you begin, you will need the right tools. Aside from the boards that you are assembling for each room (as described in Chapter 1), a handy toolbox will ensure accurate measurements that translate from the planning page to real, three-dimensional space.

You might want to have two tool kits:

◆ A mini-toolbox should contain both a steel tape measure and a cloth tape measure (steel for hard goods and room measuring; cloth for fabric measurements such as slipcovers and curved soft furnishings), pencils, erasers, and paper for sketching. When you are doing research in stores and showrooms, bring along this mini-toolbox to help you measure furnishings, write down prices, and sketch good designs that you will want to try out in your house.

◆ A complete tool kit should be kept together in a bag or basket that can be easily carried from room to room. Stock it with a ruler, tape measure, yardstick, calculator, pencils, erasers, and graph paper (there's some provided in Appendix B) for quick drawings or notes. Also carry a glue stick in your tool kit along with paper clips, so that you can neatly attach any pamphlets or information in your sketchbook for neat reference.

# Priorities: Matching Your Plans with Your Wallet

Based on how you live and what you need, you can decide how much you can afford and which room to start with. Specific ideas for each room can be found in Part 3. Researching prices and money-saving possibilities will yield a realistic budget for each room—ultimately a grand plan budget for the entire house. This one-room-at-a-time philosophy can create a logical and affordable schedule. Commonsense precautions (and asking yourself "Can I afford this?" over and over) can save you a lot of wasted time and money.

# Tackling the Tough Questions

You need to ask yourself a few basic questions before you begin your decorating plan:

◆ Do you rent or own your home? Don't put money into permanent or custom-made items if you rent your home.

Movable furnishings are the way to go! (Ikea catalogs carry stylish, inexpensive furniture, perfect for renters who want movable furniture at a good price. See Appendix A for details.)

◆ Do you have repairs that need to be done before any decorating? You must have any plumbing, heating, or other repairs done before any fabulous furnishings are bought or painting is done. No amount of decorating can be enjoyable if your home has leaky plumbing (which can only get worse) or is uncomfortable without proper heat or air conditioning.

◆ How long do you plan to stay in your house? If the answer is less than three years, you may want to limit your changes to cosmetic enhancements, like paint and wall coverings. On the other hand, major renovations in kitchens and bathrooms, while often costly, generally increase the value of your home. Let your wallet be your guide.

◆ What can you sell your house for? If you do permanent improvements, be sure that the range of local market prices will allow you to recover the money you have put in.

**Style Pointers**

Trying to stick to a budget? Follow these tips:

◆ Do it yourself whenever possible.

◆ Use what you have, renovate, and refurbish.

◆ Buy flea market items, not new furniture.

◆ Learn how to paint!

◆ Decorate around a natural focal point that comes free with a room, like a fireplace or window with a fantastic view.

# One Room at a Time: Where to Start

The best place to start is the room that you use the most, always prioritizing, reviewing budgets, and revising your plan so the priorities fit your budget. A room that shows off your treasured possession best could be a good starting point. Or maybe it's the room in which you engage in your favorite hobby. Do you have an urgent need for a home office? You might want to convert the den or spare bedroom first. And as always, a room that needs basic repair and structural upgrading is put in the neediest room category.

All of these invaluable reviews give you an idea of where to start and what you can accomplish before you even pick up a paint brush. One room at a time ensures steady progress and a sense of accomplishment. But after you finally make the decision of which room to begin with, further prioritizing within the room needs to be addressed.

# Prioritizing Projects: Essentials or Options?

This is the step that will really open up the world of decorating to you—and get you to open this book to many different sections. For whatever room you have chosen, your job is now to critique and prioritize the needs and possibilities for that space. You must list the absolute essentials first and continue through all of the optional accessories that can enhance the room.

To find out what is possible for materials, Part 2 lists potential options, whereas Part 3 lists room-by-room ideas. Part 5 lists quick makeover projects that can give some of your rooms easy do-it-yourself pick-me-ups.

But first you must assess the need for repairs (this can't be stressed enough!)—this is the top priority in every room. Check your walls, ceiling, and flooring. Are they in good shape, or does the ceiling need patching? Is the heat source working? Are there enough lights and outlets? Do you have wiring for a ceiling fixture?

Refer to the boards on style that you were inspired by in Chapter 1. Build a list of favorite items that you desire, items that you love. If you already have a fabulous rug and some classic Windsor chairs, plan your dining room around them. What size dining table can your room accommodate? Which wall for a table or buffet? How about a mirror? Again, refer to your dining room board for visual assurance that you are moving toward unified decisions.

**Pro Workshop**

An inexpensive way to refurbish an old sofa is to throw a painter's cloth over it, available at your local hardware store. They are large enough to cover a good-sized sofa with great style. Add some colorful toss pillows or a throw, and you're set!

# Planning Like a Pro

Ever wonder how professional decorators approach a room? Quite similar to how you are learning. They assess the client's personal style, coming up with ideas to match the client's lifestyle, then room arrangements that fit the budgets and again match lifestyles. They prioritize essentials to options considering the client's budget. Of course, they have had so much practice and are filled with so many ideas that decorating within a budget is their expertise. It comes naturally.

If your budget allows, good professional help is worth its weight in gold. Working with a professional can save you time (they know all of the resources) and money (they can keep you from making costly mistakes). Just be sure to ask the designer's pricing structure before you begin. You may just need a few hours of help to get you pointed in the right direction. Be sure to ask for three references from any decorators you're considering.

Word of mouth is the best way to find a professional designer. If your friend or aunt was pleased and you love the end result, why not call the same decorator and look at their portfolio? You can also contact the American Association of Interior Designers in your region to find decorators who have been proven reliable and qualified. The Yellow Pages also lists decorators under "Decorating" or "Interior designers." (See the next chapter for more on working with a pro.)

**Homematters**

Some professional decorators are called "fluffers." They come to your home and fluff it up a bit by using what you have and rearranging your furniture. They charge a one-time fee that might well be within your budget—and a little fluffing might be all you need to give your home a fresh look (or inspire you to try some new ideas on your own)!

What professional decorators do know is how to make rooms inviting with livable furniture arrangements. By following these steps, you can arrange a room from scratch or rearrange what you already have:

1. Measure your room on graph paper (included in Appendix B in the back of this book), using one square for each square foot of floor space. Measure each

length of wall and draw it on the graph paper/floor plan. Place a double line for windows and a blank area for door widths. (Mark the swing of the door.) Include any features that will affect furniture arrangement, such as sliding glass doors, fireplaces, stairways, and bay windows.

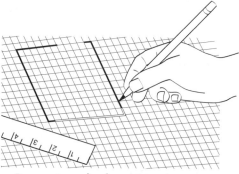

**Draw a to-scale plan on graph paper.**

2. Use the furniture templates in Appendix B to indicate furniture placement on your floor plan. (If you're not sure how to do this, see the tips at the end of this chapter.) You may want to make a copy of the templates so you can cut them out. Measure your furniture and cut out the corresponding-size template. Place on your floor plan. Trace the template on Post-It notes if you want to reposition templates.

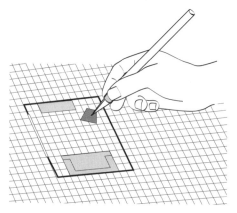

**Arrange your own cut-to-scale templates to ensure furniture fit.**

3. Build a grouping of furniture around an architectural feature like a fireplace or a piece of fabulous artwork. This is the perfect place to begin arranging a room. A pleasing visual focus naturally dominates a room, making room arrangement easy. If your room lacks focus, use an armoire, bookcase units, or a boldly colored wall to center a group of furniture around.

4. Be sure your arrangement allows for good traffic flow, placing furniture so there are pathways that are at least 2½ to 3 feet wide. Furniture acts as traffic guides arranged so a room can be easily passed through.

Here are some tips for using templates for arrangements:

◆ Large room? Break the room into two or more groupings for a cozy feeling. More than one seating arrangement promotes several conversations at the same time.

◆ Small room? Use vertical pieces that raise the eye to assume a grander feel. An armoire or unexpected overscaled piece will also lend a look of grandeur.

◆ Narrow room? Create an illusion of width by angling the furniture on a diagonal.

◆ Think outside of the box. Place furniture where it fits, not in the room where you think it should go. If your buffet fits better in the living room, place it there. It can serve as a table for showcasing accessories and storing your favorite CDs.

◆ Balance your furniture with varying sizes and heights (see Chapter 2). Distribute the various weights and shapes around the room as opposed to placing all tall or small pieces on one side for a lopsided look.

◆ Don't place all the furniture around the perimeter of the room. It will look like a waiting room. Arrange cozy groupings instead.

◆ Each area of seating should allow room for a table or a piece to hold a drink, a book, or a pair of reading glasses. An end table is fine, but many clever items like a stack of vintage suitcases, books, or a small bench can fill the need with panache. Measure those items and make your own properly sized template to include in your plan.

## The Least You Need to Know

◆ A basic tool kit makes home decorating projects and planning efficient and easy. Keeping a kit handy while traveling can help you save inspiring ideas and measure possible purchases.

◆ Budgeting consists of constantly matching your plans with your resources and going ahead if possible or making revisions if necessary.

◆ Evaluating your lifestyle and prioritizing wants and needs is a good place to start your decorating plan.

◆ Learning the basics of measuring and arranging furnishings takes the guesswork out of what will fit and won't.

◆ Consider working with a decorating professional to get you started. He or she can actually save you money!

# In This Chapter

◆ Leafing through catalogs, magazines, and books

◆ Watching makeover artists on television or video

◆ Browsing or buying online

◆ Rooms on view at chain stores or home tours

◆ Tips on consulting or hiring an interior decorator

# Chapter 4

# Help for the Novice Decorator: From Magazines to Cyberspace

Feeling the need to further your quest to learn more about decorating? Then this chapter is for you! From free catalogs to charge-by-the-hour professionals, education beyond the basics is as easy as leafing through, reading from, watching, walking through, or calling up!

Most of these resources are closer and more easily obtainable than you think. And the whole world of Internet websites allows you to do all of your shopping without even getting out of your chair! There's lots of help out there for the novice decorator. (See Appendix A for details on specific catalogs, magazines, and books.)

## Mail-Order Catalogs: Great Ideas for Free

It probably comes as no surprise, because many automatically appear in your mailbox, that home mail-order catalogs are free (well, most are) and full of all kinds of goods for decorating your home. From drawer pulls to draperies, futons to fabrics, and paints to pillows, catalogs are packed with treasures to round out every style of décor—and often at very reasonable prices!

Aside from the merchandise, most mail-order companies have helpful services, from gift boxing to express or air delivery and customer-service hotlines to liberal refund policies.

The downside of catalog merchandise is that it is geared toward the masses. That means your neighbor might have the same living room furniture. To avoid the cookie cutter look, buy furnishings and accessories with discretion. Don't duplicate room setting detail or buy all of your furnishings from one style of catalog. Use your imagination and combine new items with older pieces you already have and arrange them in a style that works for you!

**Style Pointers** _____

When ordering from a catalog, be sure to note the company's shipping charges. Pricing is based on size, weight, and destination. Sometimes that cute "little" table at a bargain price may not be so affordable after you tack on the freight charges. If you order from out-of-state suppliers, you most often avoid state sales tax (which can often offset the price of shipping).

Most catalogs are presented artfully and can actually help you see how their goods are incorporated into well-done interiors. To help you find a catalog to suit your needs, consider some of my favorites for kitchens, linens, furniture, rugs, curtains, and garden accessories.

The Pottery Barn catalog is one of my favorites.

# Magazines: Interiors by the Pros

Most magazines offer total room settings that are professionally executed. They also feature articles on home decorating by talented owners who are worthy of praise. The room furnishings, colors, textures, and shapes are shown with attitude. Furniture arrangements are clever, and details are brought to an artistic level. You can increase your decorating skills by analyzing what you love and weeding out styles that don't suit you. The best part is that the resources that the designer has used are usually listed (including where to purchase some of the furniture, accessories, or even paint). The information is usually listed in the back of each magazine.

**Homematters** _____

Here are some unexpected places to glean ideas:

◆ Movies sets—for room styles and arrangements
◆ Flea markets—for uses of simple items for display
◆ Fashion magazines—for color and fabric combinations
◆ Children's artwork—for humble and charming ways to create wall art
◆ Museums—well-planned shows that feature decorative arts

# Books: Interiors for Reference and Redos

Books catering to the home abound at your local bookstore or at book-selling giants like Barnes & Noble or Borders. They inventory a wide variety of books on decorating your home, regional and international styles, and do-it-yourself redo projects. (See Appendix A for some of my favorites.) It makes sense to buy a book that caters to your taste, budget, and lifestyle. And, of course, some of the pictures are good coffee table material. If your local small bookstore does not carry a large inventory of books, they can order any book you may desire. Also, book clubs advertised in magazines that cater to the home decorator offer books at discounted retail prices.

Books are also available at your local library, and the price is right, usually free with your library card. Magazines and videos on the home are available as well. The only drawback with the library is that you can only hold on to materials for a certain amount of time. And you are not allowed to cut up materials for your style boards! But if there is an idea you want to emulate, most libraries have a photocopy machine so you can copy a page to attach to your boards. If you want a copy of any library publication, for your permanent collection, be sure to note the ISBN (International Standard Book Number) on the back. You can order a copy through a bookstore or online (as discussed later in this chapter). Most magazine publishers are happy to send you back issues as well.

# For the Serious Amateur: Back to School?

If you still feel you need a bit more formal education, try taking a night course at your local adult education center. Times often cater to the working person, with classes often held at night. A class in basic art, elements of design, oil painting, pottery, even perennial gardening can heighten your awareness of color, texture, balance, and scale—the elements that make good design.

# Media: Television and Home Videos

Don't change the channel if you see a show on cooking or travel. Some cooking shows may be shot on location showcasing various regions and different nations. Customs, foods, and entertaining may be discussed and photographed with native interiors. Travel shows often point out national museums, interior shots of places to eat, and homes of interest. Both types can provide a study in regional tastes and décor.

Lifestyle and learning channels abound on television. They are full of how-to's and tips, redos and renovations, and simple to grandiose styles to help make your home a prettier place to live. The shows are on at all hours of the day and night on HGTV (Home and Garden TV), BBC America, The Style Channel, Discovery, as well as many others.

**Pro Workshop**

Tune in to the many gardening programs or shows that feature outdoor decorating that are on television these days. The same principles of design apply to the exterior as well as the interior!

Videos can be a great source of extra education, and you can view them at your leisure. Libraries or bookstores carry how-to and do-it-yourself videos. They can also be purchased online, as discussed in the next section.

# The Online Age

If you are adept at using a computer and are hooked up to the Internet, you can shop online right from home! With specific website addresses (a page for a company's online info and goods), the company comes up on your screen to allow you to view merchandise. Some companies even have online staff to help answer questions. Most have "shopping baskets" in which you can place desired goods with the click of your mouse, a retail form to fill out, and a confirmation of purchase. It's an easy way to go if you don't mind viewing items in virtual reality! And don't worry about using your credit card to purchase goods over the Internet. Reputable companies set up secure sites for that very reason. Many catalogs have websites as well.

Here are just a few of the sites you can peruse for home goods:

◆ www.marthastewart.com

◆ www.furniture.com

◆ www.anthropologie.com

◆ www.pier1.com

◆ www.amazon.com

Not only are there stores online, there are auctions on the "net." If you are a collector of antiques or a collector of any kind, a good site to look up is eBay online auction house at www.ebay.com. It is by far the busiest and largest online auction house. You need to register, then browse around the site for that certain item you are interested in, from china to crafts and armoires to art. Almost anything and everything is auctioned on eBay. Just be careful that you really want what you are bidding on, because your bid is legally binding and if you are the highest bidder, "you own it"!

# Rooms on View: Retail Stores and Home Tours

The great thing about model rooms in large department stores is that you can see and touch the furniture. Big chain stores like Bloomingdales, Neiman-Marcus, and Macy's offer well-appointed furnishings set up for purchase. Critique the rooms. If one catches your eye, find the name of the decorator. He or she will be glad to help you with some selections, although you may have to make an appointment. Smaller boutique furniture/decorator shops (maybe in your own town) are often owned by a seasoned and talented designer who can give you personal attention.

Some large stores devote themselves to a particular look and clientele. Ralph Lauren's Home Store in New York City, for example, boasts floors of luxurious furnishings, wallcoverings, fabrics, and decorative accents—all with a well-bred air. His rooms are arranged in themes or eras and are intriguing and thought-provoking.

The Laura Ashley Company owns chains of home shops around the world. It specializes in collections of furnishings with simplicity and style, using a skillful mixing of color and pattern. A home book is available for a small charge (refundable with purchase) that details ideas and products.

ABC Carpet and Home in New York is also a visual delight. Fantastically classic and offbeat items mesh to make some of the most artistic displays around. Its inventory includes table linens, rugs, lighting, and indoor and outdoor furniture.

See Appendix A for information on obtaining catalogs.

### Style Pointers

Don't buy an entire room setting from a retail store with all new furniture. It will look like a department store vignette with someone else's style. Buy pieces and add some that you own, or pick up some flea market items to complete the look for a more personal look.

Department store room settings allow you to touch and feel fabrics and finishes, measure pieces, compare price tags, and imagine the look in your own home. *(Photo by Laura Ashley)*

Another option is to view how others decorate at local house tours. They are usually held during holidays and festive occasions. A group such as a garden club chooses a home, decorates

it, and charges a minimal fee for charity purposes to the general public for viewing. Not only do you see seasonal décor and accessories, but also a well-appointed home! Your chamber of commerce will know when the next house tour is scheduled in your area.

Professional tours are usually held in major metropolitan areas. They consist of polished interiors, orchestrated by highly skilled professional designers who combine unusual colors, fabrics, and furniture.

Here are some tips for getting the most out of a professional viewing:

◆ Bring along your mini-toolbox (see Chapter 3). If you see ideas that appeal to you, make a sketch.

◆ Be sure to study the before and after pictures often displayed in the showcased room. Good designers know the art of disguising exposed pipes, ugly radiators, and so on.

◆ Imitate simple ideas or modify flamboyant ones.

◆ Check out the resource list filed at each showroom. Some may be "to the trade only" but can be purchased through professional designers. It lists suppliers that have been specified by the designer for the showroom décor and often are available through designers and home tradesmen. If you liked a specific drapery fabric, for example, the company can list what professionals it is available through and the designer can order it for you.

◆ If a particular room has "your name all over it," ask for a consultation with the designer. Be sure to ask about the hourly rate!

# Calling on a Pro

Taking on a decorating project can be daunting, even if you understand some basic concepts, know your favorite colors, and have a general idea of what you are looking for. Sometimes an opinion or a total partnership with a professional decorator is a good way to help you complete a small-scale or total home project.

Professionals range in skill, style, and price. A good designer will make your decorating project successful by expressing your tastes and interests on your budget, with style. Consider the following good hiring advice:

◆ Word of mouth is always reliable. Was your friend satisfied with the work? Do you like her rooms?

◆ If your project is detailed and quite expensive, it's best to hire a knowledgeable and reliable designer who has years of experience. They know most of the pitfalls and can save you time and money.

◆ Always interview as many designers as you can. Don't be afraid to ask to see some of their work and to hear about their education and experience.

◆ Always ask for references.

◆ You have to feel comfortable with your designer. Do your personalities work together? Long projects involve long hours spent together, so you'll want to make sure you're compatible.

◆ Does the designer listen to your ideas?

◆ Is the designer passionate and enthusiastic about your project?

◆ Can the designer work within your budget and on your schedule?

◆ Do you have a written agreement on pricing, including details on down payments and completion times? Never pay all costs up front. A down payment is standard and should be agreed upon—in writing—by you and the designer.

Professionally decorated rooms cleverly mix styles of furnishings. *(Photo by Lee Industries)*

## The Least You Need to Know

◆ Catalogs offer a plethora of goods for the home.

◆ Books and magazines feature well-appointed homes by professional decorators or talented homeowners. You can study them for good pointers and ideas.

◆ Home shows and videos are great resources for do-it-yourself projects.

◆ Online stores, sites, and auctions offer merchandise for purchase without leaving your home.

◆ Large retail chain stores and home tours offer room settings that are put together by decorators for purchase and inspiration.

◆ Working with a professional interior decorator can help you express your ideas while saving you time and money.

# In This Part

# Decorating from the Floor Up

Today, more products and materials are available for the home than ever before. If you have trouble making decisions, you might actually find yourself wishing for fewer choices—maybe even a cave to hide in—when facing the multitude of possibilities for every room.

Just the surrounding surfaces—floor, ceiling, walls, and windows—bring dozens of decisions. And when you turn to filling the interior space with the necessary furniture, your mind might be boggled by the range of selections. What to do? Get the basic info on all your choices in the following chapters before you head out to do your shopping. It will make it all easier and more economical. And don't forget to review the designer tricks of the trade for adding real pizzazz to all of those surfaces, furnishings, and materials. These are tried-and-true … and fun ideas from a pro.

# In This Chapter

- ◆ Wood, bamboo, and cork—nature's inventory
- ◆ The soft touch of carpet and area rugs
- ◆ The new look of vinyls
- ◆ Solid flooring with tile, stone, and concrete
- ◆ Creative ideas for your floors

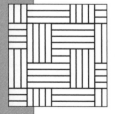
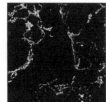

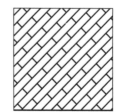
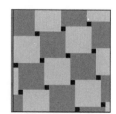

# What's Underfoot?
# Oh, the Possibilities ...

Because floors are the foundation of any room, they need to be chosen with decorative and practical reasons in mind. You want the best look in the appropriate material, a style that is within your budget, and a floor that is durable and won't need constant maintenance, right?

Many possibilities are available today with patterns, colors, textures, and pricing to fit anyone's taste and pocketbook. In this chapter, we take a closer look at the many choices available to you.

## From Nature's Store: The Warmth of Wood

Wood floors are natural beauties that add warmth to any style or décor. Traditional hardwood flooring made from oak is popular, but your floor could be made from birch or maple. Softwood floors are made of pine, fir, cedar, or spruce. Hardwood boards are available in various widths, but the standard is a 2½-inch strip floor with a tongue-and-groove edge. Softwoods come in random widths in a square edge. You can also find reclaimed wide pine boards through the specialty companies that advertise in the back of magazines such as *Fine Homebuilding* and *This Old House* (see Appendix A).

Many wood floors are sealed and finished with a clear, hard urethane in either gloss or matte finish. If the urethane is maintained and consistently stripped (removed) and reapplied, wood floors are easily cleaned.

Wood floors can also be stained, bleached, or painted. Painted floors have risen to an art form, with many paint techniques available in kits from art or craft stores, home catalogs, and museum stores. From faux marbling, complete with imitation veining to painted-on area rugs with fringe askew, the options are endless. "Spattering" and a checkerboard pattern are the easier do-it-yourself techniques. Stencil kits also aid the novice with a variety of precut patterns and instructions. Stay away from ditsy stencils that look common and unsophisticated in styling. Hire a professional for intricate details. More paint techniques are listed in Chapter 6.

Parquet is another kind of wood flooring composed of thin strips of wood arranged in various patterns. Light and dark woods may be joined to emphasize a pattern. Twelve-inch tile squares are also available with ready-made patterns for easy installation.

**Parquet patterns create simple visual texture or intricate floor art.**

**Pro Workshop**

If you're looking for a floor option that has been used in homes for more than 100 years, consider cork. Although not the least expensive choice, cork has natural beauty, adds warmth to a room, and bounces back from any indentations, making it a good choice for high-traffic areas. Cork is derived from the outer bark of oak trees from the Mediterranean area.

# Grass Is Greener

You probably never thought of using grass as a flooring material. Well, actually, bamboo is a popular choice today. It is not wood, as some think, but a grass. It is strong, hard, and stable, making it a perfect choice for flooring. Bamboo is considered a green building material because it regenerates without replanting, matures in three years, and requires minimal fertilization. Round shoots are sliced into strips and boiled. The bamboo is laminated into solid boards which are then milled into standard strip flooring with a tongue and groove on all four sides. Finished bamboo floors have rich textures with thin strips of varying color enhanced by bamboo nodes (that part or joint of a stem from which a leaf starts to grow). Bamboo flooring is generally about 20 percent more costly than oak flooring.

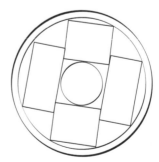

**Bamboo strips are cut lengthwise around the center of a stalk. The boards have the characteristic bamboo nodes.**

# A Comfortable Choice: Carpet

Wall-to-wall carpeting is the perfect choice for adding a splash of color, pattern, or texture to a room. It is soft on your feet, adds warmth to a cold room, absorbs sound (great if you live in an apartment or condominium), and is relatively inexpensive. But a carpet's real talent is camouflaging floors that are damaged, stained, or of low quality.

**Pro Workshop**

Make magic with carpet! Make a room seem ...

- Smaller—Use a dark-colored highly patterned carpet.
- Wider—Run a linear pattern the width of the room.
- Larger—Use a solid, light-colored carpet.
- Longer—Run a linear pattern the length of the room.
- Cohesive—Use one small patterned carpet without area rugs.

Some carpet types to familiarize yourself with include the following:

- **Berber.** A popular tufted carpet today that is a multi-level loop, durable, and specified in all styles of décor. Usually is made of "tweedy"-looking yarns.
- **Broadloom.** Any carpet made on a wide loom. Most wall-to- wall carpets today are made 12 feet wide or more.
- **Axminster.** A patterned woven carpet that adopted its name from a European factory that specialized in its manufacture.

- **Sisal.** Sisal carpet is a natural carpet woven from plant fibers in many textural patterns and is a great alternative to traditional carpeting. From beach cottage to stately mansion, sisal, seagrass, or coir (all different plant fibers) fit in naturally with every style of decorating. Mostly used in its natural color, sisal can be dyed or hand-painted with color and patterns. It is a truly classic choice.

# Art Underfoot: Area Rugs

Aside from being soft and warm, area rugs add color, pattern, textures, and pizzazz to any room décor. From expensive Asian rugs to affordable dhurries, antique to reproduction, area rugs are available at every price. Their attributes are limitless:

- Create a focal point for any style of décor
- Provide warmth underfoot
- Can be easily transported from room to room, house to house
- Be made in styles for every budget
- Protect wood flooring
- Unify a mishmash of furniture
- Define seating and conversation area

Various types of area rugs to familiarize yourself with are ...

- **Aubusson.** A French classic that is usually hand-woven in muted colors with a center design.
- **Bessarabian.** Flat-weave rugs depicting geometrics and florals, usually of Russian or Turkish origin.
- **Braided.** Strips of cloth braided and stitched together to form rugs with casual, rustic charm.

◆ **Dhurrie.** Flat-weave rug hand woven in India, usually of muted colors and numerous designs in wool or cotton.

◆ **Flokati.** Rug with a thick, rough nap, that originated as a hand-woven white wool rug in Greece.

◆ **Kilim.** Similar to a dhurrie, but colors are usually richer.

◆ **Hooked.** A nubby pile rug made with yarn or fabric pulled through a backing. Colors and textures vary with the maker, whether by hand or machine.

◆ **Needlepoint.** A rug stitched on canvas with woolen yarns that form many floral, geometric, or scenic patterns.

◆ **Oriental.** Truly the king of carpets, hand-knotted orientals are prized possessions. Their patterns are usually named after their place of origin. Their rich colors, beautiful patterns, and durability make the most traditional and eclectic schemes come to life!

Wood floors and an oriental rug are a classic choice for this informal library. The traditional patterned fabric on the armchair and ottoman complements the geometric pattern of the rug. *(Photo by Brunswig & Fils)*

◆ **Rag.** Flat-weave rugs are made with cotton or wool strips on a loom and create a charming, handcrafted look.

◆ **Sisal.** A natural-fiber rug woven into different textural patterns that can be decoratively bordered, hand-painted, or dyed.

**Style Pointers**

You can make carpets and bare floors more interesting by using area rugs in different textures and patterns. Link them through color or similar overall effect.

# The New Artistic Use of Vinyls

Vinyl, known for its durability and low maintenance, is a good choice for heavily trafficked areas like a kitchen or bath, where spills may occur. And it is reasonably priced. Sheet vinyl is available in wide rolls, which allows installation without seams. The newer patterns imitate brick, stone, or tile and are more realistic than ever.

Vinyl is also available in 12-inch by 12-inch tiles. You can customize your floor by designing your own patterns and textures with a wide variety of colors. Both types (sheet and tile) are available in many grades and price ranges, some as intricate as if looking through a kaleidoscope!

**Homematters**

If you are a quilt fan, you may want to duplicate your favorite pattern in colored vinyls as the kitchen floor!

Curlicup inlaid
border

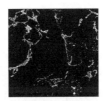

Checkerboard and
spot design

A marbled effect gives
a richer, more
interesting texture

**Here are a few patterns that you can artistically arrange with vinyl tiles (from left): inlaid border, checkerboard design, marbled pattern.**

# Durable Choices: Tile, Brick, Stone, and Concrete

Tile is available from quarry style to highly polished marble. Nothing can compare to its durability and beauty. The different kinds of tile include the following:

◆ **Ceramic** tile is fired clay that is glazed or unglazed and available in a bounty of colors, patterns, and sizes.

◆ **Quarry** tile is also fired clay but is less refined than its ceramic cousin. It is sometimes irregular in shape and earth-colored like terra cotta. It makes for a most handsome, informal floor, reminiscent of old European country homes.

◆ **Mosaic** tiles are made of glazed or unglazed clay or glass tiles. They are small squares that are attached to a backing for ease of installation. They range from soft to very vibrant colors.

There are advantages and disadvantages to consider when using tile as a flooring material. First, the advantages:

◆ Extremely durable
◆ Minimal upkeep
◆ Beautiful to the eye
◆ Excellent pattern and color selection

Disadvantages include the following:

◆ Cold underfoot unless radiant heat installed underneath.
◆ Costly.
◆ Slippery when wet.
◆ Items dropped can break tile easily.
◆ Hard surfaces may cause leg strain if standing on them for long periods.

New and old brick is another solid option for flooring. Its rugged texture can form some very exciting patterns that exude a rustic, informal feeling. Although it is "used," old brick is more sought after and expensive today. Typically, it is common red block, recycled from old houses and chimneys. New brick is available in different finishes and colors.

Marble, slate, and limestone are quarried. Although all three are expensive and more difficult to install, marble and slate are available in tile form in different colors to make beautiful patterned floors from foyers to bathrooms. Stone is easier to install and is especially unique. Granite or flagstone can add a timeless quality to any kitchen.

Concrete is the latest designer look for flooring. It is relatively inexpensive compared to stone and brick and adds a clean look to a modern country kitchen. Concrete is the perfect substitute for expensive limestone flooring. It's very durable, but of course, as with any hard floor surface, glassware will break if dropped upon it. Although gray concrete is the industrial look that many designers want, concrete can be tinted different colors with dyes, such as terra cottas, pinks, and other earth tones.

Marble tiles in a geometric pattern add interest to this rustic cottage kitchen. *(Photo by Smallbone)*

# Tricks of the Trade

Most designers have signature ideas that they love to use over and over. Flooring allows a broad array of fun ideas. Here are some of my favorite uses of different flooring materials:

◆ **Wood.** Pine flooring, painted in stripes of two different colors, one plank natural, the next black!

◆ **Parquet floor.** A stenciled border on the perimeter in black on natural wood.

◆ **Do you have an old oak floor?** Paint right over it in a bright color. Red is a lively choice!

◆ **Carpet.** Wall-to-wall wool petit-point pattern is a great backdrop for furniture.

◆ **Sisal.** Wall-to-wall carpeting is a perfect foil for bad floors. A good clean basic look.

◆ **Area rugs.** Use flokati rugs in any interior from traditional to modern. Timeless and elegant.

◆ **Concrete flooring.** Concrete offers an inexpensive and unexpected way to go for a solid, stonelike appearance. I like to encrust shells or pebbles in the perimeter. This adds a handmade decoration that is charming. Be sure that you seal it several times before walking on it!

◆ **Vinyls.** I love checkerboard vinyls, especially in putty and ivory. This hardworking floor works well in a foyer, kitchen, or bathroom. Why not create a giant checkerboard, backgammon board, or hopscotch board on the floor of your children's playroom?

## The Least You Need to Know

◆ Flooring choices require practical as well as aesthetic consideration.

◆ Nature provides some of the warmest looks in flooring with traditional wood, bamboo, and cork.

◆ Carpet and area rugs should be selected with room use in mind.

◆ Vinyls are an inexpensive and very durable flooring choice. They are available in an array of patterns that imitate the look of brick, stone, or other materials.

◆ Tile, stone, and concrete can provide dramatic floors in select spaces.

# In This Chapter

- ◆ Paints: a practical and inexpensive way to change the look of a room

- ◆ Wallcoverings that work

- ◆ Woodwork, from simple to ornate

- ◆ Tile, brick, and stone for enduring beauty

- ◆ Imaginative wall treatments

# Chapter 6

# Walls with Wallop

Because walls are the largest surface of your home, careful consideration should be taken when planning a decorating scheme with them!

Whether plain or covered with paint or wallcoverings, fabric or wood, stone or tin, there are many options to add flair to walls that can work for every room in your home. Let's take a closer look at some of them.

## Paint, for the Perfect Complexion

With paint, the possibilities are endless! It is the most popular, durable, and practical wall treatment. Why? Painting the walls is quick, easy, and generally the least expensive way to give a room an instant "makeover." Like cosmetics, paint can call attention to fine details or mask less-than-perfect ones.

There are two types of paint: latex and oil. Latex is water-based, washable, and quick to dry. Oil-based paints take longer to dry and need solvents for cleaning up, but have rich colors and are durable. Both come in finishes that range from high gloss to flat. Gloss paints have a sheen that intensifies their colors, and cover more area per gallon of paint (approximately 600 square feet). Flat colors are more subdued, do not shine, and cover about 400 square feet per gallon. Your local home store such as The Home Depot has knowledgeable employees who can answer your paint queries.

**Homematters** _____

Wonder how much paint you need for that room? Multiply the height of your walls by the perimeter of the room. In the following illustration, A × B equals the area of the room in square feet. For example, if the wall height is 9 feet and the perimeter of the room is 56 feet, that equals 504 square feet. A gallon of paint covers roughly 400 feet, so you would need two gallons.

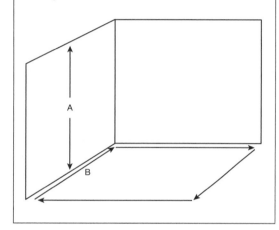

Paint colors should always be tested. Paint a piece of wallboard and drape the fabric over it that you plan to use in the room. Place the board in the room where you plan to use the possible color and view it in the morning, during the daytime, and in the evening. Be sure the color suits your taste; color changes with different lighting.

If it is easier, you can use some of the pre-tested colors such as Benjamin Moore's historical palette or Ralph Lauren's line of designer paints, available through The Home Depot. Martha Stewart carries an extensive color palette through Sherwin Williams. These affordable paints are widely available at home, hardware, and paint stores. Benjamin Moore's colors reflect classic

historic décor, and Lauren's "go together" palette presents colors of regional décor and sporting lifestyles. Martha Stewart's colors, with names like Ladybug, Rope, and Snowball, reflect nature's bounty, with garden and seascape colors grouped in compatible room colors. If you are uncertain of your color-combining sense, using pretested paints is a good way to avoid costly mistakes. Don't be afraid to try some color on your walls. Here are some tried-and-true colors from Benjamin Moore that I use over and over:

- BM 172 (neutral stone)
- BM HC 87 (medium dark taupe)
- BM HC 85 (sunny yellow)
- BM 1268 (shell pink)
- BM HC 115 (medium green)
- BM 70 (linen white)
- BM 06 (clean white)
- BM 74 (gray white)
- BM 974 (putty)
- BM 976 (stone)
- BM 127 (pale peach)
- BM HC 1 (pale green that changes with the light)
- BM 1323 (warm red)
- BM HC 135 (library green)

From easy-to-do touch-ups to those jobs that require high-level skill, there's more to painting than just brushing. Paint effects are unusual ways of giving ordinary walls great impact. There are many how-to books and videos available to help you learn these methods. (See Appendix A for resources; you might also check your library, home improvement stores, and bookstores.) Many home improvement stores offer classes and free literature supplied by paint companies.

Some popular techniques include the following:

◆ **Combing.** Dragging a tool with "teeth" through a wet topcoat to create various "combed" patterns.

◆ **Rag rolling.** Applying or removing color with a bunched-up rag. Wet or dry cloths may be used, but a wet cloth will produce softer patterns. Also, the weave of the rag will affect the pattern. A bit of practice is required to execute this procedure.

◆ **Spattering.** Spotting an area with flecks of different-colored paints by running your fingers over the bristles of a wet brush or flicking the brush to "spatter" paint.

◆ **Sponging.** Applying small amounts of paint to a wall with a sponge. Textures will vary with the pattern of the application: A subtle effect is achieved with sponging done close together, whereas greater visual texture is achieved with widely spaced sponging.

◆ **Stenciling.** Paint dabbed on a wall, ceiling, or floor through a plastic stencil that is cut in various shapes and motifs. Home stores offer precut kits, or you can make your own pattern. This is a quick-and-easy method.

◆ **Trompe l'oeil.** The "fooling your eye" paint technique that creates the impression of marble, stone, wood, or other surfaces, as well as painted architectural details. Use this technique for landscape murals that bring the outdoors indoors—or even place painted books or other rare objects on your trompe l'oeil shelves!

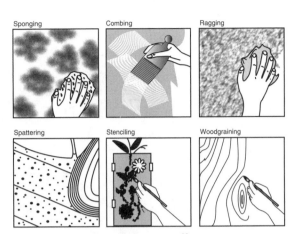

Decorative paint effects.

# Plethora of Paper: Wallcoverings for Every Taste

Wallcoverings are available in every pattern, color, and texture imaginable. The most common wallcoverings for the home are machine-printed paper with vinyl-coated surfaces that are clear in pattern and rich in color. More expensive choices include hand-printed papers with one-of-a-kind patterns or reproductions of antique patterns. Also natural-looking coverings such as burlap, linen, or grass cloth are paper-backed and can be used to add texture and dimension to walls. Designer-trademarked papers can be costly but are among the more beautiful patterns and choices.

**Style Pointers**

Use paint effects with discretion; too many used in a home can look amateurish and overdone. A kitchen with sponged walls, a dining room's walls that are rag rolled, and a living room that has stenciled walls reveals an overuse of an idea. The paint effects are no longer special.

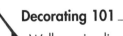

**Decorating 101**

Wallcovering liner is a stiff wallcovering that is applied the same way as vinyl wallcovering but is an undercoat to cover flaws before the printed wallcovering goes on for a smooth look.

You can use wallcovering to …

◆ Camouflage stains and defects in walls.

◆ Enliven hallways, foyers, stairwells, and even closets that might go unnoticed.

◆ Unify eclectic furniture and a mix of artwork.

◆ Make rooms "grow" or make them appear cozier (depending on the wallcover pattern).

◆ Transform a room quickly, easily, and affordably.

◆ Create a look of dimension in a sparsely furnished room or a room without architectural details.

◆ Add visual excitement, texture, and color to an ordinary room.

And here are some uses for wallcovering that you may not have thought of:

◆ Paper a ceiling.

◆ Paper the back of a cupboard or bookshelf.

◆ Cut out a wallcovering border in scallop form and attach to the front of a shelf or bookshelves.

◆ Measure 6 feet above the floor in a child's room and put a wide border around the room.

**Style Pointers**

Don't throw away those wallcovering scraps! Use them to wrap gifts, make paper holiday ornaments, create gift cards, cover a notebook, decorate a box or small table, and many other uses.

**A child's room lends itself to a whimsical border.**
*(Photo by Laura Ashley)*

**A kitchen wall is given dimension with a triple row of wallcovering borders that simulate a set of shelves with jugs, pitchers, plates, and bowls.** *(Photo by Gear)*

# Fabric Walls with Flair

Fabric applied directly to walls has a special beauty: Its textures not only provide a visual excitement, but a tactile one as well. You can actually feel the softness or roughness of the material, creating a mood for the room. Fabrics can be applied flat and tailored or shirred to create luxurious folds for a soft, sensual effect. Both add a marvelous ambience as well as hide wall imperfections! Fabric can be glued or stapled in panels cut to fit your wall space. Shirring— a gathering made in cloth by drawing the material up on parallel rows of short, running stitches—can be accomplished by stapling or attaching widths of fabric gathered on dowels.

# Woodwork: From Molding to Boards to Wainscoting

Wood applied to walls can be modest, like moldings or plain boards to better define a small space. Or wood can be elegant, with *wainscoting* or completely paneled rooms. Wood is a natural choice. Wainscoting adds structure and division to walls, and moldings immediately give a room a craftsmanlike character. Wood walls can be rustic, paneled with rough boards, or polished with smooth woods. They can be stained or distressed. Many restoration projects recycle old boards that can be used to lend an instant sense of history to a new room. You can find these at architectural salvage shops in the Yellow Pages under "Architectural Salvage."

Can't afford custom paneling? Scour the flea markets for old doors that can be installed like paneling with an aged patina.

**Decorating 101**

**Wainscoting** refers to wood panels or boards that cover the lower part of the wall (typically about 3 feet up from the floor) and set it apart from the finish of the upper wall. This is a traditional decorating technique that is many centuries old.

# Dramatic Walls with a Solid Feel: Tile, Stone, and Brick

Tile, stone, or brick brings warmth to walls that only natural materials can. These materials are highly decorative in a subtle way and easy to maintain, although they can be expensive. Use them to dramatize select areas in a room, such as a fireplace or a cookstove or alcove, or to give a wainscoting effect. Be sure to view large samples at a tile or masonry store.

Stone and wood walls are natural combinations for everlasting beauty.    *(Photo by Lee Industries)*

Brick is often used in kitchens or family rooms to give a sense of permanence and to vary the monotonous texture of sheetrock walls. Old brick is used to show off its natural earthy texture and to emphasize its aged character.

Tile is ideal for bathrooms and kitchens, where spills can be wiped. Solid or patterned squares can add striking visual impact behind a stove, around a kitchen fireplace, or above a bathroom sink or throughout the entire bathroom. Mosaic tiles make some of the most interesting patterned walls with their small size and vibrant color.

# Tricks of the Trade

Professional designers love to use a few signature looks in each project that they decorate. When it comes to walls, try these interesting and imaginative ways to treat your walls:

◆ Paint the ceiling of a room a different color than the four walls. Try a pale blue, pale pink, or sunny yellow.

◆ Wallcover your walls in fabric. Hang a large-scale, buffalo-plaid fabric in red and black for a great hunting cottage look.

◆ Stencil a love letter to your one and only around the perimeter of the top of the walls in your private dressing area.

◆ Paint an entire wall in a child's room with "chalkboard" paint, available at The Home Depot. When applied and dried, the paint resembles a chalkboard that can be written on and erased!

◆ Hang a quilt on a wall—perhaps one that has an unusual modern pattern, or bright colors, or one made from humble fabrics of household clothing. For maximum effect, be sure it is an overscaled quilt that has clout (a small design can be nondescript and have no effect). The more unusual the quilt, the more interesting wall art it makes.

◆ Recycle old pressed ceiling tin, complete with rust stains, on the lower half of a wall for interesting texture.

◆ Wallcover a room in bakery kraft paper for a unique neutral paper bag color.

◆ Apply a favorite motif or word with a rubber stamp on the walls of your bathroom. Try black ink on ivory paint for a classic look or red ink on pink walls for an energized contemporary feel.

◆ Mirrored walls can visually expand a small room and double the visual effect by reflecting the furnishings and light.

## The Least You Need to Know

◆ Paint and wallcovering are the least-
expensive materials to quickly transform
a room.

◆ Pretested colors are a good choice to
eliminate worry.

◆ Fabric adds unmatched texture to walls.

◆ Tile, brick, and stone add a sense of permanence and coziness to a room.

◆ Professional decorators and designers
know imaginative ways to treat walls.
You can emulate them in your home.

# In This Chapter

- ◆ Furniture to last forever
- ◆ Seating that is comfortable and stylish
- ◆ The case on case goods
- ◆ Designer's alternatives

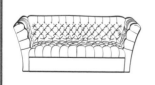

# Chapter 7

# Home Furnishings with Flair

One of the best ways to begin a furniture-buying plan is to purchase pieces that appeal to your sense of beauty and individuality. Designs, colors, and textures must harmonize with the mood of the room and with other pieces you own. And of course, the styles must be appropriate for your lifestyle.

Another factor to consider when purchasing new furniture is cost. Does the price of your furniture fit within your budget? New furniture should be purchased with the idea that it will be used for a long time. Does the quality match the price? With the variety of furniture available today, quality can range from poor to excellent. And from "off-the-floor goods" to custom-made seating or handcrafted cabinets, dressers, and tables, the styles can run the gamut from mediocre to superbly designed.

Be a better consumer by taking your time to read this chapter and learn about furniture quality and style tips so that your money will be spent much more wisely!

## Furniture: The Original "Software" and "Hardware"

In the home furnishings world, furniture is classified as soft or hard goods. Soft goods include upholstered sofas and chairs and bedding. Hard goods are called "case" goods and generally include tables, desks, chests, chairs, and benches. Let's look at the soft goods first.

### Sofas and Chairs That Sit Well

Plan your home around a few good investments like quality upholstery and you can never go wrong! Well-made upholstered sofas and chairs can last a lifetime.

Aesthetics and design are usually the first things that attract you to a piece of soft goods, but it is equally important to consider comfort, construction, and fabric when purchasing any upholstered chair or sofa.

The comfort of an upholstered chair depends on its size (can you fit comfortably on it and is it deep enough to relax in it?), construction (will the springs hold up?), fabric (do the fibers feel good against your skin, and is the fabric appropriate for the chair's intended use?). Knowing how a sofa or chair is made and what materials were used may help answer these questions.

### Style Pointers

Don't forget to use the templates in Appendix B to make sure your purchases fit your rooms. Measuring allows for well-spaced traffic patterns to ensure rooms that work.

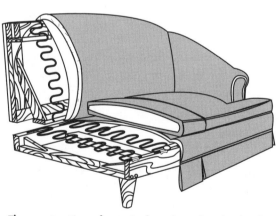

The construction of a typical moderately priced sofa. The use of more expensive materials and hand work creates a higher-priced or "custom" sofa. The use of softer inferior woods, weak joints, and low-grade fabrics reflects cheaper sofas.

The framework of an upholstered sofa or chair should be made of hardwood, such as ash, birch, oak, or maple, that has been kiln dried (moisture content reduced by the manufacturer

for greater stability). Acceptable joints on sofa frames are double-dowel construction reinforced with glue and corner blocks. The blocks should also be fastened with glue and screws.

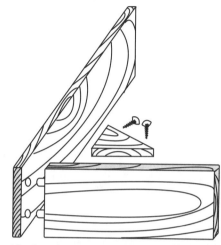

Double dowels are inserted into grooves on intersecting pieces to create a strong joint, reinforced with glue and screwed corner blocks.

The spring construction should be at least eight-gauge S-shape wires that attach to the frame to provide proper back cushion and sufficient seating support. The higher-quality construction coil springs are placed close together and tied in place with good-grade twine. An "eight-way," hand-tied spring system (each coil is hand-tied eight times), properly done, provides excellent resiliency.

Filling ranges from down (duck feathers) to polyfill. Cushions filled with down are the most expensive and softest. A foam-core cushion wrapped in down is perfect for softness and firmness, and its quality is surely felt, and is actually visible from across the room. The cushions *look* luxurious. Less expensive but still very acceptable are foam-core cushions wrapped in polyester batting. Depending on the foam core, cushions can be soft or firm and are primarily used in moderately priced sofas of good quality.

All sofa manufacturers offer fabric selections classified in different grades. The grades refer to the price of the basic sofa, usually starting with the letter "A" (the least expensive) and on through the alphabet, depending on how many grades are available. Price depends on what type of fabric is used and how much it costs to manufacture. Durable fabrics and stain-resistant finishes are usually available in all grades. Check for the cleaning codes to be sure the fabric that you choose is appropriate for its use.

### Style Pointers

Consider buying a quality sofa that's within your budget and spending less money on humbler items to fashion around it, such as flea market finds, inexpensive office lighting, and throw rugs. If your budget allows for foam only, toss some pretty down-filled throw pillows on the sofa and chair. Those will look smashing and last forever! If you can't afford down-filled throw pillows, substitute a mix of down and feathers around a foam core or purchase ready-made forms with feathers.

Here are some tips on choosing a good sofa or chair:

◆ Make sure it's comfortable—not too soft, not too firm.

◆ Look for soft pillows—no hard foam.

◆ The piece should have good "bones"— lines of the design are well-proportioned.

◆ Check that the feet, if exposed, are substantial enough for the size of seating.

◆ If the piece is upholstered, make sure it is nicely tailored—seams are straight, cording in the right place.

◆ Look for upholstery that will last—fabric appropriate for use.

Don't buy a moderately priced sofa and keep the matching pillows (especially if they are firm foam ones). Add some feather or down-filled pillows in a contrasting fabric and pattern and position them askew on the sofa, not in the corners. This will impart a more eclectic look.

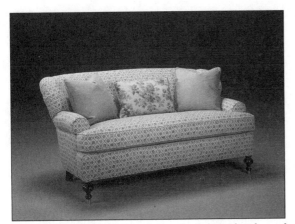 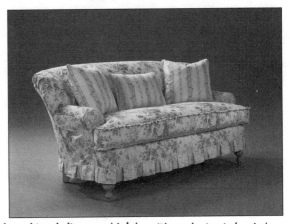

**Change the look of a plain sofa (left) with a loose box-pleat skirted slipcover (right).**    *(Photos by Lee Industries)*

A variety of sofa styles.

A variety of chair styles.

Maybe you've picked out a lovely sofa, but now you're not sure where to put it in the room. Try positioning your sofa on an angle in the corner of the room. It will be a very intimate spot. Add a folding screen behind it, a live plant or two, or *torchiere* lighting. This arrangement can make a room feel bigger, and the folding screen conceals unexpected storage space in the corner.

### Decorating 101

A **torchiere** is a floor lamp with a reflector bowl (inverted shade) for casting light upward so as to give indirect illumination.

## Slip-Covered Seating

Do you love the sofa or chair you have, but not the fabric? Before you replace it, consider a slipcover. It will improve the look of the piece tenfold and can save you money. Depending on the slipcover fabric you choose, the slipcover could be much less than the price of a new sofa or chair. Slipcovers can be baggy and loose for a relaxed, informal look (and machine washable!) or tailored and snug for a traditional feel. Custom-made slipcovers are the way to go for precision fit and best style, but slipcovers can also be purchased through catalogs. They are reasonably priced, but don't have the cachet that a custom-fit slipcover does.

If you want a luxurious look but don't have the budget, try throwing a painter's canvas cloth over a sofa—instant and chic slipcover! Another idea is to search flea markets or junk shops for vintage sofas that have "good bones" and are in good shape. Restuff the cushions with feathers or a mixture of down and feathers. Have a slipcover made, and you have a unique sofa with style! Or you can attempt to sew a slipcover yourself. (See Chapter 8 for directions on how to make a slipcover, as well as more information on using slipcovers.)

# The Case for Case Goods

Case goods—armoires, tables, dressers, desks, or benches—can be made of many materials. Wood is still the most popular choice for furniture today. It's timeless, durable, and beautiful for all styles of decorating. There are many types of wood—and different descriptive terms—that you should be familiar with when choosing wood furniture:

◆ **Hard woods** include oak, birch, cherry, mahogany, and maple, to name a few. They are generally more expensive than soft woods and are selected for the beauty of their grain. They are the most durable woods.

◆ **Soft woods** include pine and fir, both less expensive than hard wood. Soft wood dents and scratches easily but is favored by designers for its coarser grain and humble beauty. Cedar, although a soft wood, is more expensive but durable and is usually used for outdoor furniture.

◆ **Wood products** is a term that refers to wood-based substitutes for solid wood, such as particle board. This common product is manufactured from small wood fragments that are bonded with synthetic resins. Wood products are less expensive than solid wood. Built from wood waste

products, they are more environmentally sound. They are specified to lower costs and save trees. It is a stable product (doesn't warp) and paints well, but it is not as strong as solid wood.

**Homematters**

Many designers are specifying MDF (medium density fiber) board, a wood product for a wood substitute for custom-built bookshelves, cabinets, and other furniture. Although less expensive than wood and more stable (it doesn't warp), MDF should be painted to conceal its fabrication. It is also not as strong as wood, but it is easily worked.

Case good styles.

Be sure to check out the sales tag on wood furnishings and know what the terms mean:

♦ **Solid hardwood.** The exposed parts on furniture are made of a hardwood such as mahogany, oak, maple, birch, or cherry, but this doesn't mean the entire piece is hardwood.

♦ **Veneers.** These are thin slices of wood adhered to a core of solid wood, plywood, or particle board that allow for inlaid pattern surfaces. Hardwood veneers and all-wood furniture include a veneer of hardwood bonded to a wood product.

♦ **Solids and veneers.** Can be some solid wood parts and wood veneers or laminates bonded to particle board.

♦ **Finishes.** "Fruitwood," "cherry," or "oak" finish is the color of stains used, not the type of wood.

♦ **Distressed wood.** A process used to give an old look to new woods; the surface is beaten with light chains and rubbed to develop a patina.

## Learning the Local Joints

The types of joints used in joining furniture parts are crucial to a piece of furniture's quality, durability, longevity, and appearance. Take a look at the following kinds of joints:

♦ **Butt.** A simple joint made by nailing or gluing two ends together. It is the weakest of joints. Furniture made with these joints would be of the lowest quality. Butt joints are not used for structural stability.

♦ **Tongue and groove.** A projection of one edge that fits into a matching groove. This is a strong joint that is used on drawers and wood flooring.

♦ **Doweled.** One or more small pegs used to join two edges. This is a strong joint that's used on upholstery frames and chairs.

♦ **Mortise and tenon.** One of the strongest joints, a groove (mortise) on one edge is cut to fit a projection (tenon) on the other edge. Glue and screws may be added for extra strength. This type of joint can be used to join the frames of chairs and tables.

♦ **Dovetail.** A series of fan-shaped projections that fit into a series of grooves. Fine craftsmen use these to secure joints on drawers.

TYPICAL JOINTS

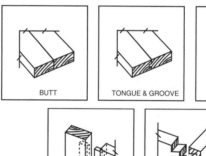
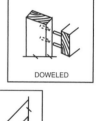

**The way wood is joined affects the durability of a piece of furniture.**

## More Than Wood for Case Goods

Wood has for centuries been the primary material used in constructing hard goods, but in recent times, new manufacturing and design processes have given us furniture made in a host of solid materials. Who knows what the next century will bring?

♦ Plastics provide sturdy, durable, lightweight, and easily maintained pieces that are impervious to moisture. Outdoor use of plastics makes great sense, but high-tech laminates are still popular for indoor use because of their slickness and moderate price range.

◆ Glass is used to protect the tops of wood furniture or to make coffee table and dining table tops combined with metal or wood. The size, thickness, and shape of the glass determine its price. Marble is used in similar applications.

◆ Metals such as brass, steel, wrought iron, copper, and aluminum are used to make furniture for inside and outside use. The increased appeal of artificially aged materials has made for a wider range of choices, with imitations of verdigris, pewter, and bronze. Rusted metal is all the rage for eclectic interiors.

◆ Wicker is actually a weaving process, but its use as a material for furniture for indoors or outdoors is popular today. Fibers of willow or rattan are woven around a frame. Quality wicker that will last is sturdy and tightly woven. Styles vary from simple and natural to quite ornate and lacquered.

◆ Faux bois is a false wood look that can be made from clay, stone, or concrete with an applied wood pattern. It is an artistic form of furniture used for mirror frames, tables, and accessories.

A set of pretty wicker porch furniture could also work in an indoor sunroom or other casual area.
*(Photo by Brunswig & Fils)*

# A Handy Buyer's Check List

Now that you've learned everything from the different types of woods and soft goods available to the importance of knowing the quality of joints used, here is a rundown of the kinds of questions you should be asking yourself before buying any piece of furniture:

❑ Does the furniture wobble?

❑ Does the furniture grain match?

❑ Is the finish applied evenly and is it of the same color? Are the corners and carving free of drips and runs?

❑ Is the distressing too fake-looking?

❑ How is the piece joined together?

   If the furniture is wood, is a strong joint used?

   If plastic, is it smoothly molded?

   If metal, are the joints solid and secure?

   If glass, are the edges smooth?

❑ Do the drawers slide in and out easily? Are the insides snag-free and free of excess glue?

❑ If the piece has cabinets, do the doors swing correctly and do they align?

❑ Is the hardware securely fastened? Are the pulls on the drawers attached with screws?

❑ Is the upholstery durable enough for the intended use? Chintz, for example, will not hold up in a children's playroom.

❑ Are the pieces in colors that work for the intended use? Hot pink painted wood might not be the right choice for your husband's office!

❑ Do the styles match your lifestyle? If your life is casual, a delicate gold-leaf table might look out of place and not be useful.

# Tricks of the Trade

Did you know that a sofa can be made from a twin mattress and box spring? Place the mattress on top of the box spring on the floor. Place the length against a wall, add some roll style pillows on the ends for "arms," and place some large toss pillows along the wall side for an instant sofa that looks stylish, intriguing—and a great place for a nap!

I often use upholstered chairs for seating in a living room instead of sofas. This way each person has a comfortable seat. I also love to use dressers as end tables. They serve double duty as storage and add height to an arrangement by being taller than the sofa backs. I also place a low table at the foot of a bed in a master bedroom. This allows for impromptu casual dinners, favorite books to be displayed, and a place to hold a bathrobe until morning. This way your night table doesn't get crowded with clutter.

To add sentimental meaning to my husband's ordinary desk, I painted a facsimile of a love letter addressed to him. You can stencil any case goods with meaningful motifs that you will treasure for a lifetime.

**A twin mattress and box spring make a chic sofa.**

## The Least You Need to Know

◆ When choosing any piece of furniture, remember that comfort, construction, and materials are as important as aesthetic design.

◆ The comfort of upholstered furnishings depends on their size, fabric, design, and construction. Make sure the furniture is made of hardwood framing and has solid construction.

◆ Case goods can be made in many grades of wood, metal, plastics, glass, and wicker. Construction quality varies.

◆ Alternative uses of seating and case goods makes for individualized rooms.

# In This Chapter

- ◆ The basics of fibers and weaves
- ◆ Decorators' favorite fabrics
- ◆ Using fabric throughout your home
- ◆ How to make a pillow and a slipcover
- ◆ Tips for mixing patterns and fabrics
- ◆ From the decorator's desk

**Chapter 8**

# Living in a Material World

Fabric makes a house a home. It brings texture, pattern, color, and warmth (or coolness) to living spaces. It softens the angular lines of furniture and architecture, making a room look and feel comfortable. With unlimited colors and patterns, fabrics can set varied moods for all the rooms you live in.

Knowing a bit about the wide range of fabrics used in decorating and their construction will help you select the best fabrics for your design and functional needs. Get to know the many fabric personalities, even those you may not initially be attracted to. Look at a large selection. Feel each fabric. Picture how it will work in your home. Becoming a more informed decorator will help you create a warm, personal ambiance in your home.

## Getting to Know Fibers and Weaves

Fabrics are made of natural or manufactured fibers. Natural fibers, such as cotton, linen, wool, and silk, are derived from plants or animals. Some manmade fibers are derived from materials found in nature, such as cellulose. Rayon is regenerated cellulose from materials like wood chips, whereas acetate is chemically changed cellulose.

Most manufactured fibers, called synthetics, are created from chemicals that are formed into strands or filaments by machines. Familiar synthetic fibers include polyester and acrylic.

The properties of different fibers determine their strength, their *hand*, how they feel, and how durable they are. The type and weight of fibers used and the way they are woven affect their appearance and performance. For example, a tightly woven fabric with highly twisted yarns will have the strength to upholster heavily used furniture. A loosely woven fabric, on the other hand, will be best for drapery, bedding, or light decorative uses.

**Decorating 101**

**Hand** refers to the drapability of a fabric. A good hand is a fabric that falls or drapes easily when placed over your hand, such as a faille, washed cotton, unglazed toile, or fine muslin. This kind of fabric is easy to work with.

Most fabrics are variations of three basic weaves:

◆ A plain weave is the simplest. One fiber is carried over another in a regular pattern, usually at right angles, similar to the weaving of a potholder made by a child. Changing the weight or texture of the fibers creates a unique material.

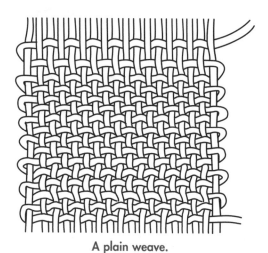

A plain weave.

◆ Twill weaves form diagonal lines. Twills are sturdy fabrics that have better draping quality than plain weaves of the same fiber. Many jeans are made with this weave.

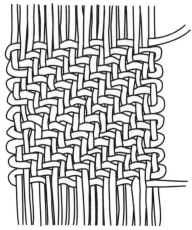

A twill weave.

◆ Satin weaves are very smooth in construction and allow light to reflect from their surfaces.

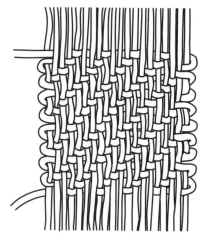

A satin weave.

# Decorators' Favorites

There are fabrics for every style, budget, and use. To help you make the right choices, take a look at the following decorator favorites:

- **Brocade.** A heavier-weight fabric, richly decorated with raised patterns that resemble embroidery. Brocade was historically made of silk, but now is made of synthetics and cottons.

- **Burlap.** A loosely woven, coarse fabric of jute that is simple but very textural, used for shades, drapes, dust ruffles, and table skirts. Burlap is popular in today's interiors and is very inexpensive.

- **Canvas.** A heavy, tightly woven cloth of cotton or linen that is perfect for shades and outdoor cushions. Sailcloth is similar but lighter in weight and great for draperies, cushions, slipcovers, and shower curtains.

- **Chambray.** A lightweight cotton in a close weave that has a "frosted" appearance. Popular today is a blue denim that resembles lightweight denim. Good for light slipcovers, pillows, and draperies.

- **Chenille.** A fuzzy-surfaced cloth that is produced by clipped, twisted yarns, it is popular today for soft upholstery, throws, trims, and accessories.

- **Chintz.** A fine cotton in a glazed finish in solids and popular florals. Used primarily for light slipcovers, pillows, and draperies.

- **Damask.** A reversible, flat fabric richly patterned by a combination of weaves. It is a sturdy and lustrous fabric. Once made of silk, it is now available in various fibers. At one time considered formal, it is now combined with homespun fabrics in eclectic combinations. Damask is used primarily for upholstery and decorative accessories.

- **Denim.** A coarse, twill, sturdy cotton cloth used for jeans but also as contemporary sturdy slipcovers and pillows. It was first made in Nimes, France, hence *de Nimes* (from Nimes).

- **Faille.** A plain, woven fabric that has fine ribs with good draping qualities and a luster.

- **Gingham.** A lightweight cotton cloth with a checked pattern, usually of two colors, typically red and white or blue and white. Great in informal interiors and pleasantly unexpected in formal interiors. For curtains, cushions, and lightweight slipcovers.

- **Lace.** Delicate, open-weave cloth made by hand or machine of cotton, linen, silk, or synthetics. Often used for draperies, table covers, and pillows to add an informal, romantic atmosphere.

- **Matelasse.** A double-woven fabric with puckered surface effects. Used for draperies, upholstery, bedspreads, and slipcovers. Especially popular today in natural cotton.

- **Muslin.** A plain cotton that varies in weight. Unbleached muslin is natural with brown flecks, and bleached muslin is much whiter. It is inexpensive. Muslin makes good slipcovers and plain draperies for a relaxed interior.

- **Silk.** A lustrous natural fiber that varies in appearance. Some silks are woven with their natural slubs, which enhance their appearance. Dyed silks are usually of bright, beautiful colors that are stunning for draperies and lightweight upholstery and slipcovers.

- **Tapestry.** A heavy cloth (even heavier than brocade or damask), woven by hand or machine, that shows pictorial scenes or floral patterns. Tapestry is typically used for wall hangings or as upholstery fabric and made from cotton, wool, or cotton blends.

- **Terrycloth.** An absorbent cotton cloth made with a pile of uncut loops used in toweling. Often used for bathroom or vanity slipcovered seating and pillows.

- **Ticking.** Heavy, closely woven fabric of cotton. Usually in a stripe such as blue and white, black and white, or brown and white. Great for upholstery, slipcovers, and decorative accessories. Fits into many styles of décor.

This toile de Jouy fabric features eighteenth-century fantasies of the Far East with chinoiserie sailboats, pagodas, birds, and Oriental figures. *(Photo by Schumacher)*

An elegant toile de Jouy fabric covers this chaise. *(Photo by Lee Industries)*

◆ **Toile de Jouy.** Traditionally, an ivory cotton with scenic designs of pastoral life in red or navy. Originally made in Jouy, a town in France. Today toiles are made in vibrant background colors with various contrasting colors. Perfect for slipcovers, draperies, bedding, and fabric walls.

◆ **Velvet.** A heavy-weight fabric with a soft pile made of silk, cotton, or rayon. Used for upholstery, slipcovers, and draperies. Velvets that look aged and faded are popular today.

**Pro Workshop**

To add softness and sensuality to a bedroom, try using a skirted round table for a night table or drape a vanity with stylish fabric. (Be sure to read Chapter 23 for more tips on giving your bedroom a romantic look.)

# Fabric Throughout Your Home

The most common fabric uses in a home are for dressing windows (see Chapter 9) and to cover new or old furnishings. Sofas and chairs can be coordinated into any design through reupholstery or slipcovers. Reupholstery requires a fabric selection appropriate for your piece. The materials are stretched and tacked on the frame, providing a neat and tailored look. In general, reupholstery is more costly than slipcovers.

As I mentioned in Chapter 7, slipcovers are covers that go over existing upholstery. They can miraculously hide unsightly, worn, or outdated fabric and increase the longevity of a prized piece. You can buy slipcovers or have them custom made. If seasonal slipcovers are made—one for summer, one for winter—you get double the wear of your covers. Slipcovers can easily vary with your personal style. Wrinkled and loose, or neat and tailored, they adapt to all lifestyles. You can customize a cover by choosing contrasting trims and braids, mixing patterns, or adding buttons, ruffles, or bows.

Here are some do's and don'ts when it comes to choosing a slipcover:

◆ Do choose a fabric that will suit its purpose. Delicate fabrics won't work in a family room.

◆ Do purchase more fabric than required in case you need to replace a stained area.

◆ Do select an appropriate style for your personality. A ruffled skirt for a romantic bedroom? Boxy and tailored skirt or no skirt for a minimalist?

◆ Do slipcover footstools, ottomans, or old hassocks. Just a yard or two of fabric is all you need.

◆ Don't slipcover sofas or chairs that have carved wood along the top or arms.

◆ Don't slipcover structurally unsound sofas, ones that wobble or that have springs that are shot.

◆ Don't feel you must have welting, the cording that is sewn in the seams that outlines the seating. You can save a lot of money if you don't specify it (and a lot of work if you sew the slipcover yourself). A linen slipcover fabric looks smashing without welting.

If you are considering new furniture, manufacturing firms usually offer a basic muslin-covered sofa with your choice of slipcover. Mail-order catalogs like Pottery Barn offer attractive selections (see Appendix A). Some manufacturers will also accept your fabric to upholster on their frame. A price is calculated on a "customer's own material" (COM) grade. It can be a cheaper way to go. You may find a bargain price on fabric at a yard sale and, thus, save money instead of buying a similar fabric from the manufacturer's selections.

**Here are two popular slipcover styles for sofas.** *(Photos by Lee Industries)*

**Here are some popular slipcover looks for chairs.** *(Photos by Lee Industries)*

Check the Yellow Pages for professionals who make slipcovers or do reupholstery. Be sure to ask to see some of their work. Or you may want to try doing a small upholstery project yourself. If you are a beginning seamstress, start by looking over the following instructions on how to make a pillow; if you are an advanced seamstress, you may want to try sewing a slipcover on your own.

## Making a Pillow

Pillows are fabulously decorative. Their plushness adds visual softness as well as tactile beauty and comfort to any room setting. They require minimal yardage and are easy to make. Pillows made in a variety of patterns and textures give a room a casual, inviting appearance, whereas pillows placed "just so" reflect a somewhat stiffer atmosphere. If you have a basic sofa, try adding a couple of overscaled pillows about 20 to 28 inches square covered in a luxurious fabric and filled with feathers and down. Embellish with cording, fringe, or special closures. This will add drama and much-needed opulence to an otherwise bland sofa.

Make a few sketches with some of your ideas. Then follow these simple instructions.

Here's how to sew a pillow:

1. Measure both the width and the length of your pillow form.

Measure the pillow form.

2. Add ½ inch all around.
3. Cut two pieces of fabric to these dimensions.
4. With right sides facing, stitch the two pieces together all around ½ inch from edge, leaving an opening on one side wide enough to stuff the pillow form through. Clip the corners.

After stitching the two pieces together, clip the corners.

5. Turn right side out and press.
6. Insert the pillow form through the opening, making sure to fill out the corners.
7. Along the opening, turn in ½ inch and slip stitch together using long stitches so that they will undo easily when removing covers for cleaning.

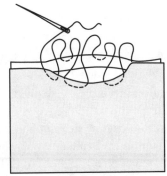

Slip stitch the opening.

**Style Pointers**

Because you need so little fabric to make a pillow, try to splurge on more luxurious fabric. It's an affordable luxury!

## Sewing a Slipcover

If you can sew a pillow, you might want to learn how to sew a slipcover. Once you know how to make a pattern for cutting out the fabric, making a slipcover doesn't take much more effort than sewing a lot of pieces together.

Here's how to make a loose slipcover for a chair:

1. Measure each section of the chair (both the front and back) at its maximum points and cut a rectangle of muslin to correspond. Be sure to allow extra material for seams and tuck-ins.

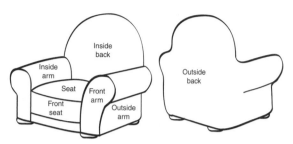

**Measure the front and back of the chair.**

2. Remove all the muslin pieces and add 1 inch all around each piece for seams and 6 inches for tuck-ins on the inside of arms, seat, and back pieces.

3. For a flat skirt with a kick pleat, measure A-B, from the bottom edge at far left to the bottom edge at far right and cut a strip of muslin to the same length by about 8½ inches wide, plus 1 inch around. Repeat this for each side of the skirt and the back piece of the chair. The pattern for the pleat (the additional length to make a pleat) should be 12 inches by 8½ inches deep, plus seam allowances.

**For a flat skirt with a kick pleat, measure A to B plus 12 inches for each pleat by 8½ inches deep. Be sure to add seam allowances for both length and depth.**

4. If there is a cushion, make a muslin pattern for this as well, the same way you did for the chair.

5. Once all the pattern pieces have been made, pin each piece in place onto the chair, wrong side out, and then pin the pieces to one another, right sides facing in the following order:

> Outside back to inside back
>
> Inside back to seat
>
> Seat to front seat
>
> Seat to inside arm
>
> Inside arm to outside arm
>
> Pin the front arms in place

6. Before unpinning the pattern, mark on each piece its identity, the direction of the fabric, the wrong side, top, bottom, the pinned seamline, and along each seamline, indicate which section it is to be joined to.

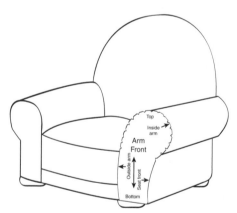

**Marking the pattern.**

7. Lay out the fabric, right side up, and pin the pieces on it, also right side up. Keep all the grain lines parallel with the selvedges (finished edges). As each piece is cut out, pin a label to it for identification and mark the top and bottom.

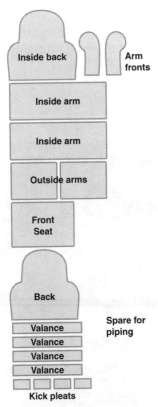

Inside back

Arm fronts

Inside arm

Inside arm

Outside arms

Front Seat

Back

Valance
Valance
Valance
Valance

Spare for piping

Kick pleats

**Lay out the pattern pieces.**

8. Pin the pieces together on the chair to check to see if they fit, working in the same sequence as for the pattern. Remove the cover and baste the seams together. Stitch the pieces together leaving an opening of between 12 inches and 18 inches on one of the back seams for a zipper or hooks and eyes at 4-inch intervals.

# Artful Combinations

Just as you can mix colors and textures, you can learn how to mix fabric patterns and colors by following these simple ideas:

◆ Get the largest samples of fabrics and observe them together with your carpets or rugs and paint colors.

◆ Study photos in wallcovering books from top designers. See how the pros coordinate their fabrics.

◆ Study existing color combinations in rugs, antique textiles, and historical décor.

◆ Try patterns that are the same but with different colors (for example, blue-and-white gingham check and red-and-white gingham check).

◆ Reverse colors often work, too. Try blue floral on a white background with white floral on a blue background.

◆ Mix opposite textures—coarse and soft, flat and nubby, plain and luxurious. (For example, a blue-and-white cotton toile with a blue damask combines simple textures with more ornate textures.)

◆ Vary the scales of patterns with large, medium, and small prints.

◆ Link patterns with color, mood, and weight.

◆ Mix geometric patterns with florals.

◆ Combine unusual fabrics like denim and velvet or silk and burlap.

◆ Study well-designed ready-made coordinates by home furnishing companies like Ralph Lauren, Martha Stewart, and Laura Ashley.

◆ Experiment until you are happy!

**Pro Workshop**

Stuck on only one print? Relax. It's okay. At least there is no worry of mixing and matching! Try these helpful tips to make your room sing:

- ◆ Spread the pattern around the room.
- ◆ Vary textures in furnishings with glass, metal, and wood for added interest.
- ◆ A bigger statement is made by using a bolder print.
- ◆ Paint walls a strong paint color to equal the bold print.
- ◆ Add vintage textiles or a patterned rug for a bit of contrast.

The dark solid and checked pillows are a nice contrast to the neutral sofa. *(Photo by Lee Industries)*

# Tricks of the Trade

Decorators often use fabrics to add unusual textures, infuse color to interiors, and cover unsightly furniture. Here are some of my favorite ways to use fabric:

- ◆ Make an interesting curtain from burlap (available at garden stores). The light filtering through shows off the rustic weave.
- ◆ Create a patchwork quilt or pillow out of old blue jeans.
- ◆ Slipcover the backs of dining or side chairs.

**Slipcovered side chairs.**

- ◆ Use fabric scraps as gift ties, to bundle notes or letters, and for other creative uses.
- ◆ Use fabric as a wallcovering (see Chapter 6).
- ◆ Cover a lampshade with fabric (refer to Chapter 9).
- ◆ For an instant airy canopy, run a length of 60-inch lace on a four-poster bed from the posts at the foot of the bed along the bed frame, behind the headboard to the floor. Or hang mosquito netting from the bed frame for a romantic, *Out of Africa* look.

Drape a bed with lace for a romantic look—no sewing required!    *(Photo by Gear Home, Bettye M. Musham, Chairwoman/CEO)*

Chandelier chain cover.    *(Photo by M. Hackett)*

◆ Create a custom-made shower curtain.

◆ Cover a chandelier chain with a piece of fabric ribbon.

## The Least You Need to Know

◆ Fabrics add an essential element of comfort to every room, as well as patterns, color, and textures.

◆ Furniture can be revived with fabric, through reupholstery and slipcovers.

◆ You can learn the art of combining fabric patterns and colors through samples and observation.

◆ Decorators use fabric in unusual ways. You can be just as clever by learning their tricks of the trade.

# In This Chapter

- ◆ A gallery of glass-type windows
- ◆ Curtain possibilities with panache
- ◆ The fabulous final touches
- ◆ Curtain magic demystified
- ◆ Tricks of the trade

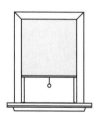
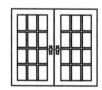

# Chapter 9

# Windows That Say Wow!

Our eyes naturally turn toward light, but windows are more than an important focal point of any room. Window styles and their coverings play a big role in decorating as well as a practical purpose. Well-dressed windows emphasize the distinct architectural style of the windows and the room. If necessary, the dressings can also disguise a window that has been oddly placed or a window style that is unappealing. Window dressings also introduce dramatic design elements that can transform a space, whether you're using long and flowing curtains or simple, trim shutters.

There are window covers that complement every décor; therefore, you can coordinate surrounding furnishings and wall coverings. Finally, window coverings serve many practical purposes, such as control of light, added privacy, and important thermal insulation. Learning the many options in windows and window dressings—including the right terms for the many different elements—is the first step in choosing the right window treatments for your home and lifestyle.

## A World of Windows

Just the way a window is shaped and how it functions are the first factors to consider when you're deciding on your options. Some standard windows styles include …

- ◆ **Double-hung.** The most common window, with sashes that slide up and down.
- ◆ **Casement.** Windows that are hinged at the side and swing in or out.
- ◆ **Picture.** A large, fixed pane of glass with possible movable sections at the sides.
- ◆ **Awning.** Horizontal panels of glass with possible movable sections at the sides.

◆ **Bay.** A group of three or more windows set at angles that project to the outside. Window seats are often built in.

◆ **Bow.** A curved window that projects to the outside with a possible window seat built in.

◆ **Palladian.** A curved arch at the top of a window.

◆ **Jalousie.** Narrow strips of glass that open out to the desired angle.

◆ **French doors and sliding glass doors.** French doors are double doors with glass panes that swing into the room. Sliding doors are double doors of glass that glide on a track, one over the other when open.

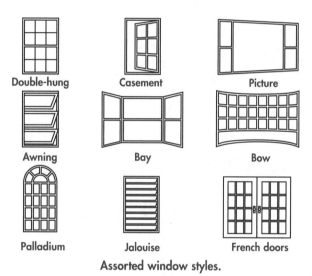

Assorted window styles.

# The Well-Covered Window: Draperies or Curtains?

Draperies are window dressings that open and close on a rod that is threaded with a pulley cord system. They frame the window when they are open and completely cover the window when closed. Drapes are usually at least the height of the window, and often are longer.

Curtains are simpler covers, opened and closed by hand and attached to a rod with pockets, ties, or rings. Curtains can vary from café, window, or floor lengths.

Clockwise from top left: café curtain, sill-length, tier, and floor-length curtains.

### Style Pointers

Full-length curtains in a living room or dining room look elegant and formal if highly constructed with linings, tiebacks, and ornate top valances. Stiff traditional chintzes or damasks take on a Bohemian feel if left unlined, loosely hung, and unadorned of muslin, silk, or sheer fabrics. Sill-length curtains in casual fabrics of florals, ticking, denim, burlap, or toiles are good choices for more casually styled rooms.

Here are some ideas for dressing various windows:

◆ Casement windows open in or out. Be sure to consider the cranking mechanism when mounting curtains; they should mount on the outside so that the curtain falls over the cranks. Individual swing arm or fixed curtain rods work well. For windows that swing in, consider a curtain style that does not interfere with the window's operation. Curtains mounted on the inside of each window, mounted shades, or blinds above the molding allow easy operation.

◆ French doors share the same problems as casement windows that swing in. You must affix curtains, blinds, or shades to each door panel or mount draperies so they draw completely to the side or top. Make sure the rod extends beyond the frame so they can be drawn out of the way of doors. Sliding glass doors need to be treated with coverings that allow easy access to the door opening. Blinds, shades, and draperies are all viable options. Be sure to mount them far enough above the frame or have draperies draw off to the side.

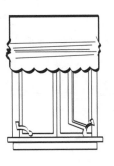 

Casement windows swing in or out.

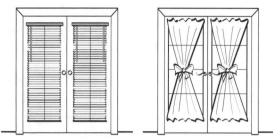

**French doors/sliders must be treated with window coverings that allow the doors to operate.**

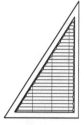

**Windows with circular, triangular, or arched shapes require custom fitted coverings or can be left unadorned.**

◆ Windows with circular, triangular, or arched shapes need to be custom fitted with blinds, shades, shutters, or shirred fabric coverings. If these windows do not pose a privacy issue, they are often best left untreated to enhance their architectural beauty.

◆ Corner windows can be treated individually but cohesively to look like continuous windows. Be sure window treatments don't interfere with the window's operation.

**Corner windows can be covered identically to look like one continuous set.**

◆ Bay and bow windows may need separate coverings for each window. Shades, shutters, and blinds give a neat appearance. Full draperies can be mounted on the outside frame across the window, giving the illusion of more depth to the bay or bow. Curving bow windows can be covered in draperies with a flexible rod that mounts along the top curve of the window.

Sliding windows.

**Bay and bow windows can be covered in many different styles.**

◆ Sliding windows require window coverings that allow privacy and light control. Blinds, shades, draperies, and valances each present unique looks. A combination of blinds and drapes allow control of privacy and light during the day. If privacy and light are not an issue, the view from the window might be all the adornment you need!

**Single windows can be dressed in many different styles to match your room décor.**

◆ For single windows, consider where the window is placed in the room. Should it be dramatically dressed or minimally covered—or not covered at all?

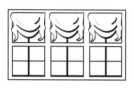

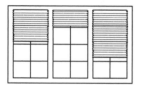
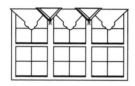

**Multiple sets of windows allow the outdoors in!**

◆ Multiple sets of windows, those identical windows placed side by side, are usually in a room to increase light during the day. If privacy is not an issue, left untreated they make a strong architectural statement. If the windows are covered, they can be treated individually or with one set of full draperies. If minimal dressing is wanted, a valance placed on the top frame softens edges.

**Homematters** _____

Curtain and drapery lining protect your fabric from the sun, block light, give body to fabrics and provide insulation. Often sheer fabrics do not need lining and drape beautifully without them. "Tea-stained" linings in particular are extremely popular today. These linings are instantly "aged" with tea colors to take on an antique appearance.

# Neat Windows: Shades, Blinds, and Shutters

A shade is any window treatment that closes from top to bottom and that covers from casing to casing. Fabric shades vary from inexpensive plain roller types to more expensive and often custom made festoons operated with a cord system. Shades are perfect for windows that have very little wall space on either side for full draperies.

Blinds are slats made of metal, plastic, or wood that also raise and lower with a cord system. All blinds can be used alone for minimal dressing or under curtains or draperies for a layered, textured look. Some blinds have slats that can be angled for desired light and privacy.

Shutters are mounted wood panels that can be opened and closed. They add dimension to any window. They are mounted in half-window or full-window lengths, again depending on light and privacy needs. Louvered shutters enable you to control light by raising the slats up and down; solid-paneled shutters control light by being opened or closed.

Here's a closer look at your options:

◆ *Roller shades* are a simple and neat treatment. A piece of cloth the size of the window is wound and attached to a roller, to be raised and lowered with a simple pull. When raised, roller shades take up a minimum of space. Roller shades are available in ready-made linenlike fabrics or can be customized with your own fabrics and decorative edges.

◆ *Roman shades* are sewn with horizontal tucks that stack neatly when drawn with a system of cords and drawstrings. They offer a softer look than roller shades but are still neat and tailored.

◆ *Austrian shades* are raised by a series of cords and drawstrings into generous and billowy folds. Trims, fringes, and ruffles add to the extravagant style.

◆ *Pleated shades* are made of permanently pleated paper or stiffened polyester fabric. They are operated by cords and drawstrings as well. Generally quite inexpensive, they are either used alone as a minimal dressing or under full curtains and valances for privacy and light control.

◆ *Venetian blinds* are made of 2-inch slats—usually plastic, metal, or wood—that can be raised or lowered with cords and tapes and tilted to desired angles. Mini and micro blinds are similar, but their slats are inch or less in width.

◆ *Matchstick blinds* are made from split bamboo, woven together with a series of strings to roll or pleat up when raised.

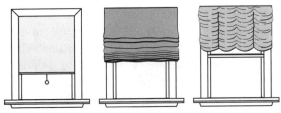

Left to right: pull shade, Roman shade, Austrian shade.

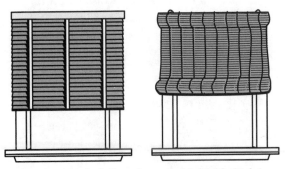

Venetian blinds (left) and matchstick blinds (right).

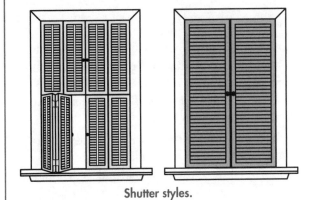

Shutter styles.

# Final Touches: Trims and Tiebacks

As you have learned throughout this book, the final touches on any decorating project are those that make the room sing! Don't neglect details that make your curtains go from fine to fabulous without much fuss, such as the selection of a curtain rod, trim on the curtain, or the style of the tieback. Each selection can add significant style with charm or polish depending on the materials.

Select curtain rods with a decorator's eye. Rods are an integral part of the overall design of curtains today. Some are works of art on their own with special metals or woods and added finials made of glass, metal, or wood in shapes and jewel-like colors.

### Pro Workshop

Create finials that reflect your personal style! Use your glue gun to apply pinecones, shells, or stones to the ends of a curtain rod.

Trims are used to accentuate the lines of a particular window covering and act as an integral part of the overall design. Braids, ribbon, and cording can border the leading edges or hems of a shade, drape, or blind. Ruffles, fringe, and tassels add soft dimension.

Tiebacks hold curtains on either side of a window. They can be straight or contoured pieces of fabric of the same material as the drape, or they can be made of contrasting fabric. They can be trimmed with various cording or ruffles. Solid or multicolored tassled cords or braids can hold a curtain back with a decorative effect. Metal hooks, usually made of brass, act as stationary tiebacks. They are attached to the sides of the knobs that attach to the sides of the windows and protrude from the wall to hold the curtain fabric. Tiebacks can also be "built-in" curtain panels with strings that are pulled tightly to form a tied-back look.

A tieback's placement affects the overall look of the curtain: Placed high on a window, a curtain will be tighter-looking at the top; placed low, a curtain will drape fuller at the top.

A curtain without conventional tiebacks is "tied back" with invisible cords sewn into the back panels.

Curtains and draperies can enhance window features and disguise less-appealing ones by proper placement. Here are some ideas:

◆ Make a window look wider by extending your curtain rod beyond the window so the curtain can be completely pulled off the window, allowing in more light.

Make a window look wider.

◆ Make a window look taller by mounting your curtain rod 8 to 12 inches above the window frame. If you add a valance between the top of the window and the rod, the illusion is maintained even when the curtains or draperies are drawn.

**Make a window look taller.**

◆ Disguise architectural irregularities such as a window placed next to a door. Treat the window and the door the same with full-length draperies that cover both the window and door when drawn.

**Disguise architectural irregularities.**

◆ Make a window look shorter by using a trimmed and elegantly shaped valance. The more ornate the valance, the grander the effect.

**Reduce the height with a valance.**

◆ Make a window look narrower by using tiebacks and joining curtains at the top.

**Reduce the width with tiebacks.**

◆ Ensure curtains do not obscure a beautiful window. Use a rod wide enough so the curtains clear the window when open.

**Enhance a beautiful window.**

### Pro Workshop

Some windows need no dressing or enhancement. If they are architecturally pleasing and privacy isn't an issue, leave them uncovered!

# How to Measure a Window

To make shopping for draperies easier, it is smart to have several measurements on hand so that you can ask salespeople for estimates on custom-made draperies, or so that you'll know whether ready-made draperies (usually in standard sizes) would fit your windows. Always use a metal tape measure for accurate measurements. You will need to know a number of dimensions to see which window treatments can work for you.

To measure lengths, do the following:

A. Measure the width of the window from casing to casing.

B. Measure the length of the window from the top of the casing to the top of the sill.

C. Measure from the top of the window to the bottom of the sill.

D. Measure from the top of the window to the floor.

E. Measure the inside of the window from the sash to the top of the sill.

F. Measure the inside of the window from jamb to jamb.

G. Measure the lower portion of the window from the top of the lower sash (if there is one) to the top of the sill.

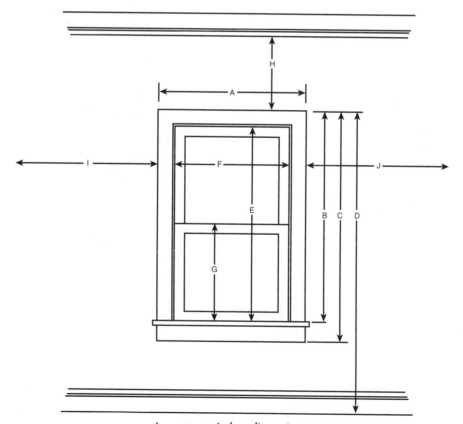

Important window dimensions.

H. Measure from the top of the window to the ceiling or ceiling molding.

I. Measure the wall area from outside of the left casing to any obstruction, such as a radiator, corner of the walls, or another window. (If there are any light switches, draw them on your illustration.)

J. Measure the wall area from outside of the right casing to any obstruction, such as a radiator, corner of the walls, or another window. (If there are any light switches, draw them on your illustration.)

If a rod is present, you will need to measure the width of the rod and how far it projects. All lengths are measured from the top of the rod to the desired length, unless it is a rod with rings. In that case, measure from the bottom of the rings.

## Tricks of the Trade

Some of my favorite signature details with windows include the following:

◆ Set off an ivory or tan painted room with black shades.

◆ Use school-green roller shades in a red library room for an interesting contrast.

◆ Tack a lace tablecloth in a window for an unusual, romantic look.

◆ Make a half curtain with old drawer or cabinet fronts. Hinge the old drawer or cabinet fronts together and place it vertically in the window to form shutter-height panels. The hinges allow you to open and close them.

◆ For a charming look, hang weathered outdoor shutters indoors on the frame of an interior window. If you only have one set, hang them in a bathroom with one window, or a single window at the top of a stairwell or at the end of a hall.

◆ Make over a room by fitting children's artwork into the window panes.

**A child's artwork makes a fun window covering.**
*(Photo by M. Hackett)*

◆ Use garden burlap as curtain material.

**Simple garden burlap transforms a window.** *(Photo by M. Hackett)*

◆ Add old drawer hardware as pulls for roller shades.

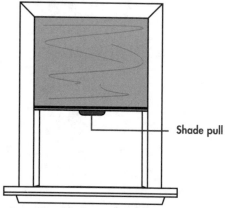

Drawer hardware for shade pulls.

◆ Lean a series of pretty paintings on the window sill as a "curtain" to "cover" the lower half.

◆ Use plain white organdy panels to imitate a summer cottage look. When the breeze blows, the curtains imitate sails on a boat.

Art stacked against a window makes a clever cover-up.    *(Photo by M. Hackett)*

◆ For a simple way to drape a new window, use clip-on rings, available at any home store, to hang panels of fabric. The clip-on ring (similar to a shower curtain ring) is a metal circle that when squeezed together opens a clip that clamps on fabric easily. Use approximately one every 6 inches on each panel. Mount the curtain rod, run the rod through the rings, and voilà, instant drapery panels, no sewing required! A flat panel of lace or a length of sheer fabric can be hung in the same manner.

## The Least You Need to Know

◆ Critiquing the shape and style of window will help you to select a proper curtain or drape.

◆ Window dressings include many styles of drapes and curtains and such dressing "extras" as trims, tiebacks, and rod accessories.

◆ By selecting the right window coverings, you can enhance features or mask less-appealing ones.

◆ Add pizzazz to your windows by following designers' tricks of the trade.

# In This Chapter

- Lighting design 101: types of lighting and fixtures
- Today's lighting styles
- Lighting ideas throughout the house
- A do-it-yourself lighting project: making your own lamp
- Lighting tips from a pro

# Chapter 10

# Putting Your Home in the Right Light

Interior lighting not only illuminates dark rooms, creating mood and atmosphere, it emphasizes areas of importance and highlights prized possessions. But selecting the best interior lighting for both practical illumination and as a powerful decorating tool isn't automatic. You need to develop a lighting plan for each room that serves your lifestyle and complements your personal decorating style.

Note the activities that are performed in each room, the ambiance you want to create, and the activity "zones" or decorative elements you want to spotlight. Define the type of lighting you need, and then select the style of lighting fixture and bulb that fits the lighting purpose and enhances the character of the room.

## The Basics of Lighting Design

Your lighting plan should include several types of lighting: general, task, accent, decorative, and kinetic. Most spaces will incorporate all five types, working together to optimally light your home. Let's take a closer look at these options.

### General

This is a home's basic replacement for sunlight: It's the overall illumination for regular activity at nighttime. General, or ambient, lighting provides a comfortable level of brightness, allowing adequate vision to safely function in a room. It is usually produced by ceiling- or wall-mounted fixtures, in the specific form of chandeliers, recessed lighting, or track lights. General lighting is fundamental to a lighting plan.

## Task

This is the illumination assigned to help you conduct specific tasks such as reading, cooking, performing hobbies, or playing games. More focused than general lighting, task lighting should be bright enough to prevent eyestrain and not cause distracting glare and shadows. Varying with the kind of task or activity it serves, this lighting can be provided by recessed and track lighting, pendant (hanging) lighting, and portable lamps.

Task lighting can often be adjustable and can be positioned directly on the work at hand. And the brightness levels can vary with different tasks—for instance, the area and amount of light you need to play a card game with four or more people around a table.

## Accent

This is an important type of lighting for decorating, because it focuses on elements of visual interest, emphasizing the aesthetics of a room. Accent lighting can spotlight paintings, house plants, sculpture, china, and other prized possessions; or it can emphasize the stylish texture of a wall, drapery, or outdoor landscaping. These focal points add to the drama of a room.

To be effective, accent lighting requires at least three times as much light on the focal point as the room's ambient lighting provides. It usually comes from track or recessed fixtures on a ceiling or wall-mounted fixtures. Traditional picture lights and spotlights are common accent lighting fixtures.

## Decorative

Decorative lighting is used as a contrived statement by many architects and decorators as part of the total room design. It could be anything from a spotlight on a sparkle disco ball that shines an artistic array of ceiling lights to a neon sign or sculpture. Decorative lighting often is the whimsical lighting in a room.

## Kinetic

Kinetic light is the "moving" light that candles or a real fire provide. Both seem to satisfy that need for the glow that only a real fire can fulfill. Even a television switched on with its neon light is moving light in a room. The most dramatic kinetic light is of course the sun, the eternal living flame that shifts its light effects throughout the day in your home.

 **Style Pointers**

Be careful when placing candlelight. I almost burned my cabinet after overzealously placing small votive candles throughout shelving. And never leave a burning candle unattended!

## Sources of Lighting: Fixtures

After knowing the type of lighting you need in a room, you can begin to choose the fixtures. Let's take a look at the options:

◆ **Portable lamps.** Fixtures such as table lamps and floor lamps used for generalized task lighting that can be moved where needed.

◆ **Pendants.** Lighting that hangs from the ceiling.

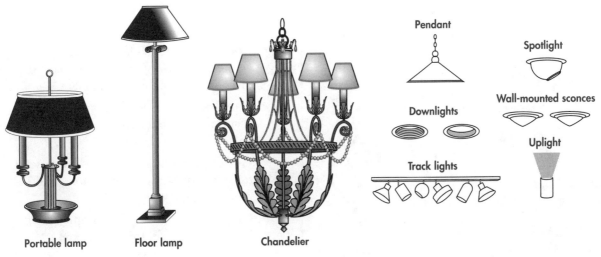

Portable lamp     Floor lamp     Chandelier

Pendant

Spotlight

Downlights

Wall-mounted sconces

Uplight

Track lights

*Several types of lighting fixtures.*

◆ **Chandelier.** Decorative pendant fixture.

◆ **Downlights.** Inconspicuously mounted on ceilings that cast light downward.

◆ **Spotlights.** Can be recessed into ceilings, mounted on tracks, wall mounted, or used individually with clips.

◆ **Track lighting.** Provides a flexible arrangement of spotlights and down lights attached to a track mounted on a ceiling.

◆ **Uplights.** Direct light at the ceiling or wall and "bathe" a surface with soft illumination.

# Today's Styles and Shapes of Lighting

Your lighting plan will probably combine at least two or three or all of the lighting types. Aesthetics as well as light quality are equally important in making choices. Study some of these traditional and contemporary choices for your home.

Contemporary table lamps include these choices:

◆ **Fontana Arte lamp.** Small oval lampshade and base both from glass with light source in base. Good accent lighting.

◆ **BestLite.** Designed by Robert Best in 1950 and still considered a classic modern lamp, a most elegant practical task light.

◆ **Miter lamp.** Metal cone secured with rivets on a modern base. Interesting shape for decoration and as an uplight.

◆ **Tango desk lamp.** Lamp whose form is as important as its function. It is a perfect task light.

◆ **TA table light.** Designed in the 1960s, a cool minimal task light with adjustable light and swivel for position.

◆ **Jielde work lamp.** A classic French industrial bench lamp, perfect for task lighting, similar to a pharmacy lamp.

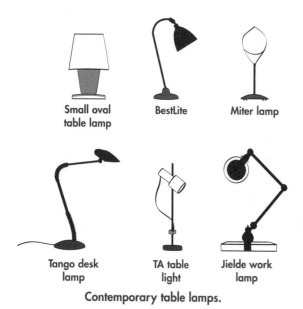

Contemporary table lamps.

Traditional table lamps include these choices:

♦ **Storm lantern.** A curve-shape glass bell used as a shield for candles.

♦ **Tole lamp.** A metal lamp (popular in the eighteenth century) with metal shade that gives localized light with no glare.

♦ **Candlestick and shade.** A pierced tin shade allows the flicker of a candle to "dance" all over the room.

♦ **Gothic lamp.** A perfect stylish and useful tall lamp to place on a worktable to illuminate a large space.

♦ **Corinthian.** A classically designed table lamp that is useful for general and task lighting.

♦ **Chinese table lamp.** A classic lamp made from the base of a Chinese urn.

♦ **Desk lamp.** A versatile and handsome lamp that is a perfect task lamp.

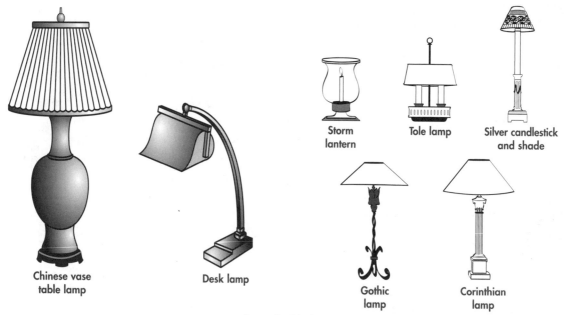

Traditional table lamps.

Contemporary wall lights include these choices:

◆ **Uplight.** A highly ambient uplight designed to direct the light reflected in the bowl onto the ceiling.

◆ **Bathroom fixture.** The light bulb is sealed in a unit, making it safe for areas with water. A fluorescent tube casts a soft and low-glare light.

◆ **Luci Fair.** A simply designed light that projects an angle into the room like a horn. A slit in the glass directs the light upward.

◆ **Can uplight.** A pipelike light that sits on a table or floor and shines the light upward for interesting ambient light.

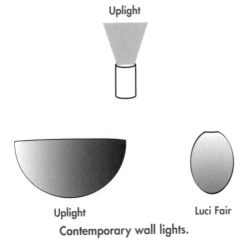

Uplight

Uplight          Luci Fair

**Contemporary wall lights.**

Traditional wall lamps include these choices:

◆ **Leaf sconce.** Wall-mounted uplight with a classic leaf pattern that shines the light upward and throughout the patterned leaves.

◆ **Gothic uplight.** Period style uplight that shines light directly onto the ceiling.

◆ **Girandole.** A sconce light with a mirror on the back fitted for a candle or bulb.

◆ **Gothic sconce.** Sconce with Gothic detailing outfitted with low-wattage bulbs. Shades reduce the lighting source but add to the design.

◆ **Exterior wall lantern.** Lantern-style light usually seen on the outside of homes, but eclectic interiors often use them on the inside outfitted with candles or low-wattage bulbs.

◆ **Rococo sconce.** Small classic design outfitted with a candlelike bulb.

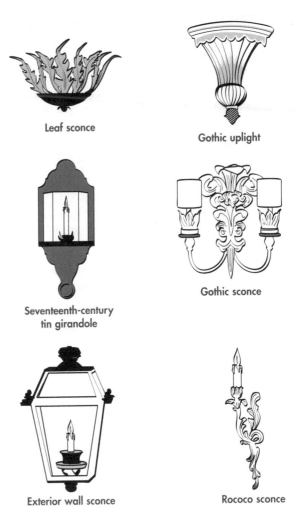

Leaf sconce

Gothic uplight

Seventeenth-century tin girandole

Gothic sconce

Exterior wall sconce

Rococo sconce

**Traditional wall lights.**

Traditional decorative chandeliers include these choices:

◆ **Armillary sphere.** A decorative modern design based on seventeenth-century models of the universe. It is a loose thematic interpretation of a traditional form.

◆ **Crystal.** Crystal *electrolier* that reflects light with its prisms. The higher-quality lead crystal creates dazzling effects.

### Decorating 101

**Electrolier** is the correct term for an electrically fitted chandelier. Today we loosely use the term "chandelier" to refer to any decorative light fixture with several arms that hold light bulbs and hangs from the ceiling. Actually a chandelier holds candles for illuminating and is not fitted with electrical wires and sockets for light bulbs.

◆ **Flemish chandelier.** A traditional Dutch design from the seventeenth century with many reproductions today.

◆ **Montgolfier.** A decorative and thematic chandelier that captures the spirit of ballooning.

◆ **Lantern.** A style based on Near Eastern hanging lamps. Often used in older homes for a period effect.

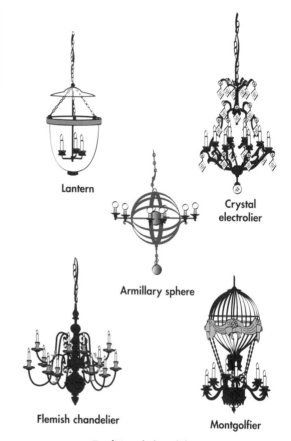

Lantern

Crystal electrolier

Armillary sphere

Flemish chandelier

Montgolfier

Traditional chandeliers.

Contemporary ceiling lights include these choices:

◆ **Modern Crisol pendant.** Hangs from ceiling low over desk or table for an effective downlight and a glowing pendant.

◆ **Track.** Arrangement of spotlights and downlights that can be positioned where light is needed

◆ **Downlights.** Lighting that is mounted into ceilings and that casts light directly down. They can provide ambient, task, and accent lighting.

◆ **Spotlights.** Can be recessed into ceilings, mounted on tracks, wall mounted, or used individually in clips. Some have exposed bulbs, whereas others have a cover.

Downlights          Spotlight

Track lights

**Contemporary ceiling lights.**

Floor lamps include these choices:

◆ **Traditional bridge lamp.** A classic design with a pleated shade that diffuses the light.

◆ **Brera.** A modern minimal lamp that provides task or accent lighting by illuminating the area around it. The shade is frosted so that the light is diffused for a nonglare appearance.

◆ **Footlight.** A very versatile light that can be placed on the floor, a table, or behind furniture to provide accent lighting.

◆ **Low-voltage floor lamp.** A modern floor lamp that is great for task or accent lighting. It can be easily moved around where light is needed.

◆ **Torchiere.** Floor light that has a shade to direct light toward the ceiling as an uplight. If shade is translucent, extra light is added to the room.

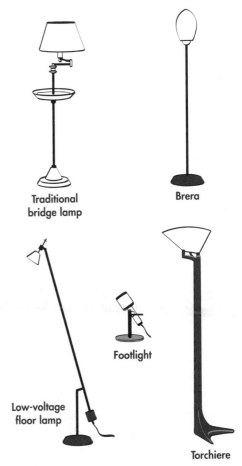

Traditional bridge lamp

Brera

Low-voltage floor lamp

Footlight

Torchiere

**Floor lamps.**

**Pro Workshop**

Still have your lamps from your college dorm? Revamp them by gluing rope, shells, or pebbles on the base and adding a new shade.

# Selecting the Source: Types of Bulbs

The ultimate impact of any light fixture depends very much on the essential light source: the bulb. Its brightness of the light and its quality—its color and "warmth" or "coolness"—will vary with the bulb choice you make.

◆ **Incandescent bulbs.** Common light bulbs that come in general-service and reflectorized versions. General-service bulbs are inexpensive and come in a variety of wattage and shapes. They produce a yellowish-white light that is emitted in all directions, suitable for general lighting in table, floor, and pendant fixtures. Available in clear or frosted bulbs, which give a more diffused light. In general, incandescent bulbs are inexpensive but need frequent changing. They also emit heat and are not as energy efficient as halogen bulbs.

◆ **Reflectorized bulbs.** Incandescent bulbs that use a reflective coating inside the bulb. The coating directs light forward, giving you better beam control than general-service bulbs. Floodlights spread light, and spotlights concentrate light. Reflectorized bulbs can put approximately double the amount of light (measured in foot-candles) on a subject as can a general-service bulb of the same wattage.

◆ **Tungsten-halogen bulbs.** These bulbs produce a bright, white light. They have a longer life and provide more light (lumens) per watt than incandescent bulbs, but are more expensive.

◆ **Fluorescent bulbs.** This is a common type of bulb that often casts a bluish light, which changes the appearance of colors in a room. "Warm white" fluorescent bulbs are expensive, but these bulbs use one third to one fifth as much electricity as incandescents and last up to 20 times longer. Compact fluorescent bulbs, which can be used in conventional fixtures, are great for energy-efficient residential use. All fluorescent bulbs are cool to the touch.

**Homematters**

Remember that the type of shade you choose for a lamp will dramatically affect the lighting. Translucent or opaque, each casts light differently. Never purchase a lamp without turning the switch on first to see the overall effect.

# Lighting Tips Throughout the House

Making a lighting plan for each room eliminates the guesswork of wondering where to place plugs and fixtures. Review some of these tips for some ideas about the lighting in each room of your house.

For the living room/family room …

◆ Decorative lighting is fun for entertaining. For a soft, glowing look, replace your regular white bulbs with pink ones. Or use holiday tree lights year round on an indoor ficus tree to cast low lighting in a corner of a room.

◆ Put several types of lights on dimmer switches so you can control the amount of lighting in different areas.

◆ Be sure there is enough general lighting in various areas for watching television, reading, or just relaxing.

◆ Mix incandescent and halogen bulbs for varied warm and cool lighting.

For the dining room …

◆ The dining table is not the only area that needs to be lit. Don't forget the sideboards from which food may be served.

◆ Chandeliers and candles create an intimate and welcoming atmosphere. In case the dining area is a multipurpose room, be sure to have auxiliary lighting such as table lamps or spotlights or downlights on dimmers.

◆ Use kinetic lighting, such as candles or a fireplace, and use decorative lighting to create mood and perhaps even a topic of conversation. Don't forget task lighting for specific functions, such as reading the newspaper at the dining room table.

For the bedroom …

◆ Create a mood with uplights that direct light toward the ceiling. Be sure these are placed on a dimmer switch to adjust the amount of needed light.

◆ Use side-table lamps with opaque shades so light is drawn down.

◆ A decorative chandelier is always fun and a point of interest when lying in bed. Be sure to have it on a dimmer switch so you can control the amount of light.

◆ Place candles on the nightstand and dresser to cast a romantic glow. (Make sure you extinguish them before going to sleep!)

◆ Long-necked reading lamps can be stylish and functional.

For the kitchen …

◆ Kitchens require both task and general lighting.

◆ Spotlights add functional task and general lighting. If you entertain in your kitchen, be sure to place all lighting on dimmer switches.

◆ Reflective surfaces such as stainless appliances, glazed countertops, and glass shelves all boost the lighting.

◆ Match lighting style and function. If you will dine in your kitchen, add decorative lighting to create a mood.

In the bathroom …

◆ Bathrooms require both task lighting for applying make-up or shaving and general room lighting.

◆ Kinetic lighting with candles or a decorative chandelier simulates a spa atmosphere for a soothing romantic atmosphere.

◆ Lighting will be reflected with surfaces of glass, water, and mirrors. Try to position lighting to enhance the surfaces.

In the den …

◆ Use both task and general lighting, and both should be nonglare.

◆ Halogen bulbs provide the closest feel of natural light for reading, writing, and working on the computer.

◆ A pharmacy-styled lamp is a versatile choice for a den desk, providing style as well as proper adjustment for light requirements. It is a sleek metal lamp with an adjustable arm that provides good task lighting.

In the hallway …

◆ Lighting a hallway creates warmth and welcome.

◆ Hallways can be lit with many forms of lighting: general (ceiling fixtures), accent (spotlights), decorative (sconce), and kinetic (candles).

**Pro Workshop** _____

You can also use light as an accent in your yard. Lighting specific plants or architectural details will throw silhouetted light on the walls of your home, creating a mysterious and enchanting atmosphere.

# Do-It-Yourself Project: Make Your Own Lamp

Consider function, style, and size when selecting a base for your lamp. You can make a one-of-a-kind lamp with vintage silver teapots, trophies, old tea tins, large glass jars filled with shells … really the sky is the limit. And what fun! Try to find a base that has holes on both ends, but if your base cannot be drilled (or you do not want to devalue it), you can let the cord hang from the socket. After all, the beauty is in the base and shade and the pride comes from making it yourself. A trip to the hardware store and you can begin.

Here are the materials you will need:

- Base for the lamp
- Threaded rod
- Washers and lock nuts
- Harp and harp retainer
- Light socket
- Electrical/appliance cord
- Bulb
- Shade

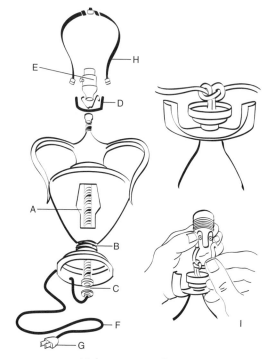

**Make your own lamp.**

A. Slip rod through the center of the base.

B. Secure each end of the rod with a lock nut and washer.

C. Place a harp retainer on the rod at the top of the base.

D. Remove the base from the socket and screw it to the rod.

E. Push the appliance cord through the rod. Split the cord at the top of the lamp and tie with a knot as shown. Do the same at the base of the lamp.

F. Strip the appliance cord at the top and attach the lead wires to the socket and add the plug.

G. Put the socket back together, place the harp on the retainer, and add the bulb and a complementary shade.

H. Customize the lamp even further by placing a finial that reveals your personality.

# Tricks of the Trade

Some of my consistent decorative as well as practical designs with lighting include the following:

◆ Placing a lamp on a table in a hallway says "welcome" when lit at nighttime.

◆ For an inventive chandelier, attach a wire egg or clam basket (tied with decorative wire with a wide candle in the base) to a ceiling hook and place a candle in the bottom of the basket.

◆ Place kitchen, master bedroom, master bath, and dining room ceiling lights on dimmers to adjust the mood of the room.

◆ Paint whimsical scenery on children's lampshades or love notes on your partner's bedside lampshade.

◆ Alter the look of a plain shade with pompoms by gluing them in a scalloped fashion around the bottom edge of the shade.

**Decorate a shade with pompoms.**
*(Photo by M. Hackett)*

◆ Use a variety of candles to create a spalike atmosphere right in your own bathroom.

## The Least You Need to Know

◆ The five types of lighting are general or ambient, task, accent, decorative, and kinetic. Most spaces need a combination of these types.

◆ A lighting plan for each room determines the type of lighting needed and the fixtures that will enhance the room's decorative style.

◆ Lighting fixtures come in several forms—portable, ceiling and wall mounted—and within each category there are fixtures for every style of décor.

◆ Lamps can be made out of a variety of bases such as china pots, silver teapots, tea tins, and so on. Use your imagination and you can make your own lamp.

◆ You can learn imaginative ideas for lighting by emulating the pros.

# In This Part

# Part 3

# One Room at a Time

Comfortable with your personal style? Confident with color, texture, and other principles of design? Certain you want to put your decorating talent to work—know your budget and where to find the items you are looking for? If you answered yes to these questions, you are ready to tackle a room for real.

In the following chapters, I'll discuss all the elements a decorator finds interesting and important to make your rooms unique. The general challenges are the same: Which furnishings are necessary and which make your room individualized? What furniture arrangements maximize their utility, what are the lighting needs of the room, and how can you use the quirkiest spaces to your advantage? Each room also presents special challenges and opportunities to make it a personal statement. The flea market finds sections in these chapters will help you do just that.

# In This Chapter

- ◆ Furniture to match your lifestyle
- ◆ Furniture arrangements for living
- ◆ The living room as a "great" room
- ◆ Making the most of a small living area
- ◆ How to create intimacy in a large room
- ◆ Flea market finds for coffee tables

# Living Rooms You Can Really Live In

There was a time when the living room was the best-dressed room in the house. But today's lifestyles dictate that the living room serves as a family room as well as a place to entertain guests—it's the daily site where you read, listen to music, watch TV, play games, and celebrate special occasions.

Today's living room, then, has to be decorated and arranged for both aesthetics and practical use, for your personal style. Furniture must be comfortable and fabrics must be durable and appeal to your aesthetic sense. Room arrangements must be set up for easy conversation and good traffic flow and to accommodate a lot of different activities. One-room living must accommodate the "living" area as well as the kitchen, dining, and sleeping area. Dual-purpose furnishings must be selected and creative dividers added. Alternative furniture may be used as something else!

In this chapter, you will learn to create an intimate and usable living room, the goal for any good decorating plan.

## How Do You Live? Assessing Your Personal Style

In Chapter 1 you learned about personal style; where it comes from and how to get it. You also learned about the different styles of rustic and refined, traditional, modern and slick, and eclectic along with flea market decor. It is very important to narrow down your idea of what your lifestyle is all about. You can then make proper choices when it comes to the type and style of furniture, arrangement, and fabric choices.

If your living room is the hub of your home, you will most likely want a sofa with a durable fabric like denim rather than silk. If you use your living room for sipping tea only, you may arrange delicate pieces amongst lightweight fabrics for its minimal use. If clutter drives you to distraction, a clean, modern look may be your style for living. Whatever style you choose, finding a focal point is the easiest way to begin to arrange your living room for living.

This living room plan allows for playing music, reading, or relaxing by the fire, and having an easy conversation because of its comfortable and decorative arrangement. *(Photo by Lee Industries)*

# Arranging the Living Room: Finding a Focal Point

How do you arrange a living room that you can actually live in? The best place to start is with an attractive visual focal point. It could be a naturally beautiful piece such as a fireplace, a piano, or a tall antique *armoire*—or even a spectacular window view. You might need to create your own focal point from an object that's less obvious. Maybe you have a great rug, a beautiful mirror, an extensive art collection, or a large coffee table.

**Decorating 101**

An **armoire** is a French term for a large, free-standing wooden wardrobe used as storage for clothing and linens. Today, armoires can be a wonderful antique hiding place for high-tech multimedia equipment!

Group different types of furniture of various shapes and sizes around the focal point. Balance large sofas with a couple of smaller chairs, or flank a fireplace or large armoire with two small loveseats. Have enough seating for six to eight people. For larger gatherings, supplement seating with small moveable chairs placed about the house (entry, hallways, dining area). Comfortable sofas and armchairs arranged around a focal point are the beginnings of a working living room.

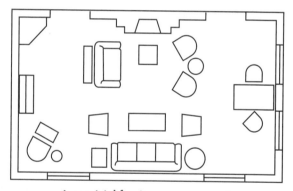

A convivial furniture arrangement.

Another principle of seating arrangements is to place your furniture so there is ample room to pass through openings. This makes it easy and inviting for people to reach seating areas and promotes a free flow of conversation. This also gives the room an appearance that is comfortable to your eye—that is, an open and inviting look, without barriers or narrow passages.

While it facilitates movement, seating, and conversation, your arrangement must also allow several activities to be enjoyed at the same time. Chairs and sofas must be placed to accommodate a group that wants to converse, but also to permit an individual to read, do needlework, write, and so on. For instance, a chair and ottoman in a corner is a great place to put up your feet and relax with a book. Add a small table for a drink, a floor lamp, and voilà—a private niche away from the main activity area is created. As you can see, your preferred activities will dictate some of your furniture selections and their placement.

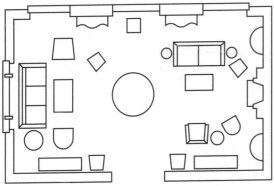

Floor plan with seating with occasional tables for style and use.

All seating should have occasional tables close by to hold drinks or books. End tables can be chests or bureaus to display accessories and hold table lamps. Coffee tables can be small or overscaled, low, or tea-table height. Large, low coffee tables are useful for displaying large books and can stand in as a dining table for an impromptu dinner. A tea table is higher than seating level and can be a nice contrast when the rest of the pieces are the same height. And yes, tea or drinks can be served easily from a higher table. Sofa tables or desks can be arranged behind the length of a sofa to hold lamps, books, and accessories. A desk or sofa table can be placed against a wall with artwork or mirrors.

If you have a fireplace, think of it as a perfect focal point and a great decorative element in itself. Framing the fireplace with decorative

tiles or marble (such as Vermont verde antique marble) adds color and texture. The mantel provides an area for creative displays of art, candles, flowers, clocks, or small collections.

Use the tools in Appendix B to sketch out some of your ideas and then transfer your plans to the graph paper with the templates. Here are some floor plans you might consider.

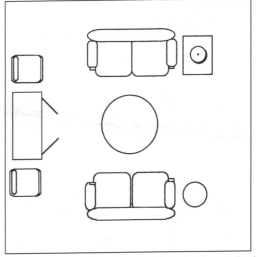

Two low loveseats balance the center-positioned tall armoire. The TV is easily viewed when the armoire doors are opened.

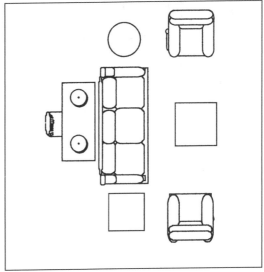

The sofa table doubles as a desk. Two lamps on the desk provide attractive design as well as task lighting.

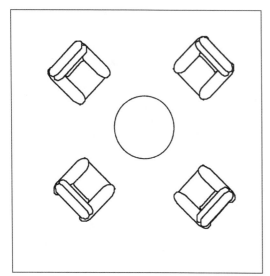

A small living room gains space from arranging chairs in a circular arrangement for a big fashion statement.

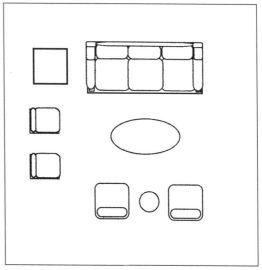

A more formal arrangement, allowing table surfaces for books or drinks.

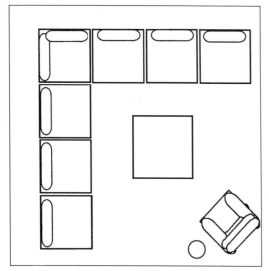

Appropriately sized coffee and side tables are useful for large seating areas.

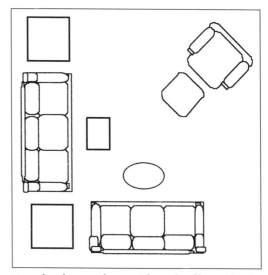

Vary the shapes of your side and coffee tables for visual interest.

**Homematters**

Mario Buatta, a prominent interior designer, is quoted as saying, "I like all the chairs to talk to one another and to the sofas and not those parlor-car arrangements that create two Siberias."

# Living Room as Family/Great Room

With nesting being very "in" these days, many of our living rooms are either family rooms or great rooms that serve many purposes. The family/great room is the center of activity today, a do-it-all space that often serves as a library, media center, dining, and relaxing spot.

Here are some tips for planning a casual, comfortable room in your style:

◆ Begin by arranging furnishings around a focal point.

◆ Select practical and stylish furniture. Select a hard, working table that is versatile for dining, crafts, hobbies, and homework.

◆ Purchase durable upholstery or slipcover fabrics.

◆ Direct traffic for function. Place furniture in ways to make paths around areas of activity.

◆ Take care when placing prized heirlooms in a much-used room. You may want to showcase them in another area of the house.

◆ Be sure lighting is versatile—general for daily and nighttime play, task for projects, and accent for mood enhancing. Kinetic lighting in the form of candles or a fire can turn a working room into a dining experience. (See Chapter 10 for lighting tips.)

◆ Display charming items that are meaningful, such as children's artwork, family photographs, or special mementos.

◆ Create neat storage for media centers, hobby supplies, art supplies, or toys that can be closed off to avoid the cluttered look. (Refer to Chapter 20 for more on storage options.)

An armoire makes an attractive and useful media storage unit. *(Photo by Gear Home, Bettye M. Musham, Chairwoman/CEO)*

The central coffee table can be accessed from each seat in this contemporary living room plan. *(Photo by Cassina)*

# One-Room Living

Many city and studio apartments consist of one room where living, dining, and kitchen are all in the same space. If the room is small, embrace your chance for intimate living with carefully planned décor. Visually increase the size by arranging dual-purpose furnishings, ones that can be used for a variety of purposes. Add grandeur with architectural elements and keep fabric choices simple and your color palette monochromatic. You will be amazed how much your space will "grow" without tearing down the walls.

## Dual-Purpose Furnishings

When selecting furniture, a sofa sleeper may be just the right choice for eliminating a conventional box spring and mattress set. If you do opt for a mattress and box spring, set it up as a sofa style for the day and for sleeping at night. An additional sofa sleeper could be used for guests. A *Murphy bed* is always useful for hiding a bed during the day.

**Decorating 101**

A **Murphy bed,** named after its inventor, W. L. Murphy (ca. 1900), is attached to the wall and folds down for use, then completely folds up when not in use. It's a popular option when space is at a premium.

Here are a few other ideas:

◆ Store throws, needlework, magazines, the remote control, and other items in an ottoman with a hinged top. They also provide extra seating as well as a place to rest your feet.

◆ Conceal videos, CDs, even small TVs, under a chair that is slipcovered or upholstered with a floor-length skirt.

◆ Choose a sturdy table that can be used for dining, food preparation, and hobbies as well as a substitute desk.

◆ Have stylish folding chairs for dining chairs so they can be folded up when not needed.

Folding chairs make casual dining chairs. *(Photo by M. Hackett)*

## Adding Architectural Character

Add a big presence with architectural features like a wall lined with bookcases from ceiling to floor for storage and decorative appeal. Build bookcases around windows and doors. These will help to draw the eye in a vertical position, giving an illusion of a bigger space.

Architectural-salvaged columns placed in the corners of a room will also raise the eye upward. Wallcoverings with Greek motifs such as columns and draped fabric and urns can add a feeling of architectural grandeur. Even a trompe l'oeil painting on a wall of a bookcase, a grand armoire, or a pediment over a door (a triangular piece over a doorway, like a Grecian-style portico) can fool your eye into thinking your room is expansive.

Here are a few more tips for adding a sense of space:

◆ Mirrored walls (or a very large scaled mirror) can reflect an entire room, visually doubling the room size and the number of furnishings.

◆ Lighting that is judicially placed to illuminate the ceiling and corners of the room gives a sense of height and separate space.

◆ Placing the sofa on an angle can provide a decorative look as well as a hidden storage area. Place a tri-fold screen behind it, adding even more storage space.

## Dividing the Large Living Room

What if your living space is so large that it feels cold and not intimate at all? The best solution is to divide it up with clever arrangements. Consider areas for intimate conversations, or viewing the outdoors, areas to relax in, areas for a reading nook, perhaps even a desk for reading mail. Place sofas back to back to create separate conversation areas and add moveable chairs to complement them. Arrange two very comfortable chairs for sharing thoughts and intimate conversations.

Other ideas for warming up a large space include the following:

◆ Unify the room with a base carpet or flooring, but add a layered look by using area rugs to anchor separate areas.

◆ Put a game table and chairs for activity in a dead corner.

◆ Use armoires on long walls to create an attractive division and add useful storage.

◆ Add small tables to all seating areas with lighting so each area can function separately.

◆ Unify the large area by choosing slipcovers in patterns or colors that are used on the walls and repeated at the ends and middle of the room on pillows, ottomans, chairs, or sofas.

◆ Harmonize the different seating areas by placing a flea market find in the different seating areas to add a unique twist with style.

**Style Pointers**

Don't try to make a large living room a one-conversation area. It will be cold and lack intimacy. Divide it up with several seating arrangements instead.

### Flea Market Finds: Coffee Tables

A decorator's greatest genius lies in the ability to transform items in ways that the home decorator may not think of by envisioning a new use for pieces that have an inherently unique design. The designer ends up with a piece costing a fraction of what a new piece of furniture would, helps the earth by recycling, and adds a one-of-a-kind touch to a decorating scheme. Most items don't need any improvement, just innovative placement! Here are some ideas:

◆ Transform an old iron gate into a one-of-a-kind coffee table by attaching legs and adding a piece of glass cut to the size of the gate. The glass is not only useful but displays the rusty scroll pattern of the gate.

◆ Position four duck decoys as bases in the corners to hold up a 42-inch by 42-inch piece of glass.

◆ Add a piece of glass to a good-sized, sturdy log that has been whittled flat on top.

◆ Make four even stacks of books (one pile in each corner) and cover with a piece of glass.

◆ Turn two metal milk crates upside down and top with a piece of glass to make individual "coffee tables," adding a modern take on an old utilitarian piece.

◆ A bench serves as a great coffee table and is usually the perfect height for holding a drink, a book, or an impromptu TV dinner.

**An old bench makes a unique coffee table.**
*(Photo by M. Hackett)*

## The Least You Need to Know

- Select furniture styles to match your personal style of living.
- Furniture in a living area is suitably arranged around a focal point like a fireplace, window view, or piece of artwork.
- The living room used as a great room needs special arranging for separate areas like reading, working, conversation, and possibly dining.
- A small or one-room living area should employ dual-purpose furnishings. Add character with architectural details like bookcases or columns for grandeur to make the room "grow."
- Create intimacy in a cold, large room by dividing it into separate conversational areas.
- Browsing through a flea market can yield ideas for a one-of-a-kind living room coffee table.

# In This Chapter

- ◆ Dining room sets, from mismatched to mass-marketed
- ◆ The dining area as a library
- ◆ Nifty ideas for small dining spaces
- ◆ Storage and display for function and beauty
- ◆ The accessories that make the difference
- ◆ Flea market finds for dining tables

# Chapter 12

# Dining Rooms: Not Just for Dining Anymore

A dining room or dining area is one of the most used places in the house—and it should also be one of the most comfortable. Whether it's a lazy Sunday morning around a table spread with newspapers or a special occasion crowded with family and friends, a dining room is the natural place for family gatherings and traditional celebrations, as well as for everyday eating.

The formal stiffness of dining rooms in earlier eras, however, has given way to the more relaxed style of contemporary eating and entertaining. In many homes today, the dining area may be a part of the "great room"—a living room/dining room combination—or it might be part of a kitchen or other dual-purpose space.

Whatever space is devoted to the dining in your home, you will want to decorate it with a focus on comfort and festivity and your personal style. Start by sitting on creative chairs whether they are mismatched, updated ones from your grandmother, or a personalized set from a mass-marketed style.

## The Beauty of Diversity

Of course, the literal center of your dining room will be taken up with a table and chairs. Whether they are made to match or come from different styles and materials, the table and chairs must work together, both aesthetically and to allow comfortable seating for eating. Matched sets of tables and chairs are perfectly suitable but not very imaginatively put together. A perfect way to add an unusual, unexpected look is to not have all the chairs match each other. You might want to place fully upholstered chairs at the head of the table to denote the host and hostess; the fabric is a nice complement for a glass, wood, or metal table. Add side chairs of wood or metal for a more eclectic look.

### Style Pointers

To add seating to a small table, have a circular piece of plywood cut to the circumference needed. Place the wood on top of the existing table and cover it with a pretty cloth. When it's not in use you can store the plywood along with extra folding chairs.

One of my favorite seating arrangements for dining is to place wing chairs (if space allows) all around the table. These provide comfortable seating for each diner in a fun and very creative way. The chairs must be proportioned correctly for the table size, and the seating must be firm enough so that you don't sink too low to comfortably eat your food!

This dining room arrangement defies convention and exudes marvelous personal style by the placement of upholstered wing chairs around the table.
*(Photo by Gear Design)*

# Stylized Sets Without Stuffiness

Have you inherited a dining room set from your in-laws that is fine but a little too stiff for your taste or the way you live? One way to keep the set and enjoy it is to give it an updated look.

Often an older wooden dining set is either too dark or too fancy. You can remove some of the stain, paint, or varnish with a remover and use milkpaint (available at woodworking stores) to give the chairs a mottled, rustic look. Leave the tabletop alone and paint the legs for contrast!

Another way to refurbish a set is to paint all the pieces a white enamel for a more contemporary look—yes, even that heavy dark furniture. Although the chairs and table are the same color, the high gloss and whiteness will lighten the heaviness and add a modern look to the somewhat outdated style. Using a pale yellow paint color can achieve a similar effect with a softer look. Painting a set black is also a style setter. Black is dramatic and visually "paints out" odd styling or outdated shapes. The color black has actually been used since colonial times but when used in high gloss and on both the dining table and chairs, you can achieve a more current look.

Does the set have a retro look with a table of chrome legs and a glass top? If you like wood, remove the glass top and put a wooden one in its place. The chrome chairs will blend well with the wood and you don't need to buy a new table. Save the glass top and make a desktop from it, or have it cut to fit an existing desktop.

# The Mismatched Set: As Varied as Your Guests

Again there are no rules when it comes to chairs and tables. A mismatched set with all different chairs can be a decorating "breath of fresh air." This relaxed approach is easy to achieve. Many chairs can be purchased at flea markets for as little as $20. You want to keep in mind the elements of design with color, scale, and texture. All wood, different-shape chairs could be the cohesive bind that makes them all work together. Or is it the shape of the backs of the chairs that are all unique but have similar styles? A mismatched set all painted one color allows for a greater range of diversity. Tall straight-backed chairs could actually work well near shorter, rounded-back chairs if they were painted the same color. The color is the thread that pulls them together.

A set of mismatched chairs adds a relaxed attitude at this dining table.     *(Photo by M. Hackett)*

### Homematters

When considering a flea market chair, make sure you have a place in mind for the chair and that you're not just adding clutter to your life. Does the style fit your overall decorating scheme? Does it have a pleasing shape? Remember that no matter how inexpensive the chair is, if it's unusable, it's no bargain. Does it have good "bones" and strong joints? Is the seat sturdy? Repairing a cane seat can be costly, while replacing a fabric seat is relatively easy and inexpensive. If it's made of wood, check that it's not bug-infested. Lastly, ask if the owner has any more chairs of that style. It may affect your decision to purchase one or a set!

# Add Character to a Set of Mass-Marketed Chairs

If you can't take the time to go hunting for a mismatched set and have resolved to order a set through the mail, or you have been given a mass-marketed set of chairs or a coordinating dining set as a wedding gift, try adding some touches that will take the cookie cutter look away.

Try slipcovering the backs of the matching chairs. The fabric introduced adds softness and another color as well as a pattern. (See Chapter 8 for some popular slipcover looks for chairs.) Glue different prominent shells on the backs with a glue gun. Or add a motif that means something to you or is indicative of your area. You might want to stencil the initial of your last name for a monogrammed look or paint the entire set of chairs an outlandish color like fuchsia or chartreuse, not seen in any catalog.

Place two or three of the side chairs around the house as extra seating and use a wooden bench, a sofa, or a garden wrought-iron settee in their place to mix in some other textures and styles.

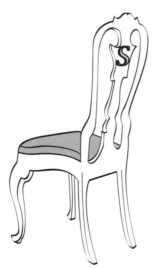

A stenciled initial gives these mass-marketed chairs a custom look.

# Chair Styles

There are many chair styles. Here are some of the classics:

◆ **Chippendale.** Named after the master cabinet maker and designer, Thomas Chippendale, this style was introduced to colonial America from England around 1755 and flourished in 1760 to 1770. The Chippendale chair combines French, Chinese, and Gothic styles, and features a claw and ball foot.

◆ **Federal.** Classicism was introduced in America gradually. Federal architecture was used to denote this classic style during the American Federal Age. Chairs reflected delicacy and symmetry, often featuring shields and heart-shape or rectangular backs.

◆ **Modern molded plywood.** Modern shapes became popular during the 1940s. Molded plywood was first introduced by Charles Eames while designing special equipment for the U.S. Navy.

◆ **Windsor.** Produced in Windsor, England, in the seventeenth century, Windsor chairs are characterized by stick legs and spindles driven into a plank seat. They were made in large quantities of various woods and hence were often painted in several colors.

◆ **Danish.** Furniture designer Hans Wegner was inspired by a little girl's Chinese chair while in a Copenhagen museum. The most famous Danish Modern style, the "round chair," was manufactured by Knoll International and debuted in 1949.

◆ **Bentwood.** Highly curved furniture of wood bent through the use of steam and pressure was used by Samuel Grass of Boston but later popularized by Michael Thonet in Austria and Hungary during the nineteenth century.

◆ **Shaker.** This style of furniture created by the Shakers, a religious sect, made a significant contribution to American design. Founders came to America from England in 1774 and settled in New York, New England, and Kentucky, among other regions. Shaker style is characterized by functional furniture devoid of ornamentation, revealing graceful lines and delicate proportions.

◆ **Mission.** Mission furniture is a style of the Arts and Crafts movement. Gustav Stickley of New York produced furniture that was made of oak, with square lines and visible mortise and tenon joints. The design was meant to be a functional mission; hence the name.

Chippendale    Federal    Modern molded plywood

Windsor    Danish    Bentwood

Shaker    Mission

**Chair styles for today's lifestyles.**

**Pro Workshop**

Dining seating can be more than chairs! Try using a bench, a love seat, or a garden settee. Use your imagination—just make sure the chair is comfortable and at the right height for the table.

# The Dining Room as a Library

The most memorable meals have always been in rooms that are filled with personality, such as a dining room that doubles as a library; the walls lined with bookshelves exposing the owner's tastes in various subjects. Most homes today do not have the room for a separate library room, so why not make one in your dining room? You can sit, eat, and linger to read—all in the same space. Bookshelves are a great organizer, as well as a decorative architectural feature. They make a bland dining area sizzle with interest. The books can be old with aged covers or new paperbacks arranged in nifty colorful piles. A chandelier and spotlights can illuminate areas of the walls of books for added interest.

**Style Pointers**

If your dining area is part of a great room or a multipurpose space, place several types of lighting on separate switches and dimmers to illuminate the area you are using and darken the areas you don't need.

In this one-room apartment, the loft library provides a dramatic focal point for both the living area and casual coffee table dining. *(Photo by Roche Bobois)*

# Small-Space Dining

Today's living promotes dining in so many areas of the house that we may have breakfast standing in the kitchen, lunch at the kitchen counter, a family dinner at the table, and a romantic dinner for two in the bedroom.

If your space is limited but you would like several places to sit and dine, here are some ingenious ways to squeeze a table into limited space for dining:

- **Demilune table.** A half-moon table that can fit against the wall with little protrusion into the room but big enough to accommodate two small side chairs.

- **Sofa table.** A long narrow table placed behind a sofa that two chairs can be pulled up to.

- **TV trays.** Small folding trays that come in chic styles today.

- **Low coffee table in bedroom.** A bed-height table at the foot of your bed that chairs can be pulled up to.

- **Drop leaf.** Expanding table that can be reduced in size when not needed and the leaves opened up when needed.

- **Fold down.** A table that is a top that is hinged to the wall or bookcase (on a porch or part of a wall unit of shelves) that can be unfolded for use and stored when not needed.

- **Kids table.** Pull out a child's table and sit on large floor pillows for a very casual dinner.

- **Two chairs or stools next to the kitchen fireplace.** Use the hearth as your table and enjoy the fire.

- **In the kitchen.** Stools under the baking table pulled out for breakfast.

- **Small table in front of a window seat.** Add a cushion to the window seat and dine in comfort.

## Style Pointers

A great way to add flair as well as storage to your dining room is to attach a wide shelf at picture-rail height around the room (approximately one foot below the ceiling). This can store and display large plates, pitchers, or collections of flea-market china. Spoon racks can also hold special silver spoons or baby cups.

# For All Your China or Pottery: Storage and Display Pieces

Storage units in a dining room serve multiple purposes. Attractive and utilitarian, they can properly store china, linens, and silverware, and provide surfaces that can be used for serving or display. A sideboard or buffet piece is especially hardworking. Its drawers or doors can hold trays, china, extra glassware, linens, and during a meal, drinks; or food can be served from it. When you're not dining, the sideboard can display special trays, dishes, crystal, candlesticks, or decanters. A serving cart can do much the same but is smaller and has legs with wheels to allow it to be moved around for easy serving. (For serving from behind a chair, position your cart or buffet at least 48 inches from the table.)

A breakfront, china cabinet, hutch, or corner cupboard can hold extra china, glassware, and vases in its lower half and display bowls, dishes, and plates on the upper shelves. A curio cabinet may hold delicate collections behind its glass doors. These pieces do not have to match your dining room table or chairs; blending traditional with modern or old with new makes a strong personal statement.

Review the following storage pieces in a dining room so you know your hutch from a highboy!

- **Sideboard.** Long low cabinet usually placed against a wall or as a divider between a living and dining room. May have drawers and compartments or combinations of both or a lower shelf.
- **Highboy.** Tall chest that appears to be in two sections.
- **Breakfront.** Tall unit that usually has glass-enclosed shelves on top of a drawer cabinet, with a projecting center section.
- **Hutch.** A tall cupboard or sideboard that usually has open shelves on the top section and cabinets below.
- **China cabinet.** A cabinet designed for display of china or glasses. Usually has a glass front or sides.
- **Curio cabinet.** A cabinet with glass doors and sides to display various types of collections.

# Accessories for a Festive Atmosphere

Accessories, as everywhere in your house, make the difference in a dining room. A buffet piece, mirrors, formal tea service, and candlesticks are classic dining room accessories. Simple pottery or a set of flea market plates, combined with clean-lined furniture, lend a comfortable, modern country atmosphere. But nothing is more seductive to diners than fresh flowers casually placed in vases or buckets.

Walls are key in a dining room. They can be hung with an arrangement of china plates with plate hangers (available at any hardware store) or with a wall of artwork that is meaningful to you. Botanical prints and sporting artwork bring nature indoors. Unusual contemporary artwork adds interesting style and can promote conversation while dining. Here are some other special touches for walls or ceilings:

- Small brackets spaced on one wall give special attention to a favorite collection.
- Hang a mirror above the buffet, and the accessories are reflected with double the impact.
- Light candles, and the reflected flickering light illuminates polished glass or chrome surfaces and sparkles in crystal ware.
- Hang a chandelier to add dramatic lighting overhead. Enchanting!

### Flea Market Finds: Dining Room Tables

My favorite flea market find for a dining room includes two fish-bait barrels turned upside down with a piece of painted MDF (medium density fiber) board on top. It serves as a working table, a dining table, a project table, and a kitchen preparation table. I purchased the barrels at a flea market for $15 each and painted one a shade of red and one a shade of orange. Otherwise, I left them as they were, complete with hauling rope attached to the outside. They are always the first topic of conversation when guests arrive!

**Fish-bait barrels used as a table base.**

You can make your own rustic dining table with a little ingenuity and a visit to your local flea market. The possibilities are endless if you keep in mind the size of your space and the look you want to achieve. Here are a few other ideas:

◆ The table legs from an old architectural drafting table make a perfect base for a do-it-yourself table.

**Drafting table legs turned dining table base.**

◆ Carpenter's wooden saw horses just need a top (an old door can suffice).

◆ Two commercial oil drums topped with a round piece of glass are industrial chic and can seat four.

## The Least You Need to Know

◆ Dining room furnishings don't have to match, as long as the pieces work well together.

◆ The dining room can double as a library by adding bookshelves and lighting to showcase your favorite objects.

◆ With a little imagination, small areas of your home can be turned into intimate dining areas.

◆ Storage and display pieces can be stylish and functional at the same time.

◆ Accessories enhance the atmosphere of the room and the enjoyment of dining and celebrations.

◆ Flea markets offer clever alternative items for dining tables. Use your imagination!

# In This Chapter

- ◆ Kitchen plans that work
- ◆ Cabinets with style and color
- ◆ Possibilities with pantries
- ◆ Special effects to enhance your kitchen
- ◆ Adding flair with flea market finds

# Kitchens: The Hub of Today's Home

Today, most kitchens are the busiest area of the home. Because you spend so much time there, it is important that it reflect the atmosphere you like and the way you want to live. Whether you are selecting a new plan that works for you and the space or working with the one you have, you'll need to decide on wall color as well as cabinet style and finish. By using clever ideas for special effects or adding flea market pieces for charm, you can give your kitchen a sense of individuality—and that's the best kitchen style.

Explore the array of materials, colors, and finishes and refer to your files and style boards to get a better idea of the type of kitchen that's best for you!

## Planning for an Efficient Kitchen

There are many ways to arrange kitchens efficiently, and just as many pleasing designs. You will learn some of these here. A good first step is to practice making some floor plans (see Chapter 3)—measuring your own space to scale and experimenting with various arrangements and sizes of appliances and cabinets to see what will fit in your home. Try some of the following styles of kitchen layouts.

### The Work Triangle

A simple formula for the placement of appliances and the creation of efficient traffic patterns in the kitchen is based on the relative positioning of the sink, stove, and refrigerator, known as the work triangle. Some experts assert that the stove, refrigerator, and sink should be placed to enable a cook to use these elements without walking clear across the room for each one. The work triangle dictates that the sink should be 4 to 7 feet from the stove and 4 to 7 feet from the refrigerator, thus creating the triangle. The 3 measurements added together should be anywhere from 12 to 21 feet.

There are various ways to lay out the work triangle. Following are some distinctive kitchen floor plans, showing the positioning of appliances and work-area surfaces. Here's a list of what the abbreviations mean:

| C | chair |
|---|-------|
| CT | countertop |
| D and C | desk and chair |
| DW | dishwasher |
| LS | lazy Susan (revolving storage space) |
| MW | microwave |
| OV | oven |
| P | pantry |
| R | refrigerator |
| RG | range |
| S | sink |
| STO | storage |
| T and C | table and chairs |

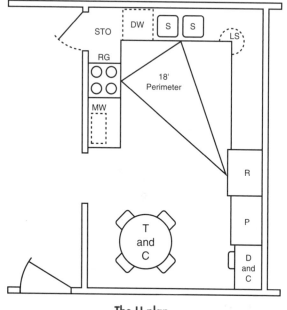

**The U plan.**

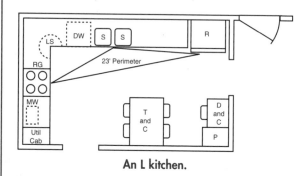

**An L kitchen.**

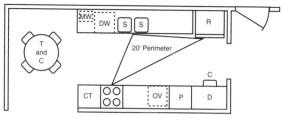

**Double-sided galley kitchen (corridor).**

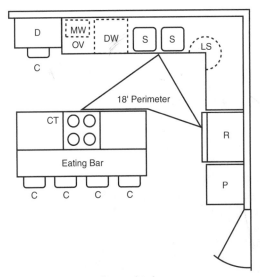

Broken U kitchen.

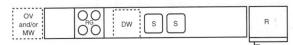

Galley kitchen.

## Zone Planning

The work triangle is one approach to organizing a kitchen. Other kitchen designers prefer to lay out kitchens according to how the room will function, the type and quantity of cooking that will be done, how many will cook, or who will serve.

Deborah Krasner, author of *Kitchens for Cooks* (see Appendix A), suggests that readers organize their kitchens by zones and create different working areas for "wet," "dry," "hot," and "cold" cooking tasks. You can find exact specifications for setting these zones in her excellent book.

Built-in cookbook shelves, a hanging pot rack, and a large island with doors and drawers provide this kitchen with plenty of storage space.   *(Photo by Smallbone)*

## Cabinets That Work for You

Cabinet style is a matter of your personal taste. Cabinets come in every shape, finish, and material, from slick laminates to distressed pine and woods such as spruce, maple, oak, beech, birch, or cherry. And of course, the shape, detail, finish, and hardware are all part of the overall design.

Factory-made cabinets come in particular sizes to create a "built-in" or *fitted* style. If your kitchen is small, built-ins can increase storage space and look streamlined for a less-cluttered look.

> **Decorating 101**
>
> A **fitted** kitchen is one with matching cabinets measured to fit along the walls and spaces of the kitchen. An **unfitted** kitchen is one with free-standing pieces of furniture that may not match other cabinets but that provide storage and decoration.

A popular choice today is the *unfitted* kitchen, one with free-standing pieces of furniture that may not match other cabinets but that provide storage and decoration. Many companies build free-standing pieces, which can be combined with open shelving and mismatched hutches or cupboards of various finishes. An unfitted kitchen style works particularly well in large country kitchens that have open wall space.

Cabinets can be built around appliances for a custom fit. *(Photo by Wolf Appliances)*

# Cabinet and Wall Paint Combinations

For the home decorator, one of the most perplexing issues can be what color to paint cabinets and the walls. Cabinets can be a solid color, two-tone, or painted to look aged, dark, or pastel; they can be natural wood or a transparent wash of color to show the grain of the wood. The walls can range from vibrant red to the palest green.

To make a small kitchen look larger, paint the cabinets and walls the same light color, such as a khaki or cream. If the kitchen is large and needs warmth, dark-colored cabinets of black, dark green, or chocolate make the kitchen look warm and inviting. (Read more on kitchen cabinets in Chapter 21.)

Picking out one color can be challenging enough, but choosing a combination that will work might have you shaking your head with frustration. Look at the color wheel in the center of the book, get out your paint chips, and try some combinations; remember to review your kitchen files and boards. What are the reoccurring colors that you gravitate to? Paint large samples of your favorites and paste them up in your kitchen, walk by them often to see if you are on the right track.

To help you think about the possibilities, here are some of my favorite combinations. Be sure to test some of these. You may fall in love with a couple of these combinations!

**Style Pointers**

For the busiest room in the house, choose a latex enamel when giving your cabinets a new paint color. It's easy to clean!

- ◆ Celery walls/darker green cabinets
- ◆ Straw walls/taupe cabinets
- ◆ Tomato-red walls/dark green cabinets
- ◆ Apple-green walls/white cabinets
- ◆ Manila (like the envelope) walls/white cabinets
- ◆ Off-white walls/warm-gray cabinets
- ◆ White walls/black cabinets
- ◆ Gray walls/very dark green cabinets

An island with a lowered granite surface for rolling pastry and a raised butcher block for chopping makes this unfitted kitchen a cook's dream.
*(Photo by Smallbone)*

Open shelving displays special dishes while storing them.   *(Photo by Gear Design)*

**Pro Workshop**

Give outdated wood cabinets new life by sanding them and then painting them with a semitransparent stain. This will show the wood grain but add a subtle touch of color.

# Elements of an Eclectic Kitchen

Looking for ways to add an individual stamp on your cooking space? Here are some ideas:

◆ Use an antique pastry table as a decorative and useful island.

◆ Use a stainless-steel restaurant supply table for a streamlined island.

◆ Use free-standing furniture as cabinets (such as an armoire or cupboard).

◆ Hang chandeliers made from flea market salvage—a wire egg basket, clam basket, or a wire chandelier with crystals in various shapes and colors.

Wire egg basket chandelier.
*(Photo by M. Hackett)*

◆ Place worn Asian rugs on floors. (Place a thin rug pad underneath so you don't slip.)

◆ Hang simple artwork such as children's portraits or favorite French bakery bags, or display a collection of worn cutting boards or rolling pins.

◆ Hang a piece of flea market vintage toile fabric askew in a doorway or a window.

**Pro Workshop**

Be sure you have your overhead lighting on dimmer switches. That way the mood of the kitchen can be instantly changed with soft lighting for an impromptu romantic dinner!

# The Indispensable Pantry

*Pantries* are a convenient place to store nonperishable goods that can be made into many quick dinner options for our busy and hectic lifestyles. Pantries make a perfect place to store extra dry goods and linens. Today, a pantry can be a closet in the kitchen (common in new homes) as well as a larger room off the kitchen (found in older homes).

Some pantries are on an outside wall with a window for good air flow. If there is no window, replace a solid pantry door with a screen door to keep the pantry from getting musty. Butler's pantries are usually galley-shape and outfitted with small sinks and an area for food preparation. All types of pantries can be made special with unusual paint colors, mirrors, and shelving from floor to ceiling.

Today's pantries offer room for small appliances like juicers, mixers, and microwaves to relieve countertop clutter in the kitchen. If space is limited, a pantry can be made under a stairwell with a small door for access or in a free-standing cupboard or converted closet with

shelves. Common closet pantries are found in most homes today—those closets with wire mesh shelving, used to store pet food, canned goods, cleaning supplies, and other items.

**Decorating 101**

A **pantry** (from the Latin word *panis*, meaning "bread") is an area or small room in or off the kitchen where cooking ingredients, canned goods, utensils, china, and other supplies are kept.

# Special Effects

Kitchens can be more than just a room to cook meals. Have you ever noticed how family and friends seem to congregate in the kitchen? You can give yours a cozy, warm feeling by introducing some special effects that make it unique. Whether you redo cabinets or walls using a new paint technique or install a custom-built kitchen fireplace, the ideas are endless.

## Paint Effects

Paint is the most inexpensive and fastest way to give your kitchen (or any room) a new look. Of course the cabinets or walls can be painted a new color for an instant makeover. But have you thought of the interiors of the cabinets, the parts that don't show very much? By simply painting the interior of cabinets a vibrant color like chartreuse green, lobster red, or cobalt blue, you will have a surprised look each time you open the cupboard!

In Chapter 6, I mentioned some paint techniques that you can do yourself. Whether you give your cabinets an aged look with a crackle finish or a smooth, slick, and modern finish, paint effects are a fast and fun way to give your kitchen a personalized touch. Here are some other ideas:

- If you are not an expert artist, you could hire a professional to paint a trompe l'oeil painting. For example, a blank wall can have a faux cupboard painted on it that "displays" a complete set of dishes—and they will never break!

- Wood floors can be patterned with paint in checkerboards, plaids, or stenciled around the perimeter.

- Traditional chocolate and ivory or black and ivory squares that are painted on the floor in a diamond style to resemble marble tiles are always chic, but a traditional black stencil on natural wood is lovely, too.

- Stripes of paint in lilac and white or apple green and white can add a cottage freshness. Black and natural wood stripes are handsome and classic and stylish!

- For a bow to the French country style, paint your kitchen floor in an overscaled red-and-white gingham check. Be sure to use floor enamel for durability and wear.

### Style Pointers

It's a good idea to test out a few samples of possible patterns by painting some boards in colors that you like and laying them on the floor before you make final choices.

## Tile Tricks

Tile can add color, pattern, and texture, creating a focal point on the backsplash of a stove, on a countertop, on the backsplash between upper cabinets and lower cabinets, or around a fireplace opening. Tiles can be hand-painted for an artistic effect, hand-made with uneven edges for a rustic effect, or perfectly geometric in solid colors or patterns in diamonds, squares, octagons, or rectangles for a smooth finish. A glossy finish adds extra shine that reflects light

and makes things appear brighter, whereas a matte or seasoned finish reveals a timeless, durable quality.

Tiles come in a variety of material and price ranges:

- **Ceramic.** A fired clay that is glazed or unglazed, available in a bounty of colors, designs, sizes, and price ranges.

- **Marble.** A more formal and beautiful tile that is extremely durable, it can be costly.

- **Stone.** Stone tiles can be polished or "tumbled" (for a worn appearance), offering a natural look. Stone is very durable but can be pricey.

- **Quarry.** Another fired clay, but this material is a little less refined than its ceramic cousin. It is sometimes irregularly shaped and earth-colored like terra cotta.

- **Glass.** These tiles are very popular today, especially for bathrooms. They offer brilliant colors that reflect light for a dazzling effect. Another costly tile.

**A fitted kitchen with tile for a backsplash between cabinets and behind the stove.** *(Photo by Smallbone)*

Hand-painted tiles add artistic flair to these built-in cabinets. *(Photo by Smallbone)*

## Add a Fireplace

Nothing adds more warmth—literally—than a kitchen fireplace. It is a real focal point that is decorative as well as useful. It becomes the soul of a kitchen, the place everyone gravitates toward. The flames (a form of kinetic lighting, see Chapter 10) are overwhelmingly charming and seductive. A full-size fireplace creates a homey place to pull up two chairs for fireside conversations or impromptu dinners. A raised fireplace, like those seen in European kitchens, offers a place to view the fire from all points. It can also be used for grilling food indoors in the winter. A kitchen fireplace area is the ultimate romantic spot for two to talk and dine.

If space is limited, a gas fireplace can be installed flush on a wall. With a flip of a switch, the propane flame simulates wood logs burning—very convenient and no mess. If your budget is limited, find an old mantel at a flea market, attach it to a wall, paint the opening black, and place very large candles at the base to simulate the flicker of a fire.

A hearth is built around a stovetop to resemble a fireplace. A lit candle on a plate placed atop the stove imparts a fireplace ambience. *(Photo by Wolf Appliances)*

## Concealing the Refrigerator

Special effects in a kitchen include ways to mask everyday items that we may not want to see, like the refrigerator. Because they are so bulky, they are hard to disguise. Try incorporating yours into an entire wall of floor-to-ceiling cupboards or closets so that the door is flush with the built-ins. You could then face the front of the refrigerator with bead-board paneling or the wood you are using for the closets. Or place the refrigerator in the pantry if you are lucky enough to have one that can accommodate its size. There are also under-the-counter stainless steel refrigerators that fit neatly under a standard counter height. Although very costly, they are certainly a great way to alleviate the big boxlike refrigerator.

**Homematters**

Handsome refrigerators with glass fronts that mimic those in commercial restaurants are available for the home today. All bottles, cartons, and foods are in full view. Be sure you are a neat person if you go for this option!

If concealing isn't an option, consider buying a retro-styled refrigerator in a color that calls attention to it, becoming a tongue in cheek focal point. And if all of these ideas are out of reach, maybe taping prints in monochromatic colors all over the refrigerator front and sides could make it be the art center in your kitchen.

**These double refrigerators are concealed behind cupboardlike paneled doors.** *(Photo by Wolf Appliances)*

### Flea Market Finds: Kitchen Accessories

Most interesting kitchens are not perfectly decorated so as to appear sterile and without a feeling of hominess. That doesn't mean you have to have all of your pots and pans and bric-a-brac displayed to add warmth. Even a sleek, modern kitchen outfitted in stainless steel with minimal furnishings can be warm if you include an element of surprise (like a gold-painted ornate chair in a homespun check placed by the sleek fireplace). Here are some ideas for flea market finds that can enhance your kitchen:

◆ An old bread baker rack makes the perfect cookbook holder or free-standing "pantry" for staples like olive oil and vinegars, salts, and so on.

◆ A wooden ladder hung over a center island creates an inventive rack for hanging pots.

◆ Plant stands used as drink holders can be placed next to seating.

**A great flea market find: a plant stand used as a drink holder.**

◆ Old, medium-size chalkboards can list the dinner menu, chores for the day, or sweet nothings for that someone special.

## The Least You Need to Know

◆ Do your homework! Research all of the possible plans that can make your kitchen efficient and well designed.

◆ Cabinets can be fitted or unfitted. Select those that will organize and store your kitchen goods and match your lifestyle in the kitchen. And choosing the right colors makes the kitchen a pleasing place.

◆ Pantries can be outfitted with floor-to-ceiling shelving, windows, screen doors, and even sinks and mirrors.

◆ Tile, paint effects, and a fireplace all add decorative flair to any kitchen. And cleverly masking bulky items like the refrigerator helps add to a pleasing design.

◆ Flea market finds add individual style to any kitchen.

# In This Chapter

- ◆ Planning and prioritizing your bathroom
- ◆ Space-saving ideas for the small bathroom
- ◆ Small luxuries that have a big impact
- ◆ Choosing lighting and color
- ◆ Feng shui in the bathroom
- ◆ Flea market finds to dress up your bathroom

# Chapter 14

# Bathrooms to Linger In

Like the kitchen, the bathroom is one of the busiest rooms in the house. And today's bathrooms are not only practical, they're also places for retreat to ease stress and refresh yourself. Whether you are planning a new bathroom or renovating the one you have, create a bathroom with a style that works for you. Consider colors and lighting that are flattering, learn the essence of feng shui, and add interest with unusual flea market items.

Begin as always with an assessment of how you live, what you like, and what you have. Soon you'll be on your way to creating a bathroom that works … and works and works!

## Real Bathroom Style: Planning, Prioritizing, and Pricing

If you are lucky enough to be able to design your bathroom from scratch, you will need to do some planning by prioritizing needs and wants that match your taste and pocketbook! You can draw your room to scale by measuring and drawing a floor plan on graph paper provided in Appendix B and by following the tips in Chapter 3. Be sure to denote the plumbing and heating. You can then measure the bathroom fixtures, toilet, bathtub, shower stall, and storage pieces or vanities.

If the templates in Appendix B don't exactly match your measurements, make up your own templates and try various floor plans. Keep in mind traffic, door swings, and privacy factors. Don't forget to measure any unusual flea market items you may add that take up floor space (perhaps a vintage dresser or a set of dramatic columns, for instance).

### Pro Workshop

Before you spend any money, consider whether there are items in other rooms that you can use in your bathroom. Maybe there's a nightstand in a spare bedroom that's not being used that would be handy for holding towels or bath products. Perhaps you have some leftover fabric that would make a great shower curtain, or there's a can of leftover paint in the garage that's the perfect color for the walls.

Here are some tips to get you started on planning a successful and stylish bathroom:

◆ Evaluate the state of your bathroom. You'll need to make any repairs (leaking faucets, plumbing problems) before you begin decorating.

◆ Prioritize your wants and needs.

◆ Build your bathroom around things you love.

◆ Get accurate price estimates for all proposed items by consulting contractors, home stores, and catalogs.

◆ Total up the estimated costs so you know the budget realities.

◆ Match your plans with your available resources.

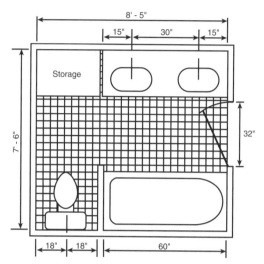

A double-sink vanity allows plenty of storage in addition to the floor-to-ceiling shelving. This layout allows adequate room at the toilet and sink areas.

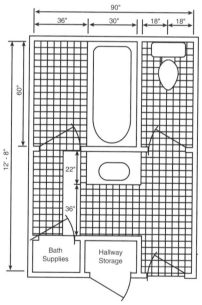

With the three fixtures in separate compartments, this large bath plan can replace a second bath, allowing more than one person to use it (and saving you the cost and plumbing of a second set of fixtures!).

Custom cabinets, architectural moldings, and large mirrors give this bathroom an elegant look.    *(Photo by Smallbone)*

# Space-Saving Ideas for a Small Bathroom

Here are some ideas if you're tight on space in the bathroom:

◆ Consider a corner-shaped shower tub.

◆ A combination tub/shower will eliminate the need for two separate fixtures.

◆ A corner-shape toilet is perfect for a closet turned bathroom or one built under a stairwell.

◆ Pocket doors (ones that slide into the wall) eliminate the need for door-swinging space.

◆ Build overhead shelving over the doors for added storage.

◆ Don't be afraid to place a sink in front of a window, if that's the only place for one. A mirror hung on the window provides natural daylight for putting on cosmetics, and the window sill acts as a caddy for supplies, eliminating the need for a built-in vanity.

The sink is positioned in front of the window. The curtains cut the glare of the sun and provide privacy.    *(Photo by Schumacher)*

**Homematters**

Live in the country? A raised tub positioned in front of a window is a very tranquil and natural setting. Live leafy ferns and other greenery can only enhance the atmosphere.

# Small Luxuries That Add Big Pleasure

Looking for a bathroom that serves as a spa? With today's busy and hectic lifestyles and schedules, it is super to have a room that one can retreat to for a tranquil moment. Create a bathroom with a feeling imitating what the spas create!

If you have the room, place seating in your bathroom. A chaise slipcovered in terry cloth is especially luxurious. If space is an issue, even a small ottoman or footstool provides a place to sit and meditate! Another idea is to have a shower curtain made from the same fabric as a comfortable terry bathrobe. Hang a hook or two on the wall near the shower to hold terry robes. Have comfortable slippers available. Clear out the drawers or cupboards with unused products and replace with water bottles, washcloths, and special soaps with pleasing aromas. And hang heated towel racks for incomparable warmth. Use wicker hampers, shells, rocks, and sea sponges to introduce natural elements. At the very least, use luxurious towels that are extra soft and absorbent.

# Lighting and Color Considerations

Sufficient bathroom lighting is a must. For most bathrooms, ceiling fixtures and lights on either side of your mirror (or mirrors if you have double sinks) will provide enough general and task lighting. A light placed over the toilet and/or the bathtub is a good addition for those who like to linger and read.

For the most flattering light when applying cosmetics, use incandescent bulbs in fixtures with glass shades that diffuse light, or opt for energy-efficient warm white fluorescent bulbs that can come close to the color of incandescent bulbs. (See Chapter 10 for more on lighting.)

For specific areas, you can use downlights or spotlights. And of course, nightlights are a comfort for trips to the bathroom in the middle of the night. A decorative chandelier placed over the bath is a luxurious way to light a bath, especially if placed on dimmer switches to adjust the lighting for different moods. And by using kinetic lighting through candles, your bathroom can be lit for an instant spa atmosphere.

Place candles on the edge of the bathtub and on the vanity counter. (Be sure to extinguish them when you're done!)

A typical dining room chandelier adds a glamorous touch to any bathroom. *(Photo by Gear Home, Bettye M. Musham, Chairwoman/CEO)*

Choose colors for your bathroom that show off your personality and that are pleasing to you. Each color you choose for your bath will give a different look:

- Seeking serenity? Pale pastels like pink are soothing, and ice blue is calming and refreshing.

- Love nature? Woodsy greens and natural earth tones simulate the great outdoors for a sense of tranquility.

- Greens can be refreshing and help to stimulate emotional growth.

◆ Are you a theatrical person? Deep, rich colors like Venetian red, pumpkin orange, and golden yellow paired with dark wood tones bring drama to an otherwise utilitarian room.

◆ Stone colors of grays, browns, and slate blues add a timeless, durable quality with an unequaled richness for an earthy look.

◆ White is always a clean and purifying look, whereas gray can portray a neoclassical look!

◆ Khaki and peanut shell colors are neutral and plain but have stunning simplicity.

◆ Aqua blues and greens are reminiscent of the sea for those who love the ocean.

◆ Purples in shades of lavender and lilac are comforting and spiritual for a bathroom that doubles as a retreat.

Be sure to review the discussion on colors in Chapter 2 before making your final paint selections.

**Homematters** _____

Color in a bathroom doesn't always mean bright. A neutral scheme is very effective when different shades of the same color are used to tie together flooring, walls, towels, and accessories. For example, try a palette of greens in celery green, caper, fern leaf, and khaki.

# Today's Bathroom as Retreat: Feng Shui Décor

If you are looking for a place to revive after a long day at work, you may want to decorate your bathroom using the ancient Chinese principles of *feng shui* (pronounced *fung shway*) décor. Feng shui, which means "wind and water," is a

philosophy practiced in China for more than 3,000 years that is becoming increasingly popular in the West. Feng shui promotes the building and enhancing of vital *chi* in our homes.

**Decorating 101** _____

Feng shui is the ancient Chinese art of placement; specifically, how your home and environment affects you. The Chinese believe that **chi,** or energy, is what fills the universe. It is the underlying essence of all things.

Chi is vital energy, necessary for the nurturing of our souls and our interests. You can promote good chi in a bathroom by arranging the fixtures and accessories in specific ways, living with what you love, and planning designs to promote comfort and safety. Also imparting a sense of organization through simplifying our surroundings makes any room feel energized with "good vibes."

How is chi cultivated? Through daily rejuvenation. Here are some ways you can use your bathroom to cultivate good chi:

◆ Bathing

◆ Stretching

◆ Practicing yoga (if you have a large bathroom)

◆ Reading

◆ Meditating

◆ Singing

◆ Playing music

◆ Laughing

◆ Enjoying wall art or sculpture

◆ Smelling flowers and viewing plants for a touch of nature

What are chi bathroom enhancers?

◆ Placing pleasing artwork on the walls or through sculptures

◆ Arranging flowers in a vase for the countertop

◆ Arranging living plants to view, mimicking nature

◆ Using incandescent lighting or halogen lamps, candles, a fireplace (the ultimate luxury!), or natural sunlight

◆ Hanging mirrors (not just the vanity mirror) to double the chi in a room by expanding the space, revealing activity and reflecting light

◆ Arranging natural objects like shells, rocks, and pinecones to bring the great outdoors indoors

◆ Using a miniature rock fountain or an aquarium to introduce active water that makes interesting sounds (wonderful to listen to as you soak in the tub)

◆ Hanging crystals to balance extremes in chi flow

◆ Selecting colors that please, soothe, and inspire you

**Homematters**

According to Terah Kathryn Collins, author of *Home Design with Feng Shui*, plumbing is considered a threat to chi circulating through the house (because it may, literally or meta-phorically according to the depth of your belief, be pulled down a drain like water). She suggests keeping the drains of the tub and sink closed when not in use and the toilet seat lid down when not in use. She also suggests installing the toilet so it is not visible from the bathroom door. If that isn't possible, hang a round-faceted cut-glass crystal from the ceiling between the door and the toilet to help lift and circulate chi!

There are many books available on feng shui if you'd like to learn more about it (*The Complete Idiot's Guide to Feng Shui* is a good place to begin). Many books discuss feng shui throughout your home as well as in specific rooms. Browse through your local library or bookstore.

# Adding Pizzazz to the Sink, Countertop, and Vanity

Today the standard vanity and sink are just that—standard. The range of possibilities is endless, with sinks that sit atop countertops instead of being sunken in and countertops made from anything but Formica. Vanities are designed as works of art.

Most home decorators head right to the kitchen and bath stores for a vanity cabinet to accommodate a sink (or sinks) and provide storage for bathroom supplies. But have you considered using alternative furnishings for a vanity? A vintage or even a new dresser can be a perfect fit, especially one with an attached mirror! The utilitarian look of a standard cabinet is replaced with a real piece of furniture, adding a lot more style. (Learn how to turn a dresser into a vanity in the next section.)

Some vanities are exposed below the counter or sink top, actually not a vanity at all, so pipes are exposed as part of the design. The countertop can be concrete, copper sheeting, galvanized steel, or wood—all elements that age in time with varied *patinas*. Sink designs are available in many forms: pedestal style, where the bowl sits atop a column for a spare look; vintage sinks with legs; or just bowl-like forms that sit atop the counter for an artistic wash basin.

A vintage sink with legs has an open and clean look.   *(Photo by Waterworks)*

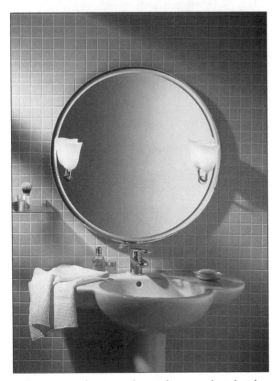

A large, round mirror, clover-shape pedestal sink, and tiled walls add up to a contemporary-style bathroom.   *(Photo by Flos USA)*

**Decorating 101**

A **patina** is any thin coating or color change resulting from age that occurs on surfaces such as old wood or silver. Patinas are highly desired by decorators. Materials or furnishings with a desirable patina can fetch high prices.

# Turning a Dresser into a Vanity

An advanced do-it-yourselfer (if you can use a drill and a jigsaw) can change the look of a standard bathroom vanity by replacing it with a dresser. You may want to consult a plumber before you start to make sure it is feasible at your site.

Here are the materials you'll need:

◆ Dresser
◆ Tag board for template
◆ Marker
◆ Drill with a ¼-inch bit
◆ Jigsaw drill
◆ Varnish
◆ Caulking
◆ High-gloss polyurethane
◆ Fine-grit sandpaper

1. If the dresser has an attached mirror, remove it. Select a sink with a rim to keep water off the surface of the chest. Draw a template of the sink and tape it to the top of the chest. Drill a ¼-inch hole on the inside of the template, and then use your jigsaw to trace around the inside of the template.

**Step 1.**

2. Cut holes in the drawers to accommodate the plumbing pipes. Seal the drawers shut or cut out wood sections (or have a carpenter's help) to replace the cutouts so the drawers are useful.

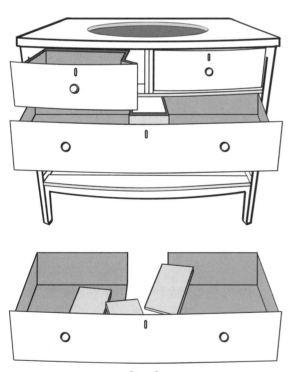

**Step 2.**

3. Clean the top of the dresser and sand very lightly. Apply a coat of high-gloss polyurethane or high-gloss acrylic if a painted finish.

**Step 3.**

4. Hook up or have a plumber hook up plumbing. Put drawers back in dresser. Cement sink to dresser with caulking. Apply a thin bead of caulk between the sink and dresser top to form a good seal.

**Step 4.**

5. Place a mirror on the wall or attach the one that came with the dresser.

Voilà! A vanity that is functional and pretty!

**Pro Workshop**

Place stones and shells in a corner of a shower stall. They will recall nature, streams, and the ocean.

## Flea Market Finds: Bathroom Enhancers

If your bathroom is as dull as a dungeon, try adding a few flea market items that can be useful, interesting, and just plain fun!

When space is limited and privacy is needed, place a decorative door as a divider between the toilet and the shower for artistic purposes and as a useful screen! No room for a door? A curtain made from a vintage textile can pull double duty as a beautiful piece of cloth and a practical divider. Hang it from the ceiling on a dowel or hooks mounted right into the ceiling.

**A vintage cloth or beloved printed sheet makes a perfect artistic shower curtain or divider.**
*(Photo by Garnet Hill)*

A large ornate mirror adds significant drama and interest to a small, dull bathroom. The mirror reflects light and visually doubles the size of the space.

Here are a few other ideas for perking up your bathroom:

◆ Old grocery-style food displays often make nifty wire shelving for tissue paper, soaps, and towels.

◆ In a child's bathroom, a vintage Barbie doll can be mounted to the wall with the arms outstretched to hold a washcloth (Ken for a boy's bath). What fun!

◆ A small table can double as a bathroom countertop. Follow the directions for "Turning a Dresser into a Vanity." Place a basket of towels underneath if you want to disguise the plumbing pipes.

**Oversized mirrors add grandeur to a bathroom space.** *(Photo by Smallbone)*

## The Least You Need to Know

◆ Before any decorating takes place, do some planning by prioritizing needs and wants that match your taste and pocketbook.

◆ The smallest luxuries can have the biggest impact on comfort and emotions.

◆ Selecting the right light and colors for your bath will have a profound impact on your spirit. They make you look and feel good.

◆ Feng shui décor works well in a bathroom as a retreat area. If you are looking for good chi or vital energy, follow some of the feng shui philosophies.

◆ Bathrooms to linger in are the ones with unusual sinks, countertops, and flea market art. There is so much to view!

# In This Chapter

- ◆ Bedroom planning for practicality and pleasure
- ◆ The all-important bed
- ◆ Choosing styles and colors
- ◆ The bedroom as home office
- ◆ Flea market finds for the bedroom

# Chapter 15

# Bedrooms to Match Your Moods

Bedrooms are our private sanctuaries. No other room so clearly reflects our personal passions and style. If you express these well in your bedroom, you can deepen your relaxation and add pleasure to your private moments. Your bedroom should be a combination of a cozy area to rest and rejuvenate, a space for hobbies or work, a place to exercise, and an area for romantic escapes. And the color choice should work to facilitate these needs.

By reviewing some of your style files and color boards selecting colors that match your personal style and furnishings that reflect the way you live, you can create a mental picture of what your bedroom should look (and "feel") like. And if your bedroom doubles as a home office, I'll show you how to make it a comfortable area that blends in with your décor so you can work in beautiful surroundings.

## Arranging the Bedroom for More Than Sleeping

Today's bedrooms serve several purposes. With proper design, you can make your bedroom a practical and private place for such varied activities as reading, writing, workouts, and enjoying hobbies. It can be a good dual-purpose site for a study or office, a dressing room or vanity area, or a crib space. Here are some important questions to ask yourself as you plan a bedroom for privacy, relaxation, and various uses:

◆ What activities or purposes does your bedroom serve now? What activities would you like to find a place for in your bedroom?

◆ If you share your bedroom, do you and your partner's personal styles click? Do you need to come up with a list of shared desires and dislikes, and consider how to accommodate both of your styles?

- What are the basic items that you need? A new mattress? A headboard? Night tables? Storage pieces?

- What size bed do you have: king or queen size? Do you need to buy a new one? Draw up a floor plan and place a bed template on it to assess scale and position. Remember that four-poster beds take up more space, both physically and visually!

- What would you love to have in your bedroom that would make it feel like a sanctuary?

- Do you need bookcases (for an avid reader), a sound system (for a music lover), or dimmable lighting (for the romantic)? Or all three?

- Can you allow at least 2 feet around both sides of the bed for easy access?

- Do you need storage space? (For some ideas on functional but stylish storage, see Chapter 20.)

- Is there room for seating? Room for a desk?

- Does the room provide adequate privacy and quiet? Do you need to add draperies to muffle noise, thick carpets for sound absorption, or soundproof walls during construction? You may want to place wardrobes or bookshelves on walls that are next to other rooms to help act as a sound barrier.

- Does your room provide adequate natural light (or too much)? Do you want to add windows, put in a skylight, or put up blackout shades?

- Where are the light sockets and switches? What are your electrical requirements? What about television or telephone jacks?

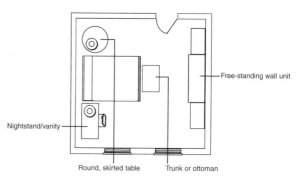

**Homematters**

The principles of feng shui state that to achieve good chi or energy, the bedroom should be located at the back of the house where chi is naturally more serene. More feng shui tips: Place the bed where you have a view of the door, and position "active" furniture like exercise equipment and desks as far from the bed as possible.

Free-standing wall unit

Nightstand/vanity

Round, skirted table     Trunk or ottoman

**An example of a bedroom layout.**

You can visually expand a small bedroom by using a few pieces of larger-scaled furniture. This is better than using a lot of small furnishings, which looks cluttered. Use vertical space for built-in storage pieces and a tall bureau for maximum storage space.

# You and Your Bed

The most important thing in your bedroom is, of course, the bed. We spend at least a third of our time sleeping. With that many hours invested, you want your bed to be not only comfortable, but also pleasing to the eye.

## Mattress Matters

Although you might not have thought of including bedding in your decorating budget, it is one of those essentials, like electrical repair or plumbing, that you need to have to form the foundation of further decorating plans.

Steer clear of bargain bedding! It's likely to be of poor construction and low-quality materials. Buy your mattress from a reputable dealer and be sure you are shown the inner construction. A dealer usually has a sample of the inner construction of each mattress available for you to look at. Look for bedding that isn't too soft, so the hips and back are properly supported; on the other hand, it shouldn't feel boardlike, without proper padding.

What size should your mattress be? Consider that most people are comfortable in a bed that is at least 6 inches longer than they are tall. Standard bed sizes are as follows:

- **King.** 76 inches width × 80 to 84 length
- **Queen.** 60 × 80 inches
- **Full.** 54 × 75 inches
- **Twin.** 39 × 75 inches
- **Twin extra-long.** 39 × 80 inches

## Creative Headboards

If you'd like to add pizzazz to your bed with a headboard, you don't have to go out and buy one from the furniture store. There are alternative and inexpensive headboard options that you may not have thought of, available at your home/garden or hardware store. A solid board of MDF painted in a gloss paint makes a contemporary statement. Cut a sheet the width of your bed, and attach with screws to a metal bed frame. It will be a spare, slightly overscaled contemporary style. Here are some other ideas:

- With the help of a skilled carpenter or as a do-it-yourself project if you're handy, use a jigsaw to cut a piece of plywood into scroll shapes to form an artistic headboard. Paint with high gloss paint.

A headboard made from MDF board cut in a scroll pattern with a jigsaw and painted in a high-gloss paint.

- Fencing makes a natural headboard, with most sections coming in 4-foot widths. A white picket fence evokes cottage style, whereas a stockade style can be modern or eclectic in various paint colors.

A picket fence headboard made from a section of fencing.

- Garden/home stores offer trellises that are premade, some perfectly sized to encase a twin or full-size bed.

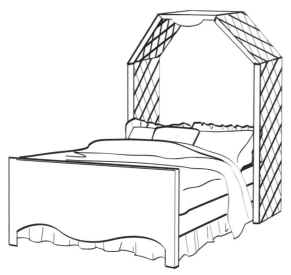

A trellis headboard made from garden lattice.

◆ A wallpaper "headboard" is easy to do. Just paper behind the bed on the wall in the desired shape (a rectangular shape is perfect) and trim with a border in the size you desire.

A headboard made from wallcovering cut to size with border trim.

# Styles and Colors for Everyone

How do you decorate a bedroom to match your personal style? By giving it a mood with the right color that works as a backdrop for furnishings in your taste. The same holds true for children's rooms. Your personal style is carried right through to the nursery or child's room. The furniture is smaller, the artwork age appropriate, but the mood is often a version of your personal taste. The one big difference is that the child's room should be able to change and develop as your child gets older.

A child's bedroom is a perfect opportunity to create an imaginative decorating scheme. Create a trompe l'oeil mural that is fantasy-filled from a time-honored classic children's story. Forego a current fad theme that your child may outgrow in a short time.

This "Bunny Business" chintz fabric is a perfect choice for curtains or bedding in a nursery or child's room. *(Photo by Brunswig & Fils)*

**Stimulating prints are ideal for a child's room.**
*(Photo by Garnet Hill)*

Whether you are a classic or contemporary type, country, creative, or downright *Bohemian*, color and furniture choices make the greatest impact on the overall style. Which type are you?

### Decorating 101

In reference to décor, **Bohemian** refers to a style that mixes many different elements into a mesmerizing, often unconventional scheme.

## Contemporary

If your style is contemporary, consider these color combinations and accessories:

◆ For a glamorous look, combine camel, ivory, or other neutral colors with a hint of sparkly fabrics in gold or silver. Add

furnishings with clean lines in Lucite (an acrylic resin or plastic that is cast or molded into transparent or translucent material), glass, or metallic finishes.

◆ A bonafide sophisticate? How about ivory walls with a gray/silvery comforter? Blend furniture in with the same or shades of the wall color. Keep a spare look with simple lines and see-through accessories like glass. Mix textures of silk, wool, and cotton in various bedding, pillows, comforters, sheets, and blankets.

◆ Use various tones of lilac and green to add freshness and vibrancy. Use airy fabrics on windows or simple blinds. A slim four-poster wrought iron bed is visually light.

◆ A monochromatic scheme of black, gray, and white gives a modern appeal. Paint walls a soft gray. Use a low, natural wooden bed with a mattress only. Keep bedding minimal in black-and-ivory patterns. Keep night tables the same height as the bed. Add lighting in contemporary styles with chrome bases and white paper shades.

**A streamlined bed with built-in night tables and pendant lighting.**    *(Photo by Cassina)*

# Classic

If you love a clean, classic look, consider these options:

◆ Combine tans, linens, ivories, and white with various textures on walls, bedding, and flooring for a calming, timeless atmosphere. Wood floors with classic flokati rugs in ivory wool scattered about add panache.

◆ Mix yellow or cream shades of straw with ivory trim and wood floors with worn Asian carpets. Try an upholstered headboard in a deep yellow suede with a burnt-orange paisley comforter. Add a chest for a night table and a large skirted table on the other side.

◆ Gray on gray is the new black! Gray is a sophisticated color that works like a pair of khaki pants—all colors seem to work well with it. For a classic aura, add ivory and natural linen colors on the bed with chocolate accessories. How about a pashmina throw at the foot of the bed or a faux animal rug?

◆ Red walls trimmed with ivory, grounded with a sisal flooring and accented with hunter green bedding, are a traditional and eye-pleasing combination.

**Pro Workshop**

Consider these decorator tips for making your bed as comfortable and stylish as possible. Add a feather bed, a mattress made from feathers that is enclosed in a fabric case that is placed on top of your mattress. Give your comforter a fresh new look with a duvet cover, an envelope case that fits right over your comforter. Purchase cotton sheets with a luxurious quality 350 thread count, the number of threads per square inch, to ensure the highest comfort.

# Country

If you like an outdoorsy country look, try these ideas:

◆ Any color of green—sage, apple, leaf—found in nature imparts a country style when painted on wide pine floors. Stencil leaf motifs on kraft paper lampshades to repeat the leaf color. Paint walls a salt white.

◆ For a fresh, modern country look that's reminiscent of the sea, combine aqua blue walls with ivory accessories. Add natural elements such as a substantive collection of sea shells, sea glass, and driftwood.

◆ Try yellow walls with combinations of solid yellow, pink, and ivory bedding for a charming country look. Slipcover headboards made from patchwork quilts of the same colors. Paint the floor ivory for a clean and fresh look.

# Creative/Eclectic/Bohemian

If your style tends toward the offbeat and eclectic, consider these ideas:

◆ Paint walls a fabulous rich color such as deep pink or red. Add silk bedding in stripes or paisley of burgundies, oranges, or pinks. Hang a colored-glass pendant-style lighting fixture over the bed. Layer the bed with comforters, blankets, throws, and pile on several down pillows.

◆ Paint the floor and ceiling the same shade of pale pink for a wash of color that makes the room feel spacious and bright. Add flea market finds in wood, bamboo, and rusty iron. Touches of fuschia continue the pink theme with silk pillowcases and a sari on the bed.

◆ Shades of purple painted in stripes or patterns on the walls reflect a creative attitude. Pair it with a period reproduction bed with headboard and footboard. Keep wooden floors worn and scrubbed. Accent the look with night tables and storage units that are modern with clean lines.

◆ A bright, leafy green color like chartreuse is smart and shocking! A grand four-poster bed with vibrant coverings in shades of green will create a monochromatic scheme.

The ultimate in a Bohemian-style bedroom ... in the out of doors!    *(Photo by Roche Bobois)*

**Style Pointers**

Need some quick changes for seasonal looks? For summer, put away heavy rugs and leave floors bare or use sisal mats. Make the bed in white or citrusy colors to visually "cool down" the room. Replace heavily draped windows with rattan blinds or gauze curtains. For winter, add cozy comforters in florals or patterns in rich colors like reds, golds, and oranges to "warm up" the room. Scatter throw rugs that are warm to the feet. Layer windows with full-length curtains to add a cozy dimension.

# The Bedroom as Home Office

No space for a home office? Why not tuck a work area in your bedroom? A long writing table placed next to or at the foot of the bed works perfectly, just pull up a comfortable side chair. Be sure you have a lamp that provides adequate lighting, and an electrical outlet handy (and a phone jack, if you need it).

If you have the luxury of having a closet that can be turned into a hidden office, place the computer equipment on a small table with casters so it can be rolled out when needed and put away when not in use. Even a small chair on casters can be wheeled in and out, keeping your bedroom free of clutter and your office behind closed doors. Use the back of the closet door for a bulletin board and attach a pocket organizer.

On a wall opposite the bed, a custom built-in closet with a flip-down desk can accommodate books as well as office supplies. When the desk is not in use, it can be concealed so the wall of built-ins is neat and attractive.

This free-standing wall unit not only provides dual closets and a writing desk for this bedroom, but architectural character as well.    *(Photo by Smallbone)*

Make your office/work area handsome by using inventive non-office-looking files such as wicker baskets fitted with hanging file mechanisms. Soften your office chair with a slipcover in a fabric that coordinates with your bed linens. Add a vase of fresh flowers whenever possible to bring a bit of color and nature in. Other ideas:

◆ Organize your desk supplies in inventive containers, such as a vintage muffin tin for paper clips, rubber bands, and stamps. Pretty wooden bowls or tin boxes also make great organizers.

◆ Keep cords for computers and printers and fax machines neat by placing some hooks underneath the table that they can be threaded through.

◆ An armoire can be fitted with a pull-out shelf that can house a computer, a printer on another shelf, and books on yet another shelf. The inside of the cupboard doors allow for note boards and hooks for hanging organizers. An armoire is decorative and functional and completely conceals the bedroom office.

**Armoire as home office.** *(Photo by Gear Home, Bettye M. Musham, Chairwoman/CEO)*

◆ A chest at the foot of the bed can house paperwork or even files.

◆ A skirted table can disguise a filing cabinet.

### Flea Market Finds: Bedroom Beautifiers

A bedroom that exudes personal style is one that has unique and inventive items displayed or reused in clever ways. For recycled headboards, use large sections of old tin ceiling screwed directly on the wall. You can repaint these or leave them as is for an aged patina. Old shutters attached together form a unique backdrop as well as iron gates, one for a twin bed and two for a queen or king bed.

**An old iron gate makes a fanciful and creative headboard.** *(Photo by Garnet Hill)*

Architectural salvage provides some of the most interesting recycled pieces for a bedroom. Porch columns make an interesting bed frame. Try placing two at either side of the head of the bed with a vintage piece of lace hung between as an ode to the Greek Revival style.

Two columns from a colonial home's porch, complete with peeling paint, make a spectacular frame for a queen-size bed.    *(Photo by M. Hackett)*

Vintage lace makes a great canopy if hung from two rods attached to the ceiling and left flowing as the "headboard." For an even simpler addition, drape a piece of vintage fabric from one post of a four-poster bed.

Vintage cloth hung in one corner of the bed makes a simple but stunning statement.    *(Photo by Roche Bobois)*

An armoire that is too big for your room can be sawed in half and made into two night tables, a top added for one side and a base for the other.

An armoire sawed into two pieces and placed as nightstands for a modern country style.

## The Least You Need to Know

◆ As a quiet private space, the bedroom has potential for many purposes besides sleeping. Think how you want to use it (as an exercise or hobby area, for example).

◆ The focal point of any bedroom is the bed. Make it comfortable, creative, and seductive!

◆ The bedroom as a home office can be outfitted with all necessary electrical outlets for computers and other equipment, stylish storage, and a comfortable chair to make working there efficient and elegant.

◆ Your favorite styles and colors should be reflected in your personal bedroom space. Your child's bedroom is a version of your taste, ever changing as the child grows.

◆ The most imaginative bedrooms include flea market items that are unique and quite clever!

# In This Chapter

- ◆ Your work style and office setup
- ◆ Desk, chair, storage, and lighting—you're in business!
- ◆ Where should you put your office?
- ◆ Special touches and luxury items for a five-star office
- ◆ Flea market finds for the home office

# Chapter 16

# The Home Office

Many people today are opting to do some or all of their work at home and have a room or space entirely devoted to it. Even if you make your living by going to a traditional workplace every day, you may need a home office for any number of reasons: to do work you bring home, work on activities or projects you're engaged in, or just keep track of household maintenance, repairs, and expenses.

Of course, you may not be able to devote an entire room to a home office. In that case, you can partition a section of the living room, kitchen, or bedroom into a separate space, using folding screens, bookshelves, or simply a change of floor coverings. Or you may find just enough room in a stair landing or nook under the stairs to set up a desk, some storage, a small chair, and lighting. Wherever you locate it, your home office will have to be a quiet, well-lit zone where you can concentrate on your work.

## Your Work Style: What's Important for You?

To create a successful method of working at home and a suitable home office environment, the first thing you should do is consider your work habits and personality. Some questions you might ask yourself are …

- ◆ Will I be using my office alone, or will colleagues, clients, or members of the household be coming in and out to use the office? How much seating do I need?

**A more formal home office is set up for small conferences.** *(Photo by the Hon Company)*

◆ Am I a neat and organized worker? A person who delves into projects with reference material on every surface? Or am I more of a *mis en place* type? After I use a book, do I return it to its proper place?

**Furnishings with clean lines add up to a contemporary, light, and airy look.** *(Photo by the Hon Company)*

**Decorating 101** _____

**Mis en place** is a French phrase that means everything is put in its proper space after use.

◆ Can all office items be left out, or do they need to be hidden when the office is not in use? Is the office in a separate room or does it pull double duty as a guest room or dining room?

**A snazzy dining room is used as a home office/ conference room with a large table and several chairs.** *(Photo by the Hon Company)*

◆ Does my work require my undivided attention? Do I need a door that I can close to eliminate distractions?

◆ Will household calls or conversations distract me? Can I place my office far away from the hub of the family gathering area?

◆ Do I need total privacy? Is my work intense? Should I think about soundproofing the room?

◆ Am I disciplined enough to work at home?

◆ Are friends or family members apt to stop by unannounced or call frequently?

◆ Are my hours flexible? Can I work when I want to?

- How much natural light is available at different times of the day? Will I be working in the early hours of the morning, during the day, or at night? What type of lighting will I need?

- Do I like working with music in the background? Is a stereo a possibility?

A well-designed office is the ultimate expression of personal choice, allowing you to create an atmosphere to meet your needs, tastes, and idiosyncrasies. A home office can have all of the advantages of a traditional workplace: furnishings, equipment, technology, communications equipment, and supplies, but the décor, colors, lighting options, and comfort level should be tailor-made to your specifications. Are you looking for a warm and homey atmosphere with personal accessories like family photographs, mementos, your children's artwork, or handmade bowls that you made in pottery class? Or a more streamlined look with plenty of storage to eliminate clutter? Creating an effective work environment will help make you an effective worker.

# Businesslike Basics

A home office without adequate space or storage or even a proper table or chair will add chaos to your life. Have a comfortable chair, a desk that works for your needs, and as much storage as necessary to organize your paper and projects. Ideally, your home office will have a desk, comfortable chair, filing cabinets, plenty of bookcases or shelving, proper lighting, and probably a computer, printer, and fax. Let's take a look at some of the basics of a successful home office.

## Furniture

Choosing the right desk and chair is the first step in applying *ergonomics* to your furnishings. Do your homework by testing out different chairs and desks before buying. A comfortable chair is a must for good posture, but it should also look attractive. Sit in it, and check whether it has good back support and a padded seat. If an office-style chair is not an option, some dining chairs can be substituted if they have upholstered backs, seats, and arms (and preferably, if they have castors, or wheels, as well).

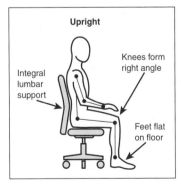 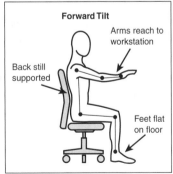 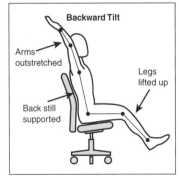

The correct chair. Upright: Sit upright so that your back is supported. Forward tilt: Be able to tilt forward and reach across your desk. Backward tilt: Be able to tilt backward and stretch your limbs.

**Decorating 101** _____

**Ergonomics** is the study of the relationship between workers and their office surroundings and equipment.

## Storage Options

Plenty of storage for files, books, office supplies, and other necessities is essential for an efficient home office. That way you can retrieve information readily and keep a sense of organization, which alleviates overwhelming feelings of chaos. Two types of storage, built-in or movable, can work, depending on your situation.

A neat office space with storage to accommodate a large number of files. The Asian rug adds warmth to the wooden floor. *(Photo by the Hon Company)*

Movable storage units are perfect if you rent your home or apartment or if you are in a temporary setup. When you move, you can take your office with you or choose a new site easily. Movable units include free-standing bookshelves, armoires, modular storage units, and stackable cubes. Modular and stackable units allow you to have a built-in look arranged in a fashion that works for your work and supplies.

For more ideas on modern and useful storage options, see Chapter 20. Also check Appendix A for mail-order catalogs like Hold Everything and Ikea, both of which offer clever storage ideas.

Built-in shelving, bookcases, file cabinets, or a flip-down desk all make for a streamlined, efficient office. Some built-in pieces can even add an architectural air. Wall-to-wall bookshelves can add much needed storage and free up floor space by using an entire wall space. Bookshelves can be custom built around seating, a desk, or a door opening. Built-in furniture is usually more costly, so assess how long you will be in your home before having custom units installed.

**Pro Workshop** _____

A plastic wire basket hooked under a desk can manage the cords from various office equipment that tend to tangle. Tags on the cords will help identify them.

A wall-hung shelving unit supplies plenty of storage and fits perfectly in a small space such as a bedroom alcove.

## Lighting

Proper lighting is essential to defining the task areas in the home workplace, and it also prevents eye strain, of course. General lighting provided by an overhead fixture is fine for normal activities but must be supplemented by adequate task lighting. Place a lamp at each area where you work. Adjustable architect's lamps are useful because of their capability to swing to any position, laterally and vertically, to illuminate your work. You may want to purchase a few inexpensive clip-on lights, which can attach to the side of a bookcase or shelf. Table or floor lamps that shine light downward are useful on either side of a seating area. (See Chapter 10 for more about lighting options.)

An adjustable architect's lamp is useful home office lighting.

## Where to Put Your Office?

Of course, choosing the right space in your home is very important. If you spend most of your day in the office, choose a space that is bright and attractive. Unless it suits the kind of work you do, a dark space will diminish your productivity and creativity. Take time to analyze your work habits and lifestyles. Which are your priorities?

- **Simple?** A basic workspace with a table, comfortable chair, filing cabinet, and outlets will suit you.
- **Warm and homey?** Part of the kitchen can be used as a desk area.
- **Bright with a view?** You'll want to have plenty of windows and natural light.
- **Mobile?** A cart can be used as a desk on wheels.
- **Concealable?** Make sure your workspace can be hidden away at day's end (behind the doors of an armoire, for example).
- **Eclectic?** Try an imaginative blend of vintage furnishings with modern technology.
- **Private?** Position your office on the quietest side of the house in an area that can be closed off (preferably one with a nearby bathroom).

### Style Pointers

If you are creating a new home office, always add more electrical outlets than you think you'll need. It's much more economical to do it in the construction phase rather than after the room is completed. Don't forget to have a couple of phone jacks installed in the room as well.

## A Specific Room?

If you have the luxury of converting an entire room as your office, locate it away from the family hubbub in a quiet area. If natural light is important, choose the room with the most windows. Air flow is important, too, and proper heating or air conditioning affect the way you work. Do they work sufficiently in the room you chose? Your choice may be the room that is most aesthetically pleasing, with paint color or wall covering you like. Is there a room that is already outfitted with bookshelves? Are there several outlets in one particular room?

Consider these aspects before you plunk down your desk.

**Homematters** _____

Did you know that if you place your home office in a bay window area, the large window view will invite expansive vision!

## A Tucked-Away Space?

If you don't have a spare room that you can use as your office, you can get creative and find a place to tuck one in. Consider these ideas:

◆ Place a slim table and chair at the foot of the bed.

◆ Use a fold-down desk that is part of a bookshelf unit.

If you are short on space, a folding table works great as a temporary home office. *(Photo by the Hon Company)*

◆ Have a combination dining table/desk. (You will also need a storage piece for files, supplies, and so forth.)

◆ Place a desk or table in a dormer space that has a window.

◆ Place a cozy office space, complete with shelves, under a stairwell.

◆ Invest in an armoire fitted with pull-out shelves.

◆ Use a closet that can hold a pull-out table with a computer and a chair on casters.

◆ Try a night table/desk combination beside the head of the bed.

◆ Convert the attic or basement to a work area. (Make sure you have adequate ventilation and light.)

A library doubles as a home office with comfortable leather seating. *(Photo by Lee Industries)*

An office tucked in under a stairwell is efficiently organized.

# Special Touches for Your Home Office

Personalizing your surroundings with comfortable and familiar objects can enhance your productivity. The more you like your work space, the more you will want to spend time in your home office. Here are some suggestions for special touches for your office:

◆ If you have any, use ancestral storage items like an antique armoire to give the office a touch of family history. Place framed family photographs on your desk and other areas.

◆ Hang your professional degrees, display trophies from sporting events, and hang your favorite flea market finds.

◆ Monogram a pillow with your one large initial, for example "M" for Mary.

◆ Have one of your children draw an Andy Warhol–ish tongue-in-cheek portrait of you. Either enlarge it to an overscaled size or copy it several times and individually frame each.

A traditional home office feel is enhanced with old books, leather chairs, and artwork.    *(Photo by the Hon Company)*

◆ If you started your own home business, frame a memento of the time that reminds you of when you came up with the "Eureka!" moment—for example, a business card from the restaurant where you talked it over with your husband, wife, or friend; or the napkin you drew your plans on.

**Style Pointers**

Have a comfy sweater à la "Mr. Rogers" that is your "work" sweater. Each time you go to work, change into your sweater. It will help get you into the work mode.

## Quiet, Please!

The home office can be made more sound-proof with smart decorating choices. Here are a few:

◆ To muffle sound, use wall-to-wall carpeting for flooring treatment.

◆ Maximize fabric use on walls and window dressing to absorb sound.

- Use bookcases filled with books to act as a functional and decorative sound baffle.
- Use oversize cork bulletin boards or cork tiles on walls. These are super sound absorbers, and a cork bulletin board makes a great place to tack up frequently used phone numbers, notes, receipts, to-do lists, business cards, and other paperwork.

## Lap of Luxury Items

Small luxuries in a home office that you can add as you go will help you to think, create, or even retreat from the outside world if you feel like it. Try some of these accessories:

- A small kitchen center in a corner of the workspace behind a folding screen. A tea or coffee maker is a nice addition that can fill the space with a wonderful aroma. A small, dorm-size refrigerator can keep cold water and drinks handy.
- A CD player loaded with your favorite music. CD racks can be hung behind closed doors or in a free-standing CD rack. A set of headphones can be used when you share your office.
- Down-filled pillows covered in fabrics that can take a beating can be placed on the sofa for a truly comfortable head- or backrest. If you want to splurge, use down-filled cushions for your chair or sofa. You'll never want to get up!
- A treadmill helps release some pent-up energy during a lunch break!

---

### Flea Market Finds: Home Office Finds

Take the office look out of your home office by using flea market items to relieve an institutional atmosphere. Be inventive with desks, accessories, and storage! Try some of these unique ideas:

- Make a desk out of an old door. Place it on a set of saw horses for an instant work table. Repaint if necessary. Add a glass top to ensure a smooth surface.
- Bookcases can be formed from stacked apple or milk crates. A set of nine makes a fabulous wall set-up.
- Waste baskets can be made from former maple syrup buckets.
- Aged wicker baskets can be fitted with hanging files to hold paperwork.
- Vintage mirrors add pizzazz to a bland office and are a nice combination with a modern desk and storage units.
- Old carpenter's toolboxes hold all desk supplies in one box.
- Silver cups, trophies, or glass jars are pretty pencil holders.
- Arrange your collectibles—a miniature car or matchbook collection, perhaps—in shadow boxes for wall art.
- Mound beach glass in very large old jars to bring in some color.

## The Least You Need to Know

◆ Home offices—even in the smallest spaces—should be created around your personal tastes, work habits, and lifestyle.

◆ The basic elements for a home office are a desk, comfortable chair, storage, and good lighting.

◆ Sound-absorbing elements like curtains, bookcases, and wall-to-wall carpeting are useful in the office area. Additional items like a music system, small refrigerator, treadmill, and personal accessories make the office an inviting place to work.

◆ Flea market items can make useful and inventive storage pieces or desks—or just add charm and personality to an office space.

# In This Chapter

- ◆ Adding pizzazz to the front entry, foyer, stairs, and hallways

- ◆ Hobby hideaways

- ◆ A quiet space for solitude

- ◆ Flea market finds for other areas of your home

# Other Significant Spaces That Might Be Overlooked

The entrance to any home is the first place you and your guests will see when coming into your home. That is all the reason you need to give it a soul! Don't disregard this space. There are many ways to make it welcoming.

Front doors, foyers, stairways, and hallways, and even cubby corners and other overlooked or odd spaces, can be enhanced with the right lighting, paints, furnishings, and decorative touches. Pay attention to these spaces when planning your décor by making them useful, pretty, and maybe even a little bit surprising!

## Making a Memorable Entryway

One of the most interesting ways to make an entry unforgettable is to embellish the front door. A door painted in an unexpected color like lavender or bittersweet orange immediately pleases you and pleasantly surprises your guests. An aged door with a rich and handsome patina reveals a home with a history. A glass door is bright and airy. A weathered door is a perfect choice for a seaside home. And a screen door is always welcome in the summer months. Be sure that if your front door swings in, it coordinates with the interior; like a story, the door is the book cover that leads you into the novel, or the rest of the house.

Other welcoming touches include placing a natural-fiber straw mat in front of the door for cleaning shoes. Create an inviting entry with lots of flowers, plants, or sculpture flanking the front door. Replace an electric doorbell with a ship-style bell with a beautiful rope or ribbon on it that hangs down. Install a creative door knocker, like a cast iron mold turned greeting knocker. A bench placed outside the door is also inviting. Reveal who you are before anyone enters your home!

A lobster cooking mold turned door knocker. *(Photo by M. Hackett)*

The most humble doorstops are often the most provocative. Try placing a good-size, nice-shape rock at the base of a door to hold it open.

A needlepoint-covered brick makes a pretty doorstop and adds a personal touch to an entryway. *(Photo by M. Hackett)*

# Fashioning a Foyer with Flair

You may forget the very first space that you and your guests pass through before coming into the home, the foyer. Often these are the last spaces that you think about when decorating your home, but they can be one of the most impressionable if they are relaxed and warm. But how to add warmth to a formal or forgotten foyer? Here are some hints of how to soften up that space (and make it useful):

◆ Place a wall-hung cubbyhole on the wall opposite the door to showcase a small collection, revealing the things you love.

◆ Paint or stencil the floor in stripes, checkerboard, or in a spattered technique.

◆ Decorate with painted floor cloths for an artistic welcome.

◆ Use patterned carpet for a soft feel.

◆ Place an area rug that is multicolored and patterned for a jolt of color and style.

◆ Cover the walls in a large-patterned wall-covering, not a tiny nondescript pattern. Choose a print with clout!

◆ Hang a chandelier that is on a dimmer switch to adjust lighting for mood. Use special light bulbs that flicker for the holidays. Lit candles are lovely, but never leave them unattended!

◆ If you are artistic (or if you know an artist), have a trompe l'oeil scene painted in the foyer, perhaps an outdoor scene with your family members painted right on the walls.

I like to drive up to a home that has a light on in the foyer. It says "welcome" to your guests—and "welcome home" to you. Place a side table in your entryway with a table lamp on a timer device so that the light turns on automatically when darkness falls. The table can also hold your keys or purse, and a guest's bag or gloves or gift that they have brought.

**Pro Workshop**

Delight the senses by arranging fresh flowers in a vase on an entry table. For a unique welcome, fill a large shallow bowl of water with floating flowers, herbs, or lemon slices. It's very inviting, especially on a warm day.

No room for a table and lamp? Why not install a wall sconce? If placed on a dimmer switch, you can adjust the mood of the entry. Hang a shelf underneath the sconce to accommodate keys, your purse, a hat, and so forth.

Mirrors—a large one, if the space permits—are perfect accessories for foyers and entryways. They reflect light, visually enlarge the space, and offer you a final glimpse of your appearance before heading out the door. They also give your guests a glimpse of their appearance as they arrive at your home—a thoughtful touch. Because mirrors expand the size of a room, they are perfect for small entryways. Placing a lit candle near a mirror offers a flicker of a romantic atmosphere making the entry very special.

Add a seat for you or guests to collect themselves before a gathering or after a long day. A bench, footstool, or two chairs create a practical and stylish foyer. A wall-hung hat rack and bench combination provides storage and helps to eliminate clutter.

**A small entry is made useful with seating and a coat rack.** *(Photo by Gear)*

A grand entryway is enlivened with wallcovering patterns of birds and flowers. *(Photo by Schumacher)*

# Stairways That Are Special

Don't just think of your stairway as a place to hurry through to get from one level to another. Enjoy that pass through. A stairway is like a thread, weaving the fabric of the different spaces of your home together. Make it special by following some of these tips:

◆ Stencil a saying on the risers that sums up your philosophy in life.

◆ Be daring with color. Instead of a safe or standard treatment, experiment with a deep and vibrant color such as apple green or deep orange that ties your rooms together. Use the same color paint for the risers and treads. You could also use a three-way combination, painting the risers one color, the treads another, and the *balusters* another! Try teal, yellow, and burnt orange; or monochromatic shades of tan, cream, and straw.

◆ Install a cushioned runner that is textured like sisal or elegantly patterned like an Oriental carpet.

◆ If your stairs are carpeted, be sure the carpet is a handsome short pile rug or one with a flat weave to avoid a bulky look.

◆ Select a carpet with a print that is a bit extraordinary, like an animal-styled print of zebra or leopard or large-scale botanicals or ferns.

A grand entry and stairway is connected through patterned Oriental carpets. *(Photo by Couristan Kashimar Collection)*

◆ An open stairwell is a perfect showcase for a decorative chandelier.

◆ Affix decorative tiles on the risers for a picturesque passage.

**Decorating 101**

A **baluster** is any of the small posts that support the upper rail of a railing. Don't confuse it with a **balustrade**, which is a railing held up by balusters.

# Hallways with Pizzazz

Hallways can be more than just narrow corridors. Like the stairs, home decorators often overlook these spaces. Again, they are the connectors of various rooms and should be pleasant and interesting to walk through. Make your hallways useful and artistic with the following hints:

◆ Frame and hang art to make your own gallery setting. Affix lighting to showcase it.

◆ Paint hallways rich, deep colors (try tobacco brown or eggplant). Instead of closing them in, the color will be so dramatic it will "open up" the space for critique!

◆ Paint doors with a motif that signifies what is to be found behind it. For example, if a bathroom is off the hallway, you might paint figures of a man and woman; a library, a saying in Latin referring to books; your son's bedroom, an image of his face.

◆ Mirrors in a hallway make lighting dance and help to make the hallway appear larger than it is. Any motion is reflected with active energy, adding life to an ordinary space.

◆ Place demilune console tables along the wall for use and added shape to a linear space.

◆ Attach a curtain that is swept up to one side halfway down a long hallway to break up a corridor effect.

◆ Use uplights as sconces on the walls that direct lighting toward the ceiling to add drama. Try lanterns that have open metal framework and clear bulbs that cast light in even more dramatic effects and patterns.

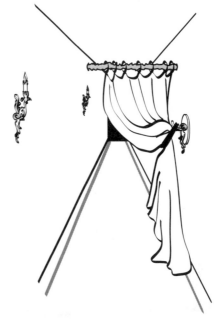

A curtain hung in a long hallway can eliminate that hotel corridor feel.

This hallway is opened up by a patterned wallcovering that features views of a country village. *(Photo by Gear Design)*

**Style Pointers**

Hang a grouping of framed pictures or china plates over the tops of hallway doors. You won't just rush through; your eyes will want to view them.

# Creating a Hobby Hideaway

Looking for a space to store your hobby paraphernalia? Try these quirky spaces:

◆ An unused pantry can be used to store gift wrap, paper, and craft supplies.

◆ Set up photography equipment in an unused bathroom.

◆ An attic can be turned into a private space for knitting, needlepoint, or a painting/art studio.

◆ A spacious laundry room can double as a sewing room.

◆ Seating at the end of a hallway offers built-in storage space for books and hobby materials.

Seating at the end of a hallway offers a cozy nook for relaxing as well as storage space for books and other materials.

◆ Under an eve makes a cozy reading nook with room enough for a club chair and light.

◆ Measure the width of a walk-in style dormer and attach brackets to hold a desk-size piece of wood. Place the desk top at 29 or 30 inches from the floor to allow for proper leg room and a comfortable chair.

◆ Add shelves in the upper half of wide stairwell walls for a book aficionado's library.

# Creating a Place for Solitude

Creating a setting where we can let go of daily demands and reconnect with our inner soul is essential to a healthy mind and home. How this area is decorated should reflect a stable and orderly atmosphere: Textures should be smooth and soft, colors quiet and harmonious. Neutral colors, earthy tones, and pastels are uplifting. Lighting is soft, and seating is comfortable. Fragrances with candles or herbs and flowers are a delight to the senses.

Some possible space to carve out to call your own could be a remodeled attic for a quiet respite. Place a mattress covered in pillows on the floor. In your place of quiet respite, you might also want a small table for candles, an inspirational statue, or personal objects.

Lighting should be on dimmer switches so that you can alter the brightness at night, and candles should be available for important kinetic movement. Hang muslin or a sheer fabric in a window to cut glare and soften the light during the day.

If you do not have an attic, a window seat with a full set of draperies provides a quiet alcove with a view! Even an arrangement in a corner with a mat, table, and floor pillows can work if it is not near the hub of a busy home. Hang a banner or mobile from the ceiling to denote your space.

**Style Pointers**

Don't throw out old porch balusters; they make great candle holders! Add a wooden base so they can stand. Glue a 2-inch nail with a large head, head side down, on the top of the baluster and place a votive candle (or any candle that is wider than the baluster) atop. You can also revive an old tabletop by using balusters for new legs.

### Flea Market Finds: Little Touches for Often-Overlooked Spaces

Flea market finds can be showcased in quirky spaces like hallways. Add a few of your favorite finds to hallways, stairwells, or foyers for super style!

◆ Panel a wide hallway with old doors that have an aged patina, emulating a traditional paneled library/drawing room but with added flair.

◆ Place columns from old porches along the hall to break up a hotel/corridor look. Columns always add a bit of architectural grandeur to any space.

◆ Purchase some vintage wallpaper with a one-of-a-kind pattern to add charm to a dull foyer.

◆ Replace a ready-made (not custom) post at the bottom of a balustrade with an old one with history, styling, and some heft!

◆ Use various accessories for umbrella holders such as galvanized flower buckets or plant stands (the kind with rings that hold small pots).

 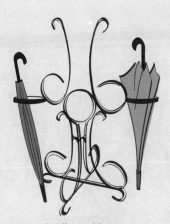

**A plant stand makes a unique umbrella caddy.**

## The Least You Need to Know

◆ Entryways, stairways, and hallways should be included in your decorating plan; after all, you pass through them several times a day. Consider the lighting plan as well.

◆ Mirrors are invaluable in hallways, making them appear larger, reflecting lighting for dramatic effect.

◆ The quirkiest spaces can make great hobby hideaways. Be creative!

◆ Scour your home for a quiet space for solitude. Everyone needs a space and a moment to wind down.

◆ Make your hallway, foyer, and other areas come alive with unique additions from the flea market.

# In This Part

# Part 4

# The Finishing Touches

No matter how much you think you have made all the right decisions planning, selecting for, designing, and arranging your rooms in your home, it's the small touches that people notice, the final touches that make the room come together. Every space can be enlivened with the right accessories properly placed, whether they are live plants or treasured collections, symmetrically arranged or deliberately askew.

These chapters will add extra decorator knowledge from the author's signature styling—decorating methods that work—including ways to create inspiring table settings, welcoming guest rooms, rooms with a view, and stylish storage. These chapters are packed with creative ways to make a personal statement in each room.

# In This Chapter

- ◆ The art of displaying accessories
- ◆ Tips for placing pictures and mirrors
- ◆ The beauty of nature's art
- ◆ Hanging the unexpected
- ◆ Signature details

# Chapter 18

# Accessories to Make Your Room Sing

When it comes to displaying and arranging accessories, adhere to the same rules of the elements of design with color, texture, balance, and scale. This will help you take your final decorating touches from fine to exceptional. Accessories show off your personal touch by stamping a room with your signature—with items that appeal to you and that work with the whole plan, just as a necklace visually completes an evening gown.

Finishing touches of artistic porcelain atop a fireplace mantel, a pillow with ball fringe, or a spray of fresh flowers—these are the accessories that make a room sing. You may prefer a clean minimal look with just a few choice pieces, carefully selected and judiciously placed or an all-out cozy atmosphere, offering many objects and collections in a warm, generous, and visually interesting display.

Whatever style and amounts of accessories you decide to choose, be sure to refer to Chapter 2 to guide you through the basics of how color, texture, balance, and scale pertain to all aspects of décor and have an effect on the whole of the room.

## The Art of Display

Coordinating, grouping, and displaying accessories throughout your home is an art in itself. All of the elements of design that you learned in Chapter 2 come into play. Whether you go for a modern or traditional look, successful display considers color, texture, balance, and proportion. There's an added element, too, because theme can be an important factor when coordinating accessories. For example, if your home is by the sea, you might display a collection of antique lighthouses or model ships. A home in the Southwest might display a collection of Indian blankets and concho belts.

Color, of course, can be a common visual connection if you are arranging unrelated and otherwise dissimilar accessory items. For instance, a quilt in shades of light blue, royal blue, and sea green and a rug that picks up one of those shades make a powerful punctuation in a bedroom. A living room's upholstery that is mismatched and of different styles is unified by slipcovering all pieces in one shade, perhaps ivory or pale pink. Texture can do the same: Similarly textured porcelain jars, even different sizes and patterns, make a unified and interesting display.

Consider balance and proportion as well. The "visual weights" of your objects must balance within the display. The shapes and sizes of objects must be in proportion to each other, and the whole display must be in proportion to the space or surface it occupies. Also, although symmetrical displays are easier to arrange, like a tabletop of two candlesticks on either side of a bowl of fruit, asymmetrical displays are often more interesting and exciting. Think of a single tall calla lily in a glass vase atop a table balanced by a plate of green pears. The different heights are balanced by the placement of the vase and plate. There's a lot to think about!

### Pro Workshop

The most interesting mixes of accessories are those that are fine paired with objects that are considered valueless. For example, place a fine piece of art in a gilt frame on a driftwood shelf, or a handmade wreath between ornate silver candelabra.

A window fitted with shelves showcases a collection of topiaries and miniature trees. *(Photo by Gear Home, Bettye M. Musham, Chairwoman/CEO)*

Use thematic displays to arrange objects of the same type, color, or shape. Small objects (stones, butterflies, bottles, toy soldiers) should be displayed together, perhaps in a case with a glass front or on wall-mounted shelves. When scattered throughout a room, they lose their impact as a collection and as a decorative element.

Large pieces of sculpture or pottery can stand alone on a floor or be a mounted on bases of stone or wood. But theme works with large objects, too. If large pieces are related in a subject or texture, grouping them together makes a particularly strong statement.

The symmetrical arrangement of china on the upper shelves is balanced by the asymmetrical display of accessories on the lower shelves.    *(Photo by Smallbone)*

A horse enthusiast prominently displays a collection of prized ribbons and statues over the fireplace mantel.    *(Photo by Gear Design)*

**Style Pointers**

Don't go for trendy accessories that go out of style and date your décor. And instant collections are not nearly as interesting as treasure troves that involve mixes of old and new, priceless and valueless memorabilia. Accessories are your most intimate statement in the room: Make it passionate!

# Hanging Pictures and Mirrors

There is an art to hanging a picture. You must consider all of the items that will influence where to hammer the first nail: the size of the frame, the color of the artwork, other frames it may be near or next to, the space of the wall, and so on. Before you get out your hammer and nails, look over these helpful hints on picture display. You will get the best effect for your room!

◆ Cut templates of the frames that you are hanging and tape them to the wall with nonmarking tape. This way you can view your grouping before pounding nails into the wall.

◆ Hang several small pictures in identical frames close together to make one large "picture" over a sofa.

◆ Unify a mismatched collection of prints with the same mat and frame.

◆ Group pictures together instead of scattering them around a room.

◆ For symmetrical arrangements, hang similar sizes and frames in rows, either vertically or horizontally (for example, a group of eight frames hung in two rows of four; a group of six frames hung in three rows of two; or a group of three, with two smaller pictures flanking one large picture).

◆ Asymmetrical arrangements often place the largest picture to one side, and smaller ones are arranged together on the other side to balance out the display.

◆ Horizontally arranged pictures make walls look wider. Vertically arranged pictures make walls look higher.

◆ Just because you are tall doesn't mean you should hang pictures high. Conversely, if you are short, do not hang them too low. Consider the proportions of the picture and wall surface area as well as the surrounding furnishings. From the bottom of the picture frame, measure 6 to 8 inches above the mantel, sofa back, or table. This is only a guideline; the size of your frames and the size of the piece over which the picture is being hung have to be considered.

**The two smaller picture frames over the sofa balance the larger center frame.**    *(Photo by Gear Home, Bettye M. Musham, Chairwoman/CEO)*

Here's another tip: Did you know that 3M makes a hook with a tape on the back that can sufficiently hold a picture frame? If you change your mind, you pull the tab on the tape and there are no visible marks on the wall. It's perfect for temporary living situations or rental apartments. This is available at most home and garden stores or hardware stores.

**Pro Workshop**

One of the most clever ways to frame just about any artwork or beloved treasure is to encase it between two pieces of glass held together with clips. This way you see the artwork! It doesn't compete with an ornate frame.

Mirrors are one of the perfect accessories to add life to a room. Their magical beauty reflects views, adding energy to any space. Mirrors are so versatile because they …

◆ Add active energy to any space.

◆ Reflect furnishings. (Place a mirror opposite an item you love, and it will be reflected for a double look!)

◆ Visually enlarge the size of any space.

◆ Add spark to a dull space.

◆ Break up long hallways into exciting passageways.

◆ Are fairly inexpensive art.

Placed behind a candle, a mirror reflects a warm flicker that adds a romantic mood to a room. You can bring the outdoors in by placing a mirror across from a window with a beautiful view. Mirrored walls are exceptionally decorative and useful. They can open up alcoves, intensify light, and visually double the room size. Or try a collection of antique mirrors grouped together on a wall in various frames and sizes to add a rich presence to any room. Place a *beveled* mirror in a fabulous frame to add a glamorous touch to your décor. Hang it over your mantel or on a wall over a sofa with a bit of a tilt in order to reflect the room and not just the opposite wall.

A stylized mirror placed over a dining buffet reflects the diners and your décor. *(Photo by Roche Bobois)*

**Decorating 101**

**Beveled** refers to a sloping part or surface, as in the angled edge of plate glass.

# Living Art: Plants and Flowers

Bring the garden into your home from nature's jewelry box with cut flowers and plants, accessories that are appropriate for any style décor. Not only do they soften hard lines in a room and add wonderful focal points, they fill empty spaces with lively color.

To display fresh-cut flowers, consider the area where your arrangement will be placed, the colors you need, and whether it should be casual or formal. Keep everything in scale: The space will help you determine the container's size and shape. And the container will determine the scale of the arrangement. Tall, geometric vases call for arrangements with height; low shallow bowls allow flowers to spread out.

One of the most intriguing arrangements is flower heads floating in a large, shallow bowl filled with water placed atop a dining table or entry table. A larger version, a shallow urn that is 24 inches in diameter placed on the floor with floating flowers, is the height of drama. This could be placed outside an entryway or in a quiet nook.

For the best effect (and recalling the design element of scale and balance) with plant displays, group small ones together and balance tall and thin plants with short and bushy ones.

Consider containers as well; balancing color adds texture. Plants can grace many interior spots: Use a pair to flank the bottom of a staircase or place a plant in an entryway or on a console table. You can hang a plant from a hook at the top of a window to add color. Large and tall plants fill an empty corner with height and color.

The large plants enliven and add height to a summer porch arrangement. (Photo by Gear Home, Bettye M. Musham, Chairwoman/CEO)

The style of your home may dictate the style of your arrangements, but the most clever ones are those that exploit the differences of style. For example, an artistically askew "arrangement" like abundant wild branches of forsythia spilling out of the container breathes fresh air into a formal room. And vice versa!

And arranged flowers bring order to a rather chaotic atmosphere. That is flower style at its best!

For maximum versatility with the flowers you bring into your rooms, it's a good idea to have many shapes and sizes of vases in various textures. Also, some of the most stunning flowers are those of one type in generous bunches. Choosing two colors of the same type also works well, such as green and yellow, pink and purple, red and orange, or yellow and orange. Flip back to the color section in Chapter 2 to apply all of the same rules of color and decoration to flowers and plants.

# Hang the Unexpected

Walls can be enhanced with more than just photographs and paintings! Hang items that you love and want to look at. Hang the unexpected for real style. Here are some ideas that you don't see in every home:

- Unfinished needlepoints with burlap backing. The texture and colors of the yarns are works of art in themselves. Group them by theme or color.

- An Asian kimono or dress. Place a dowel through the sleeves and attach to brackets on the wall for a dramatic wall hanging.

- Take that wedding dress out of its box. Hang it between two glass frames attached with clips. Hang in a hallway or over your bed. Memorable art!

- Remember that denim jacket your daughter wore when she was three years old? The one with the Parisian applique on the back? Frame it!

- Label your room with your name in driftwood or sticks. Glue gun pieces together in alphabet shapes and hang over your bed. Or emphasize your feelings in driftwood letters on the porch outside!

LOVE is spelled out in driftwood and other natural materials, lending charm to this porch.

# Signature Details

I always find myself leaning toward unusual accessories and wall art in my decorating projects. Some objects that I tend to use over and over or that I find extremely appealing are …

- **Children's art.** Take it to grand status with chic or gilded frames (overlaid with a thin layer of gold). Everyone will be charmed.

- **Handmade humble crafts.** Few things are more appealing than handmade crafts. Pottery marbles, weavings, hand-carved stick whistles, all arranged in an en masse collection in a large glass jug, woven basket, or shadowbox table.

**Various shapes of ottomans serve as seating, footrests, or even tray tables. Many also provide storage space.**
*(Photos by Lee Industries)*

- **Imperfect porcelain.** Cracks and nicks are signs of use, history, and an owner with a relaxed attitude!

- **Disco ball in laundry room.** Hang one for humorous effect. Plug in a radio and do a dance while folding the laundry. What fun!

- **Polar fleece throws.** Inexpensive, soft, and cozy fleece blankets thrown over existing upholstery (or chairs you haven't recovered yet!) for an instant change in attitude!

- **Footstools.** You can never have enough. Vary the shapes from a tuffet size to a large old hassock!

- **Cubbyholes.** Filled with personal (but interesting mementos) that reveal your inner soul, like weathered beach rocks, monogrammed baby bracelets, your parents' silver ID bracelets, red china lobster salt and pepper shakers. Your college ring that doesn't fit anymore.

- **Pashmina shawls.** The ultimate soft-colored throw for your favorite chair can be used to wrap you in a luxurious feeling.

- **Glass frames with clips.** Framing for theater tickets, playbills, the dinner menu from your wedding, or any printed matter that has meaning for you.

## The Least You Need to Know

- Decorative accessories are the finishing touches to a room. Choose them carefully for stylish displays, trying not to clutter!

- Accessory displays should be guided by the design principles of color, texture, balance, proportion, and theme.

- Collections can be eclectic and inexpensive, as long as they are artfully displayed.

- Always bring nature in to a room with living plants and fresh flowers.

- Hang the unexpected! If you treasure an item … hang it on the wall so you can view it each day—your wedding veil, a pair of your mother's baby shoes, or a collection of vintage toy soldiers.

# In This Chapter

- ◆ Making the connection: creating rooms with a view
- ◆ Making guest rooms special
- ◆ Unexpected table settings
- ◆ Signature details that turn ordinary into fabulous

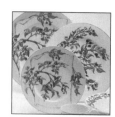

Chapter **19**

# From the Decorator's Desk ...

For all the time that I have been decorating homes for other people, some consistent styling touches always seem to show up in my decorating. I love to create rooms with "views," allowing your eye to travel through a home, making you wonder what the next surprise will be, from one room to the next. I also love to create welcoming guest rooms with all of the right touches that make a guest feel right at home and pampered! Setting the table creatively is when a real artistic side comes out. You, too, can create dinners that will have that *je ne sais quoi* feeling ... every day!

Read over some of my thoughts and specific ideas about how to go the extra mile to add interest to your home.

## Creating Rooms with a View

All rooms should have a view, even if there are no windows. Creating interior views in decorating means simply connecting one room to the other so that you or your guests are kept in anticipation of what is to come next. This can be done in several ways. One is with the correct architectural setup, having all of the doorways line up from room to room so that you can see through to the other side of your home. This is called *enfilade*, a word that means "to thread" or "string along" like one bead after another. In many older homes with traditional floor plans, rooms were laid out with doorways aligned so as to add a sense of order coming from the repetition of the same opening (and to save on heating!).

Windows near doors that are in enfilade cast light on the door openings, adding richness to rooms. Light is cast on various textures and forms such as door molding and polished flooring to create interesting shadows.

**Decorating 101**

From the French word *enfiler,* meaning "to thread or string," in architectural terms **enfilade** means "a layout in which all of the doorways line up from room to room so you can see through to the other side of your home."

A mirror and a chandelier offer a shimmering duet in the room at the end of the view.   *(Photo by Pierre Frey)*

But you don't have to own the Taj Mahal to be able to create rooms with views. If you can't afford to remodel by realigning your doors or windows or you only have a couple of rooms, you can use color to lead your eye beyond the immediate room and capture that aesthetic pleasure of connecting one room to the other. A red room leading to a tobacco-colored room, for example, provides striking contrast.

Also, hanging artwork at the end of a view is a bit like creating a full-scale shadowbox, especially if you can see a portrait or frame three rooms away. The vista is intriguing. You can't wait to get through the next door to see the object of interest.

Making the connection from room to room is also easily done with a decorating theme that is cohesive, meaning that each room is traditionally furnished or eclectically furnished, or whatever your style may be. Repetition of

accessories in various sizes, colors, and textures is one way to link rooms together. For example, a collection of oriental rugs scattered throughout leads one to want to see the rug beyond in the room next door.

# Inviting Guest Rooms

Guest rooms are an area of your home where you can pull out all the stops! Because they are not used as often as regular bedrooms, you can attend to these with special effort. Guest bedrooms should immediately say "welcome" when your guest opens the door. Think of what your guests may need while in the privacy of the guest room and try to provide it before they have to ask. A desk or table and a comfortable chair is handy for writing (don't forget stationery, pens, even a sketch pad and pencils is thoughtful); you might even have a computer available from which your guests can check their e-mail (if not, show your computer-toting guests where it's most convenient for them to connect their laptops, both the electrical power point and a telephone outlet). You want to make your guest feel right at home.

Aside from the basics of a comfortable, freshly made bed, night table, reading light, and perhaps a reading chair, here are some items you may not have thought of that really make your guest bedroom the ultimate in hospitality:

- Fresh flowers
- Bowl of fresh fruit
- Jar of treats, candy, or mints
- CD player with a variety of CDs
- Television with DVD player and a few movies
- Newspapers
- Books or magazines that would interest your guest
- Both soft and firm pillows
- Fine linens

- Down comforter or feather bed
- A selection of small soaps and toiletries
- Bottled water with a glass
- Alarm clock/radio
- Mini-refrigerator stocked with favorite beverages
- Bed tray for breakfast in bed
- Small coffee maker and an assortment of coffees
- Closet space or clothes/coat rack
- A bed draped with fabric to simulate a canopy

### Pro Workshop

Want to go beyond the basic? For the ultimate five-star experience, house your guest in a room that has a fireplace or a balcony—or both. Many older homes have fireplaces in several rooms, or arrange to have a gas fireplace installed. The only problem is your guest may never want to leave!

**Splashy printed bedding is fresh and fun for a spare room turned guest room.** *(Photo by Pierre Frey)*

Guest rooms are the perfect room to show off your sense of humor by using whimsical furniture or tongue-in-cheek items for accessories. Many flea market items that you love, but that don't fit in your main living quarters, might be the perfect thing for a guest room.

### Pro Workshop

Budget tight for guest room furnishings? Purchase various furniture from yard sales and flea markets. Paint them all one color to make the pieces have a cohesive effect in the room.

**A table lamp for reading, some fresh fruit, and a few selected books will make your guests feel so welcome!** *(Photo by Gear Home, Bettye M. Musham, Chairwoman/CEO)*

A comfortably made bed is the ultimate luxury for guests. *(Photo by Gear Home, Bettye M. Musham, Chairwoman/CEO)*

# Setting a Table with Style

You can find so much gratification out of setting the table for dinner. I always try to find unique ways so it appears I go to great effort in presentation, albeit simply but artistically. By mixing china and pottery, fine linens and cotton napkins, and crystal with everyday glassware, the meals are so much more fun, visually exciting, and aesthetically pleasing.

### Style Pointers

Don't use synthetic napkins! They are nonabsorbent and feel awful. Natural fibers of cotton or linen are preferable. Linen napkins actually improve with age. A worn appearance reveals lots of dinners!

Often, simply set tables can have the biggest impact. Here bare wood and simple flowers look clean, crisp, and pretty. *(Photo by Roche Bobois)*

Use your china! Don't keep it locked up in a cabinet never to be seen or used. Why not spice up your dinner table one evening by serving soup from a fancy tureen for the sheer dramatic impact on an everyday event? Pull out those oversized richly patterned damask napkins and pair them with your everyday china … just for the fun of it. Or hang a varied group of flea market linen towels on the back of each chair for a clever napkin display. Try using small trays as a base for a place setting, adding small varied individual bowls and plates for servings of food. Or be brave and set the table with those gaudy goblets that your aunt gave you. They may be just the right thing to get a conversation going.

### Homematters

If you're not that fond of your wedding china pieces, place them in your display shelves behind your favorite flea market pieces. The wedding china will be like mats, framing your eclectic mix of china but still revealing a part of your past.

Place traditional printed china like the set shown with solid brightly colored plates or patterns that are splashier and modern for an interesting table setting. *(Photo by Gear Home, Bettye M. Musham, Chairwoman/CEO)*

An edible centerpiece of pineapples and other fresh fruit is always eye-catching—and delicious! *(Photo by Gear Home, Bettye M. Musham, Chairwoman/CEO)*

# Signature Details

Every designer has particular methods of decorating that he or she feels are the cat's meow—whether it be their clever finishing touches or innovative designs that clearly set their rooms apart from other designers. Here are some of my favorite ideas for creating rooms with a view, inviting guest rooms, and table settings.

Rooms with a view:

- Place mirrors on walls that reflect a beautiful object, scene, or view! A collection of mirrors is always intriguing.
- Hang decorative chandeliers in rooms for capturing interest during the day and evening.
- Place a large old family portrait in clear view, as if the person in the portrait is mysteriously watching you enter the room.
- Hang modern art or sculptures that invite the viewer to take a closer look.
- Arrange a greenhouse effect in a windowed room at the end of a view with a plethora of plants and flowers (and possibly a water source). The natural décor is seductive.

Guest rooms:

- Leave a guest book and pen on the night table so guests can read about former visitors who stayed at your home and leave their own comments.
- Offer a basket of luxury snacks such as Belgian chocolates, seasonal fresh fruit, shortbread cookies, or meringues.
- Hang an oversized map of the region for wall art.
- Offer a chaise for style and comfort.
- Have beautiful music playing while your guest enters the room for the first time.

◆ Place a warm shawl such as a pashmina at the foot of the bed for extra warmth or for your guest to wrap up in on a cool night's outing.

◆ Offer cashmere socks (an especially nice touch in chilly weather).

◆ Have a child write a welcoming note with an imaginative portrait of the guest—a little memento, suitable for framing, to take home.

A chaise is the ultimate reading chair. *(Photo by Lee Industries)*

Table settings:

◆ Matching valuable and humble items on the same table; for example, stones used as place cards with antique china.

◆ Utensils with natural handles of bamboo, imitation ivory, or horn placed next to fine porcelain

◆ Colorful china in modern patterns on a rustic bare-wood table. Or try classic blue-and-white willow-ware and heirloom silver on a very rustic worn table with an aged patina.

◆ Plain brown paper (kraft paper) used as a tablecloth. Write each diner's name on the tablecloth.

◆ Red-and-white gingham napkins with a large vase of apple branches for an elegant picnic look.

◆ Different plates with a coordinating print, color, or pattern.

A pashmina shawl placed at the foot of the bed is an inviting accessory for any guest room. *(Photo by Garnet Hill)*

## The Least You Need to Know

◆ Creating interior views is a decorating art that can be practiced in any size home!

◆ Pamper your guests with special touches in the guest room, such as fresh flowers, snacks, and luxurious bed linens.

◆ Table settings can be a rewarding daily artistic event by mixing contrasting materials of glass and pottery, linen and paper, floral and fruit, and natural and manmade materials.

◆ View details of designers' rooms to try to understand how their minds work. You can emulate their designs.

# In This Chapter

- ◆ Organizing the stuff in your life
- ◆ Room-by-room storage solutions
- ◆ Small-space storage in the busiest rooms
- ◆ Signature details for clever concealment

# Chapter 20

# Functional Storage and Stylish Organization

You can eliminate clutter in every room of the house with stylish and useful storage. Start getting organized by sorting through papers, filing photographs, and arranging collections and housing them in attractive compartments or storage pieces. Begin by selecting one room at a time to eliminate feeling overwhelmed by stuff!

Whether you need to build new shelving or use what you have, some of these room-by-room storage ideas will help you get your house in tiptop shape.

## A Place for Everything in the House

Every space in your home can be utilized for attractive storage and stylish organization. Again, begin by going room by room, starting with one room, getting it organized with storage, and then moving on to the next room until your entire home is uncluttered and everything is in its place.

## Living Area

Because many living areas double as family rooms, storage is of critical importance to maintain neatness and order. Cabinetry that can hold and hide TVs, VCRs, and CDs is a godsend. Many are available in sleek, unornamented styles with bookshelves attached, forming a single wall unit. Reproduction or rustic cupboards fitted for TV and stereo cords are quite attractive for decorative as well as functional purposes.

Games, needlework, magazines, and toys can be hidden in built-in storage units like window seats that conceal storage beneath the seat, or behind doors that are fitted to the bottom of shelves. Bookshelves that surround a doorway offer architectural structure as well as organizers for books and showcases for china, candlesticks, clocks, pictures, or pottery. Glass shelves placed in windows can hold colored-glass collections that sparkle when sunlight shines through.

### Style Pointers

For a simple, inexpensive storage idea, cover a 36-inch round table with a table skirt. You can display items on the table as well as store items such as photo albums, books, and magazines underneath the table, hidden by the skirt.

There are some stylish ottomans (large footstools) that lift open for storing blankets, magazines, craft supplies, and other odds and ends. And trunks serve dual purposes when used for coffee tables or end tables.

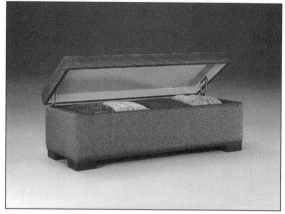

A trunk serves as both storage space for throws and blankets and as a table or seat. *(Photo by Lee Industries)*

A modern living room is kept clutter-free with sleek entertainment storage units. *(Photo by Roche Bobois)*

This large ottoman triples as seating, a coffee table, and as an extra bed.    *(Photos by Lee Industries)*

## Dining Area

Storage units in a dining room serve multiple purposes. Attractive in themselves, they can properly store china, linens, and silverware, and provide surfaces that can be used for serving or display. A *sideboard* or buffet piece is especially hardworking. Its drawers or doors can hold trays, china, extra glassware, and linens; and during a meal, drinks or food can be served from it. When you are not dining, the sideboard can display special trays, dishes, candlesticks, or decanters. A serving cart can do much the same but is smaller and has legs with wheels to allow it to be moved around for easy serving. (For serving from behind a chair, position your cart or buffet at least 48 inches from the table.)

A *breakfront, china cabinet, hutch,* or corner cupboard can hold extra china, glassware, and vases on its lower half and display bowls, dishes, and plates on the upper shelves. A *curio cabinet* may hold collections behind glass doors. A *highboy*, with its many drawers, stores linens and small accessories. Refer to Chapter 18 to learn more about the art of display. Again, the cupboard does not have to match your dining table or chairs. Blending traditional with modern or old with new adds your personal signature.

A great way to add flair and storage to your dining room is to attach a wide shelf at picture-rail height around the room (approximately 1 foot below the ceiling). This can store and display large platters or china. Spoon racks can hold silver spoons or baby cups.

### Decorating 101

A **sideboard** is a long, low cabinet usually placed against a wall. It can have drawers and compartments or a combination of both. A **breakfront** is a tall unit that usually has glass-enclosed shelves on top of a drawer cabinet, with a projecting center section. A **china cabinet** is designed to display china or glasses. A **hutch** is a tall cupboard or sideboard that usually has open shelves on the top section and cabinets below. A **curio cabinet** with glass doors and sides is used to display various types of collections. A **highboy** is a tall chest that appears to be in two sections.

A china cabinet with solid bottom and upper glass doors is the perfect combination of storage for a dining area. *(Photo by Gear Home, Bettye M. Musham, Chairwoman/CEO)*

## Bedrooms

With the variety of personal items that we keep in our bedrooms—clothing, linens, and living accessories of all kinds—finding the right storage is almost as important as finding the right bed. Consider the general choice of built-in or free-standing storage units. Built-ins maximize storage space using every possible nook and cranny and can make a room streamlined and cohesive. Built-in storage units can be expensive custom-made pieces that cover an entire wall, combining drawers, doors, and shelving for clothing and entertainment. They can be built in to surround and frame a bed, with storage space and lighting units, too.

Free-standing pieces like bureaus, dressers, armoires, and trunks are the traditional approach to clothing storage. They serve perfectly, too, as the place for dressing mirrors and for displaying personal objects. Consider some of these other ways to add storage to your bedroom:

◆ Add storage drawers that maximize space and fit under a bed with a metal frame and pull out for easy access. Or use a platform base with drawers that the mattress and box spring rest on.

◆ Use nightstands with double drawers.

◆ Skirted tables used for display can also hide storage units under the fabric.

◆ Professional closet organizers are experts who design custom storage for your closets. Maximize closet space with custom storage.

◆ Attractive quilt racks can hold extra quilts or bedding.

◆ Trunks or ottomans can be used to hold extra bed linens and pillows.

◆ Hang tie racks, shoe shelves, and mirrors on your closet doors.

◆ Vanities fitted with drawers are a great place to hold personal items, and you can display other items on the vanity itself.

An armoire acts as a free-standing closet for clothing storage.  *(Photo by Lee Industries)*

## Kitchen

Whether you opt for fitted or unfitted cabinets for your kitchen (refer to Chapter 13), they need to provide adequate storage for all of your kitchen needs. Base cabinets with double doors can hide fixed or slide-out shelves or house drawers of various depths. Open bases can be fitted to hold baskets of vegetables and fruits. Upper cabinets may have shelves with glass doors that store and display glasses, plates, or food items. You can attach shirred panels of fabric inside the door or order frosted glass if you don't want to show the goods.

> **Pro Workshop**
>
> For better organization in your cabinets, purchase plastic-wrapped wire drawers, baskets, or shelves from home stores. These come with proper hardware for installation. Some drawers already have built-in fittings for silverware and sharp-knife storage. Corner cabinets can be fitted with lazy Susans—rotating circular shelves for efficient use and space.

Consider these other storage ideas for your kitchen:

- Open shelving lets you store and stack attractive plates and glassware while displaying it. Add hooks at the bottom edge of upper shelves to hang cups and mugs.

- Hanging pot racks are an efficient way to store pots and kitchen tools.

- Store utensils, pot holders, and other items on hooks on a grid hung on the wall.

- Shelving can be installed inside a door to hold spices.

- Islands are work areas that often stand in the middle of the work triangle and can store varying amounts depending on their size.

- If you do ironing in your kitchen, consider a cabinet with a built-in ironing board that pulls down when needed.

- Place recycling/trash bins under counter space or inside a cabinet.

A custom-built kitchen island stores jarred food and bowls while the hanging pot rack keeps pots and pans in order.   *(Photo by Gear Home, Bettye M. Musham, Chairwoman/CEO)*

## Baths

There are many stylish ways to store and display bathroom supplies and accessories. Overhead cabinets above the toilet can be fitted with doors to hide toiletries, make-up, towels, toilet paper, and other supplies. Depending on placement, a towel bar can be added or built in to an overhead cabinet bottom. The top of the cabinet could hold a collection of colored bottles, oversized seashells, or baskets for small items.

Handsome medicine cabinets serve double duty, both as a place to store prescription medicines and as a fixture for bathroom mirrors. If your bathroom is large enough to accommodate a vanity table and chair, it can display perfume bottles, powders, and a pretty mirror and comb set, while other grooming supplies are hidden away in drawers.

Built-in or free-standing shelving can hold towels, and if you have enough shelves, you can assign one to each person who is using the bathroom. Children may use the lower shelves for storing bathtub toys. Pegged racks or towel racks can be topped with shelves for extra storage or attractive displays.

If your bathroom serves as a catchall for dirty laundry, install an attractive chrome or wicker hamper with a pullout, washable liner for easy transport to the laundry area. Of course, if you have more space, more shelves, tables, or cupboards are always useful. Magazine holders are handy near the toilet or tub. A small shelf placed above the sink or sinks can hold perfumes or colognes. Read on for ways to find storage in a small bathroom.

A wicker basket keeps rolls of toilet tissue close at hand.   *(Photo by M. Hackett)*

## Storage Solutions in Small Spaces

Tight on space? Looking for more storage in a small kitchen, bath, or bedroom? Find extra storage space in each room with the following ideas.

Kitchen:

◆ Use tiered pot stands to hold myriad dishes or pots.

◆ Install metal wire shelving in windows to add storage but to still allow light into your kitchen.

◆ Use open shelving over doorways or even a window.

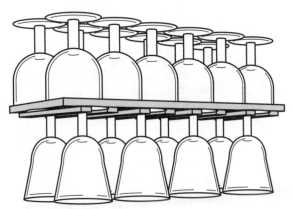

Double your storage capacity by hanging stemmed glasses under a shelf.

Bathroom:

◆ Use waterproof tub caddies that hang on a showerhead or on the edge of a tub to hold soaps, shampoos, and loofahs.

◆ Build a simple shelf above the bathroom door to hold towels.

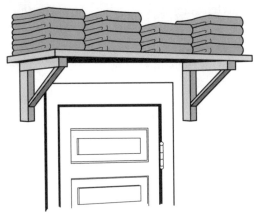

This shelf above the bathroom door holds towels.

◆ Hang a decorative and useful backpack on the wall for dirty laundry.

◆ Hang large medicine cabinets disguised as picture-framed mirrors.

Bedroom:

◆ Use platform beds with storage drawers.

◆ Install a Murphy bed that pulls down from the wall when needed.

◆ Store blankets, sweaters, and other items in under-bed storage drawers on wheels or plastic or wicker containers; conceal with a bed skirt.

A delicate iron bed doubles as a sofa to maximize space.   *(Photo by Laura Ashley)*

### Style Pointers

Clutter getting the best of you? Try these ideas for staying organized:

◆ Regularly sort through stuff and store it, give it away, or dispose of it.

◆ Keep infrequently used items elsewhere. Instead of storing holiday ornaments in the dining room buffet drawers, for example, box them up and place in a garage, attic, or basement.

◆ Move bulky winter items to another storage area for the warm months.

◆ Organize items in attractive baskets or coordinated boxes.

## Signature Details

Some highly effective and stylish storage items I have found to be clever concealers are …

◆ Wicker baskets for laundry, towels, tissue, mail, office files.

◆ Slipcovers that fall to the floor so that you can stash magazines and books underneath.

◆ Trophies to organize art supplies, office tools, cosmetics.

◆ Glass jars for grooming supplies.

**Attractive crystal bottles hold everyday grooming supplies.** *(Photo by Waterworks)*

◆ Wire shelving mounted in the bottom half of kitchen windows for organizing glassware. Light is not obscured.

◆ Ice cream sundae glassware to hold kitchen utensils.

◆ Tea cart to hold bar paraphernalia.

◆ Rail around the walls of a contemporary styled room a few inches above the floor to organize and display artwork.

◆ Simple warehouse metal shelving as book organizers and storage.

## The Least You Need to Know

◆ Assessing your needs, setting priorities, and using your imagination are the keys to successful organization and useful storage.

◆ Organize your home by beginning with one room and completing it. Then go on to the next room until your entire home is free from clutter.

◆ Small-space storage taps all of your creative ingenuity. Think of all the possibilities!

◆ Observe professional decorators' ideas for creative storage in magazines, books, and on television shows about the home. They have so much experience knowing what storage looks good and functions, too!

# In This Part

# Quick-and-Easy Room Makeovers

One of the most exciting things about decorating is the big effect of small changes. Often, when you introduce a new element in a familiar environment—a bit of fresh paint, a set of curtains, or a display of memorabilia—you can put a whole room through a magical mood swing.

In this part of the book, I'll show you how to use the power of small innovations to quickly revive some tired old spaces—the busiest ones in the house—the kitchen, bathroom, and bedroom. But in each of these hard-working areas—where your family spends so much time—you can easily implement a few changes and revive their fading energy. Put some of these ideas into practice and your home will look and feel better … fast!

# In This Chapter

- ◆ Painting: the most efficient makeover method
- ◆ Soft goods to ease hard lines
- ◆ Ten simple ways to give your kitchen a new look
- ◆ Advanced do-it-yourself projects

# Chapter 21

# Kitchen Redo: Minimal Effort for Maximum Effect!

If you have come this far in this book, you already know that decorating takes a lot of personal passion to achieve rooms that you'll want to live with for a long time. But decorating does not always have to be a top-to-bottom effort. Sometimes time or financial resources just don't allow for thorough repair, renovating, or refurnishing.

But for a busy room like a kitchen, where you spend a lot of time, you don't have to live with dingy or dull or look at the same old scenery. And you don't have to spend a lot of cash! With just a few hours of work, you can add life and new personality to your kitchen with quick and easy-on-the-budget makeovers.

## Transform with Paint

Nothing transforms a room faster or more inexpensively than paint. A new coat and color will refresh the blandest atmosphere. It's the quickest kitchen picker-upper there is! Almost every surface in your kitchen can be painted as long as you use the right type for the particular material and job. Begin with one surface at a time. And go slowly!

## Walls

Paint your kitchen walls with a semi-gloss or eggshell finish latex paint for durability and better washability. If you want color, there are standard kitchen colors that produce positive effects. White and ivory are always very "clean" colors; yellow will brighten a dull kitchen; terra cotta will give an old world appearance, whereas apple or sage green will bring in a bit of nature. Review Chapters 2 and 13 for other color ideas.

You may choose to do some simple paint techniques like sponging or rag rolling as discussed in Chapter 6. If your ceiling needs a fresh coat of paint, white will open up a kitchen with low ceilings. Rag rolling it in shades of tea color will give the ceiling an aged look and interesting texture. If you can paint like an artist or know an artist, fill your kitchen with scenes of landscapes that have special meaning to you.

### Pro Workshop

Personalize your kitchen by painting a thought-provoking saying on the walls. A memorable kitchen was painted French yellow with a saying lettered above the cabinets: "Thou hath nothing under the sun than to eat, drink, and be merry!"

## Cabinets

Reviving old cabinets with paint makes an instant impact. Use a latex semi-gloss or low-luster enamel for the best durability and washability. Flat paint will chip and wear quickly with constant use.

A handsome, unconventional look is to paint the lower cabinets a darker color than the upper ones. Similarly with open shelving, you can paint the wall background a color that contrasts with the face of the cabinet. With glass-faced cabinets (or even solid-door cabinets), paint the outside a different color than you paint the inside. One possibility for a super combination is painting a sage green color on the exterior of the cabinets and a dark black-green on the interior. Pewter grays and ivories, blacks and natural wood, or vibrant greens and yellows are just some of the many tasteful combinations possible. More on cabinet colors can be found in Chapter 13.

Whitewashing cabinets is another technique that gives your wood cabinets a fresh look. Whitewash is made from mixing equal parts of white enamel paint and paint thinner. Before applying the wash, be sure to strip any paint or stain from the cabinets. Whitewashing cabinets allows the wood grain or knots to show for a very textural effect. It will also lighten a dark kitchen.

## Floors

Try painting old wooden floors using a spatter technique, as mentioned in Chapter 5, or use any pattern that appeals to you, such as gingham plaid or checkerboard. Another decorator idea is to paint floorboards by alternating stripes of ivory and your favorite color or a combination of black and leaving the next board unpainted (natural wood). Stenciling is always a great way to enliven your floor with a pattern. Be sure the paint is a floor paint: latex with epoxy reinforcement or an oil-based paint with polyurethane reinforcement.

### Style Pointers

Painter's tape will help prevent different colors of paint from bleeding into each other and keep surfaces from getting paint on them. It is easy to place on a surface and easy to remove. Masking tape is *not* easy to remove! Painter's tape is available at any home or paint store.

## Appliances

If your appliances are old or are an outdated color, blend them in with your cabinets by painting them with a metal paint. If they are vintage pieces, paint them a color from their era (such as aqua from the 1950s) to highlight them!

## Tile

If your tile on the backsplash is not your cup of tea, your home or paint store can specify a relatively new type of paint specifically made for tile, which you can use to cover right over old tile and tile prints.

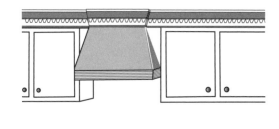

A decorative molding.

**Style Pointers**

If you paint your kitchen chairs an unconventional color—say, fuchsia—they may be the only surface that needs paint to give your kitchen that extra oomph!

An eclectically styled kitchen combines old wooden ceiling beams and a sleek island counter. *(Photo by Wolf Appliances)*

# Ease Hard Lines with Soft Goods

Most kitchens have sharp lines created with cabinets and appliances. With the use of fabrics, rugs, and textures—collectively known as *soft goods*—you can add softness with the following decorator touches:

◆ Hang a collection of vintage linens on a rack in groups of three for effect. Or expose your large collection of vintage linens in an open cupboard.

◆ Add colorful premade soft cushions to your dining chairs. Tie them on in a matter of minutes!

◆ Create your own window curtain with jute and dishtowels. Attach a piece of jute string from casing to casing at the half point of the window. Clothespin a pretty kitchen towel (or towels) as half curtains.

◆ Use different tablecloths for an instant change of atmosphere. Or make your own with a couple yards of fabric.

◆ Remove cabinet doors under the sink and replace them with a gathered split skirt for a French country effect.

- Add a simple valance or set of curtains on the sink window. (See Chapter 9 for a review of curtain styles.)
- Place small rugs at the sink area, under the table, or in front of a bench.
- Place shirred panels of fabric in glass-front cabinets.

# Ten Instant Makeovers for Your Kitchen

There are no particular skills necessary to do the following "quick and easies" to give your kitchen a fresh new look. But you may want to first review the elements of design in Chapter 3 and the art of display in Chapter 18. Then get ready to have some fun with these ideas:

- Display a collection of rolling pins in an urn like a "bouquet" and place on the counter.
- String fresh herbs or flowers with jute and hang at the kitchen window or attach a hook in the ceiling to hang garlic braids or chili peppers.
- Stamp a meaningful word or saying on the backsplash with ink stamps.
- Spice up the atmosphere. In cold weather, keep a pot simmering with a potpourri of lemon and orange rinds and spices. In warm weather, fill a bowl with lemon peels and herbs and ice-cold water for refreshing scents and hand dipping.
- Add small rag rugs or oriental rugs for summer/winter looks. (Use a rug pad to keep them from slipping.)

- Add a station for cooking and casual entertaining with a free-standing table fitted with a butcher block or a piece of marble.
- Disguise your wastebasket by placing it in an oversize crock.
- Place a handsome map depicting an area that you love on the wall near the seating area to provoke lively conversation and add to the décor.
- Use a breadbox that has a glass front to reveal beautiful loaves of bread as works of art.
- Hang a beautiful French printed linen on the oven door handle, or hang a special apron on a hook as wall art!

A generous supply of flowers dry on a rack suspended by a cord-and-pulley system. *(Photo by Smallbone)*

This kitchen is given a new look with porcelain knobs, stenciled doors, and drawer fronts.
*(Photo by Smallbone)*

### Homematters

Architectural elements add clout to any kitchen. Placing old porch columns in entryways or corners adds a sense of timelessness and drama and is relatively simple. Salvaged porch brackets can be nailed in place to add decorative supports for shelving. If you are an advanced do-it-yourselfer, crown molding placed at the ceiling and wall joint around the perimeter of the room adds significant definition to a bland kitchen.

# Advanced Do-It-Yourself Kitchen Projects

If you have some experience with do-it-yourself projects or are just plain handy, the following improvement projects will give your kitchen a new look that you can be proud of!

If these projects are out of your league, consider hiring a professional. These projects are relatively small but can yield big dividends in the enjoyment of your kitchen:

◆ Replace that dull kitchen lighting fixture. Hang a creative chandelier. Ask an electrician for help if need be. Or hang a candle-lit chandelier over the island or dining table to illuminate for festive occasions and birthdays. A simple wire wreath form with added candles hung with three ribbons works in a pinch!

◆ Replace ugly cabinet fronts with new panels. Your local kitchen and home store can offer expert advice on the how-to's. Change the hardware with new or vintage knobs and handles.

◆ Add shelving above windows and doors to display coveted pottery or china. Attach architectural brackets for added pizzazz.

White iron brackets hold up extra display shelves for large platters and soup tureens. *(Photo by Smallbone)*

◆ Decorative tiles add a country touch when installed below the kitchen counters and above the counters or behind the stove.

**Natural tiles simulate stone on this stove's backsplash.** *(Photo by Wolf Appliances)*

◆ Install a greenhouse window over the sink windows for growing herbs and other plants. A local home store will advise you on what will work in your kitchen.

◆ Cover an outdated countertop with a sheet of copper. After time it will age to a fabulous patina.

◆ Add a glass panel to a solid door that leads outdoors—or to any door—to add more light and the illusion of space if needed.

◆ Create a pass-through window in the wall between the kitchen and living/dining area to view activity from each room.

**A pass-through window creates a "from kitchen to living room view."** *(Photo by Lee Industries)*

## The Least You Need to Know

◆ For the quickest makeover in your kitchen, repaint the walls, cabinets, floors, furnishings and appliances. Contrasting colors produce lively effects.

◆ The softness of fabric, special paint finishes, and area rugs balance the hard lines of kitchen cabinets and appliances.

◆ There are many ways to give your kitchen a fresh new look that take little time and money.

◆ Some kitchen makeovers require little skill but others require a bit of experience. Most do-it-yourself project advice can be found at your local home or hardware store.

# In This Chapter

- ◆ Paint for a fresh new look
- ◆ Giving your bathroom a soft touch with fabric
- ◆ Ten simple ways to brighten your bathroom
- ◆ Tips for working with wallcoverings
- ◆ Advanced projects for the do-it-yourselfer

# Chapter 22

# Bathroom Brighteners That Won't Break the Bank

The bathroom is another room where you spend so much time. If yours is in need of a wakeup call and a complete remodeling is out of the question, consider some of the quick and easy cosmetic changes in this chapter to give it extra sparkle.

Many of the projects can be done in minutes without a lot of skill necessary; others require a little expertise. If you can sew, then you will be able to add softness to your bathroom yourself! If painting is your thing, you can give that bathroom a new fresh look—fast! So help transform your bathroom into a space that you will want to relax and rejuvenate and linger in.

## Refresh Your Bathroom with a New Coat of Paint

By now you know that paint is your quickest, most efficient, and inexpensive resource for jazzing up the dullest bathroom space. Color choices abound. Use the color of your fixtures, the sink, toilet and tub, as a starting base. If you have colored fixtures, painting walls and choosing fabrics in contrasting colors will make the room seem smaller. On the other hand, if you match the fixtures in a monochromatic color scheme, the room will appear larger. Common white fixtures actually look good in an all-white atmosphere, and you can paint the walls and the floor (if possible) for a clean, fresh look. Living plants may be all the color you need for accessories.

Looking for a cool bathroom? Paint the walls in pale blues or greens. For a warmer ambiance, choose pale pinks, peaches, or yellows. Review Chapters 2 and 14 for other color ideas.

One paint technique you can try is to stencil a motif that has meaning to you and one that will make an impact. A small stencil pattern used in only one or two spots will make no impression at all, but an overall use of the small stencil will create a significant impact. Some powerful places for a stenciled-lettered saying is around the mid-wall molding, right above the sink or above the baseboard!

Easier stenciling can be accomplished with a stamp kit. Alphabet letters, geometric designs, and fern leaves are just the beginning of what is available in stamp form. Stamp pads are available in a variety of colors like gold, silver, black, and colorful jewel tones of red, blue, and green. Another fun idea is to paint a tongue-in-cheek motif on the bathroom entry door like a face of a male and female if it is a family bathroom or a stenciled lettered "his" and "hers" above the double vanity sinks. (See Chapter 6 for more on stenciling and other simple paint techniques.)

### Style Pointers

Give an old-fashioned bathtub new life by painting the exterior with a high gloss oil paint specifically made for tubs. You can find this paint at any home/hardware store. Ask for expert advice when considering this do-it-yourself project.

# Soft Materials for Easy Cover-Ups

There are a number of ways to bring a soft look and feel to your bathroom with fabric. Consider your colors and fixture styles so you can coordinate shower curtains, sink skirt, and window coverings through pattern, color, and texture. Think about the following areas that can be softened up for visual and tactile texture.

## Windows

Simple window coverings always work well in a bathroom, but elaborate ones are a bit unexpected and can have a dramatic impact. A ceiling-to-floor curtain can visually add height to a cramped bathroom, whereas a simple soft pull-down shade is neat and trim and adds visual order. A quick way to make an ordinary roll-up shade more decorative is to attach a large tassel for the pull. When the shade is up, the tassel will make a delightful focal point of the room. For a more tailored shade, attach a vintage kitchen drawer handle for the pull.

## Banners

A clever, inexpensive way to use fabric is to create a "wall" between the bathtub and toilet with a "banner" hung from floor to ceiling the width of the bathtub. Use a transparent fabric like organdy to hint at privacy and lend an airy look to the room. The banner can be attached to a wrought iron curtain rod or dowel fastened at the top of the wall and can easily be taken down for dry cleaning.

## Slipcovers

If your bathroom is large enough, the ultimate luxury is seating. One comfortable chair gives the aura of a room that is meant for pampering. A slipcovered chair in terrycloth or soft muslin is perfect, and the cover can be removed for washing. Be sure to have the fabric prewashed and shrunk before any slipcover is made. This will allow the slipcover to be cleaned as necessary without shrinkage. A small terrycloth-covered tuffet will do if your space is limited. Some have a hinged seat for storing small items.

A comfortable chair slipcovered in terrycloth is pure luxury in a bathroom. *(Photo by Lee Industries)*

Boudoir furniture like this tuffet is a good choice when you want the luxury of a chair in the bathroom but don't have the space. *(Photo by Lee Industries)*

If you have a wall-hung or pedestal sink (or cabinet doors you would like to remove), attaching a gathered skirt is a simple project. Here are the steps:

1. Measure the sink from one side to the other and from the top of the sink to the bottom of the floor.

2. Double or triple the width of the skirt for desired fullness.

3. Turn over the top of the skirt and sew it for a neat appearance. Gather and attach the skirt to a band that is the size of the perimeter of the sink, and hem the skirt to the correct length.

4. To fasten the skirt to the sink, sew loop Velcro to the skirt band and glue (using porcelain glue) the corresponding hook Velcro to the top of the edge of the sink.

A full-length curtain, valance, and sink skirt that matches the wallpaper dress up this bathroom in style. *(Photo by Schumacher)*

For an extra special effect, add ruffles on the bottom of the skirt or have a scalloped hem made. Or sew buttons down the front to imitate dressmaker details, even attach bows. For a Bohemian-style skirt, attach an unhemmed burlap skirt with frayed hems. Fabrics for durability and washability like denim, muslins, and lightweight canvas are smart choices. Chintz, burlaps, and linens are just as good-looking but might require dry cleaning.

## Shower Curtains/Towels

The easiest way to impart softness in your bathroom is to display and arrange sumptuous towels, washcloths, and floor mats in soft textures and colors. Embellish plain towels with ribbon, monograms, and pom-pom fringes. Set out a basket of a glorious assortment of washcloths in various colors or patterns. Neatly fold or roll your bath towels and group them together on open shelves. Hang your comfy terry robes (in colors that work with your bathroom scheme, of course!) in plain sight on the back of the door. And whether you have mismatched vintage linens or new oversized towels with long cotton fringe, hang them from interesting hooks or fold them and lay them on top of the vanity.

# Ten Easy Ways to Perk Up Your Bathroom

You are only minutes away from giving your bathroom a new look. It's that quick and easy to add refreshing items to make that bathroom spa-worthy. And you'll enjoy the big payoff from investing very little time, money, and energy.

1. Clear shelves of unsightly grooming supplies and place them in drawers or a medicine cabinet. Fill the shelves with bottles of spring water for drinking after a hot bath. They will impart a clean fresh look.

2. Add a hook on the back of the door to hang your comfy robe.

3. Tie a bunch of fresh herbs on the bathtub water spout. Let the water flow on it to release the fragrance.

Flowers add fragrance and a soft visual look to a contemporary-style bathroom. *(Photo by Waterworks)*

4. Replace a heavy old plastic shower curtain with a modern clear vinyl one to open up the space!

5. Place a piece of marble or granite on top of a bulky vintage radiator for a useful shelf.

6. Create a serene atmosphere by painting the ceiling a pale sky blue.

7. Towel bars made of tree branches add a rustic touch to any bathroom. You can make hooks for towels, clothes, or robes.

8. Hang an overscale mirror over the vanity to make the bathroom look bigger. Or add a full-length mirror on a wall or the back of the door to serve as a dressing mirror.

9. Set out aromatherapy oils, perfumes, bath oils, potpourri, or scented candles on a silver tray to make your bathroom smell great.

10. Fill large glass jars with shells or sea glass. For the full effect, play a tape of the sounds of the ocean—waves rippling to shore and seabirds calling—while you relax in the bathtub.

### Homematters

The late decorator Mark Hampton wrote in his book *On Decorating:* "Bathrooms allow us to be more extreme in style than we might want to be in the rest of our house … What would be vulgar in any other room looks great in the private precincts of the bath."

# Wallcovering Tips

Working with wallcovering for the first time can be frustrating. Here are some tips that might help you out:

♦ Your bathroom should not be your first wallcovering project. The bathroom is one of the harder rooms to learn how to wallcover (along with the kitchen) because of all the doors, windows, and trim.

♦ Choose a small (but not bland) pattern repeat for less waste if you make a mistake. Pattern repeats are the distance between the exact same design going lengthwise down a sheet of wallcovering. Pattern repeats can vary from 1 inch to 2 feet. The longer the repeat, the more you will have to "waste" if you make a mistake.

♦ The busier the pattern, the less mistakes will show. Grid patterns will show mistakes easily and reveal if your room is not plumb.

♦ The seams in a wallcovering with a dark background show more than seams in a light-colored background. Go light on your first attempt.

♦ Always prepare your walls by removing old paper and priming the walls with a primer specifically made to use under wallcovering.

♦ Find a good place to begin wallcovering and where to end so you aren't left with tiny strips around doors and windows. Professionals "engineer" the room beforehand to ensure the paper is hung correctly and they are not left with odd-sized wallcovering strips that look terrible. A simple way for you to do this is to measure the width of your paper and mark where you will begin. Continue to mark the width around the room. If you have tiny strip markings left around doors and windows, move your beginning point forward or backward until your markings are at better points so you will not have to work with those tiny strips.

◆ Always order extra wallcovering, at least a double roll, in case you make some mistakes or you have a plumbing problem, like leaking water.

◆ If you feel uneasy about tackling your bathroom with wallcovering, or are not the handy type, hire a reliable professional to do the work. Be sure to get some recommendations.

**Style Pointers**

Choose a random match patterned wallcovering. A random match pattern is one that doesn't require you to match along the edges. You know those patterns with branches, flowers, and leaves that have to match so precisely? Don't attempt them on your first try!

## Projects for the Advanced Do-It-Yourselfer

These bathroom projects—a new paint technique, wallcovering, or tiling, to name a few—may require a bit more experience. But if you have the right tools, are not afraid to seek advice from experts, and have the time, each can make your bath visually exciting and a place you will want to relax in. Consider these ideas:

◆ Cover the walls in a large-patterned wallcovering for a dramatic look. A powder room is a good choice. No one will expect such a jolt of pattern in a tiny room. Read directions and take your time. Be sure your bathroom has good ventilation and you use vinyl-coated wallcovering.

◆ Heighten the drama in your bathroom with an unexpectedly elaborate window curtain that runs the full length from ceiling to floor. Instant grandeur!

◆ Tackle a small tile project by tiling the back of the sink. You may need as few as five to a dozen tiles. Mismatched leftover tiles can add an eclectic feel, and different solid-colored and printed vintage tiles can evoke a patchwork-quilt look when arranged. If you find this easy, consider tiling the walls of your bath next!

◆ Add architectural clout to a modern bathroom with ceiling beams. Consult a carpenter if you don't have advanced do-it-yourself skills.

◆ If you have the room, add shelves at the end of the bathtub wall. Display glass sculptures or attractively packaged toiletries.

**Tissue and grooming supplies look elegant in slick pewter caddies.** *(Photo by Waterworks)*

◆ For a distinctive vanity, replace yours with an old dresser and set a small sink into the top of it. (You'll find directions for this project in Chapter 14.)

◆ Insert glass shelves in the bathroom window to display colored glassware. No window? Paint a trompe l'oeil window on the wall.

◆ Cover old walls—one half to three quarters of the way up the wall—with tongue-
and-groove bead board. Add a display
shelf on top of the board. For a custom
look, you can even enclose a tub unit in
bead board, too.

Rustic beams add a sense of timelessness to a well-
outfitted bathroom.    *(Photo by Smallbone)*

## The Least You Need to Know

◆ Paint and different paint techniques can
brighten, enlarge, and warm or cool your
bathroom … fast!

◆ Fabrics can add softness to your bathroom,
so pay particular attention to your window
coverings, sink skirts, shower curtains,
and towels.

◆ Simple projects—as easy as making it
smell good—can enliven any bathroom.

◆ With a few tips and some practice, you
can wallcover your bathroom!

◆ More advanced do-it-yourself projects
such as adding tile may require some
expert advice but certainly are worth the
time and effort.

# In This Chapter

- ◆ Setting the mood with paint
- ◆ Creating cozy and intimate areas
- ◆ Soft goods for a comforting atmosphere
- ◆ Lighting styles that can define your moods
- ◆ Ten simple ways to add romantic touches
- ◆ Advanced projects for the do-it-yourself seamstress

Chapter **23**

# A Fine Romance:
# You and Your Bedroom

With our busy lives, our bedrooms often seem to be the last room on the list for remodeling, refurbishing, or refreshing. Why is that? We spend half of our life in our bedrooms, why not make them the most sought-after rooms in the house, especially if you can transform them with touches of romance? No matter what the style of your room (or the style you want it to be), some common elements that you will want to have are a comfortable and beautifully dressed bed, intimate lighting, and personal objects and pictures.

Of course, new paint color is always an easy option, as well as embellishing the windows, adding more pillows, and displaying photos of your loved ones. This chapter will help you to make some small additions to turn your bedroom into a retreat that inspires hugs!

## Painting a Romantic Story

Here we go again: Yes, paint! Paint colors can excite emotions. What paint colors excite you and stimulate your sense of romance? Maybe white reminds you of summer sensuality? Or pale colors evoke serenity and relaxation? Almost anything goes in your bedroom. Use whatever colors to create the atmosphere you are searching for. Refer to some color combinations in Chapters 2 and 15 that work for many different tastes. Here are some more suggestions for paint and wall-treatment schemes that might get you in the mood to redo your bedroom:

- Consider a paint technique such as rag rolling that produces a soft visual texture. (See Chapter 6 for more on rag rolling and other simple techniques.)

- Wallcovering is a wonderful way to add instant drama to your bedroom. Florals, soft wide stripes, or artsy geometrics are all good choices.

- Monochromatic colors inherently evoke a pleasing atmosphere with varying shades of the same color.

- It is tantalizing to have a scenic or patterned ceiling. Consider an old world master's scene or simple *fleur-de-lis*.

- Paint your ceiling in a color contrasting with the walls. Some interesting combinations are ivory walls with apple-green, pale pink, soft blue, or sage-green ceiling.

- Have an artist paint a duplicate love letter on the walls from your special loved one only viewable from your dressing room. A loving reminder every time you change your clothes!

- Use deep, rich colors to add a sense of drama, such as cocoa, red, or eggplant.

**Decorating 101**

**Fleur-de-lis** is a French term directly translated as "flower of the lily." It actually refers to three iris-type flowers bound by an encircling band. It was used as the coat of arms of the former royal family of France. The fleur-de-lis pattern is a popular motif in printed fabrics and wallcoverings today.

Old master's painted wall panels, Asian rugs, and a fireplace create intoxicating combinations, forming a very grand, elegant, and sensual atmosphere.
*(Photo by Roche Bobois)*

## Set the Mood for Romance

The easiest way to create a comfortable and romantic bedroom is to have areas for relaxation, inviting places that are cozy enough to promote intimate conversation. Here are some ways to do just that:

- Create a seating spot for two! The perfect invitation for intimate conversation, impromptu candlelight dinners, and indulgent Sunday breakfast. Pull up two chairs or a loveseat to a small dining table. Or recline together on a chaise.

A chaise is perfect seating for relaxation and intimate talk. The toile de Jouy fabric adds an old world romantic character. *(Photo by Lee Industries)*

◆ Create your own dressing area with an exotic folding screen. Add plush boudoir furnishings for an alluring atmosphere.

◆ Nothing is more inviting than an appealing bed. Create a royal setting by adding a canopy or full-length curtains to a four-poster bed. Netting or gauze is also dreamy and very inexpensive! Elevate your plain old bed on a frame by adding height with PVC pipes (available at any plumbing store). Buy four pieces at 4 inches in diameter and 13 inches in height, attach to each leg of a standard metal frame and create a bed of 29 inches in height. You'll feel like a queen (or king!)

**Style Pointers** _____

Hang an inexpensive, overscale poster over your bed of your favorite characters from romantic films like *Out of Africa* or *Gone with the Wind*.

Coordinated robes, towels, and comfortable bedding add up to a romantic invitation. *(Photo by Pierre Frey)*

# Soft Goods for a Soft Atmosphere

The key to any romantic bedroom is softness. You can enhance this feeling by covering bedroom furnishings in soft and inviting fabrics; by using luxurious window treatments that ensure privacy while still allowing in natural light (even moonlight) to the extent you want; and by covering your bed with plush cushions, pillows, and comforters. This all adds up to an atmosphere that says "Come in and let your cares slip away."

Consider these decorator touches:

◆ Create an all-white scheme with white linens, bed furnishings, window coverings, and walls. This will allow your favorite artwork, portrait of your loved one, or a cherished piece of furniture to be the romantic focal point of the room.

◆ Use dust ruffles that are a size bigger than your bed and let them "puddle" on the floor.

◆ The ultimate in comfort is a down-filled pillow or featherbed the size of your bed placed over the mattress for luxurious softness.

◆ A bed with many pillows is irresistible. Combine rich fabrics of velvets, tapestries, laces, and linen.

A simply dressed bed with comfortable pillows is the romantic focal point of this room. *(Photo by Laura Ashley)*

◆ Faded florals that have a soft, worn look create a romantic feel when used on pillows, slipcovers, or comforters. And

although florals need not—and should not—be used on every surface to create romantic ambience in a bedroom, don't rule them out. A small amount of floral fabric made up as a single pillow or used on a bench seat may be just enough to give a neutral color scheme or a plain room a fresh and soothing feel.

◆ For summertime sleeping, use sheer and filmy window curtains. They drape well and blow in soft waves with the breeze like sails on a boat. Welcome winter with heavier drapes of tapestry or velvet hanging in deep folds to emphasize their luxury.

◆ A comfortable slipcovered chaise with a down-filled seat is a lovely place to read love stories. Choose one that has a long enough seat for two persons to sit and chat.

Ruffled sheer bed drapes add a crowning touch to this elegant bed. *(Photo by Schumacher)*

**Style Pointers**

If you share a bedroom, consult your partner on his or her tastes before selecting new paint colors and fabric patterns. One may like flowers, the other abhor them. Blue might be one's favorite color and the other might find it depressing. Taking your partner's tastes into consideration will help you create a room both of you can enjoy as a peaceful sanctuary.

# Set the Tone with Intimate Lighting

Next to luxurious linens, creating intimate and mood-enhancing lighting is essential to a bedroom. It should include several different romantic light sources that work in combination so that the illumination can be adjusted from daytime throughout the night and according to the time of year. A chandelier (electrolier) over the bed and fitted with clear bulbs that flicker on a low setting is a perfect mood enhancer. If your bed is a four poster, has a canopy, or a *corona* where recessed lighting can be installed out of view as uplights, other lighting such as candlelight placed on both sides of the bed on the night tables can enhance the overall effect. The uplight fills out the dark space between the bed top and the ceiling, offering a soft wash of light overhead. If the corona is draped in a sheer fabric, a bit of the light will filter through and cast a delicate touch.

**Decorating 101**

In decorating terms, a **corona** is a crownlike fixture that is placed above a headboard. Often draperies are attached to create a flowing look at the head of the bed.

**Unusual lighting provides a sultry ambience to a tailored bedroom.** *(Photo by Lee Industries)*

There is nothing more romantic than candlelight. The flame is seductive, especially in your bedroom. Candlelight can be used to fantastic effect in candelabra, wall sconces, or in a grouping on a tray. A girandole (as mentioned in Chapter 10), a wall sconce with a mirrored back, can enhance candlelight even further by creating a reflection and doubling its effect. Place mirrors in other areas of the room and the effect will be even greater. (Enjoy the romantic mood candlelight provides, but never leave a burning candle unattended or go to sleep with one lit.)

Some other ways to create intimate lighting are …

◆ Place all lighting on dimmers.

◆ Use opaque shades on side-table lamps so light is cast upward and downward.

◆ Try using soft-yellow light bulbs to imitate candlelight or pink bulbs for a flattering glow.

◆ Filter natural sunlight through fabric like muslin curtains during the day.

◆ "Throw" light onto a floor with a downlight placed below eye level to create soft ambient lighting.

◆ Install a wood-burning or gas fireplace, the ultimate bedroom luxury.

A bed can never have too many pillows to create a "come lounge with me" setting. Placing the bed near a fireplace quadruples the fact that romance is in the air! *(Photo by Pierre Frey)*

Candlelight is further enhanced with ambient lighting set on low. This table lamp has a dimmer switch for low-level lighting. (Photo by Gear Home, Bettye M. Musham, Chairwoman/CEO)

A corona bed canopy and wall sconce lighting are seductive additions to this sumptuously decorated bedroom. *(Photo by Pierre Frey)*

**Style Pointers**

Turn off your phone, beeper, pager—anything that might distract you while relaxing in your bedroom. If you have children, consider putting a lock on your door for uninterrupted private time!

# Ten Easy Ways to Add Touches of Romance to Your Bedroom

Create easy and lovely changes to your bedroom, right now! Here are some ways to achieve an alluring atmosphere:

1. Place all electronics such as a television and CD player out of sight behind a closed-door cabinet or under a skirted table.

2. Stack your night tables with books that feature poetry, exotic travel, and classic love stories.

3. Use an Asian-printed folding screen behind your bed as a headboard.

4. Place your bed in a new position—on the diagonal or in the middle of the room—for an airy and exciting look. Or remove the frame and place your box springs and mattress on the floor for an artsy Bohemian look.

**Try a new look by placing your bed directly on the floor.** *(Photo by Garnet Hill)*

5. Remove clutter that can distract your thoughts! Stylish storage solutions such as wicker baskets or oversize old trunks contain clutter while looking neat.

6. Display family portraits, fresh flowers, and accessories that appeal to all of your senses. Add bowls of potpourri and scented candles that you love!

**Toiletries housed in delicate glass bottles look fresh and pretty.** *(Photo by Waterworks)*

7. Highlight candlelight with many mirrors on the walls.

8. Frame a love letter behind glass and hang it above your side of the bed or in your dressing area.

9. Hang a simple candle chandelier above your bed for consummately romantic light.

10. Drape sheer fabric or a beautiful piece of lace from a four-poster bed to create a magical presence.

**Homematters**

If you're a romantic at heart, you can find decorating inspiration in movies such as *The English Patient*, *Out of Africa*, and *The Age of Innocence*. All feature scenes with fabulously romantic bedrooms. Of course, you may not want (or have the budget) to duplicate the look detail for detail, but you can achieve the same romantic feel by selecting the things you love, whether it's a lacy canopy or a vintage trunk.

# Projects for the Advanced Do-It-Yourself Seamstress

Decorating changes to your bedroom can add an uplifting ambience, hopefully spurring on romantic feelings. It is the place to express your feelings and dreams. If you can master a sewing machine, you can do it with fabrics. If you can't sew, you may have a friend or know of a local seamstress who can put these ideas into play in your bedroom:

- Create summer/winter looks with seasonal fabrics for pillow cases, curtains, and duvet covers (comforter covers). Use muslin, cotton, organdy, linen, and chintz for summer, and use tapestry, velvets, and wools for winter.

- Sew a duvet cover from vintage cloth or worn, large linen tablecloths. The wear of the fabric is part of the charm.

- Add a wide ribbon of velvet to a blanket.

- Make loose romantic slipcovers for a loveseat with petticoat hems and closures of buttons, bows, or ribbon ties. For a simple artistic look, throw a painter's cloth over your present slipcover and hand fit for a tousled look.

- Cover small boudoir footstools in exotic patterns of animal prints, ferns, or flowers.

## The Least You Need to Know

◆ In the bedroom, you most likely want to create a romantic mood, and the proper paint colors are a quick way to do just that.

◆ A comfortable and romantic bedroom has cozy areas for relaxation and intimate conversation.

◆ Wonderful bedding, linens, and curtains add visual and tactile softness, creating a tender atmosphere.

◆ Candlelight is the ultimate romantic lighting, and combinations of various types of lighting can further enhance the candlelight.

◆ Anyone can impart small changes to a bedroom for quick and easy results at minimal cost.

◆ Sew-it-yourself projects for the advanced seamstress add dramatic effects to a bedroom.

# Appendix A

# Resources

## Books

Better Homes and Gardens. *The New Decorating Book*. Des Moines: The Meredith Corporation, 1997.

De Chiara, Joseph, Julius Panero, and Martin Zelnick. *Time-Saver Standards for Interior Design and Space Planning*. New York: McGraw-Hill, 1991.

Dickson, Elizabeth, and Margaret Colvin, photographer. *The Laura Ashley Book of Home Decorating, Revised Edition*. New York: Harmony Books, 1988.

Fairbanks, Jonathan L., and Elizabeth Bidwell Bates. *American Furniture: 1620 to the Present*. New York: Richard Marek Publishers, 1981.

Hampton, Mark. *On Decorating*. New York: Random House, 1989.

Krasner, Deborah. *Kitchens for Cooks*. New York: Penguin Group, 1994.

Landis, Dylan. *Elegant and Easy Rooms*. New York: Dell Publishing, 1997.

Lawlor, Andrew. *A Home for the Soul*. New York: Clarkson Potter/Publishers, 1997.

McCloud, Kevin. *Lighting Style*. New York: Simon & Schuster, 1995.

Savill, Julie. *101 Bedrooms*. New York: Hydra Publishing, 2002.

Sloan, Annie, and Kate Gwynn. *Color in Decoration*. Boston: Little Brown & Company, 1990.

Taylor, Lesley. *Inside Colour*. London: Cassell & Co., 2000.

Wolfman, Peri, and Charles Gold. *A Place for Everything*. New York: Clarkson Potter/Publishers, 1999.

# Magazines

*Architectural Digest*
High-end designs by topnotch designers

*British Homes and Garden*
British design with town and country styling

*Classic Home*
Traditional, timeless interiors

*Country Living*
Real-life, comfortable, country interiors

*Elle Decor*
Inspirational and adaptable fine design

*Fine Homebuilding*
Just as the name implies, fine homebuilding techniques and polished interiors

*House Beautiful*
Beautiful homes with beautiful interiors, variety of styles

*Martha Stewart Living*
Includes a little bit of everything: cooking, entertaining, projects, and decorating

*Metropolitan Home*
Contemporary design

*Real Simple*
Fresh approach for easy living and a stylish home

*This Old House*
How-to's and information on building and redos

*Victoria*
For the homeowner with a romantic touch

*Vogue* (international)
International designs for superb inspiration

# Mail-Order Catalogs

*Anthropologie*
Fresh and quirky accessories for the home
1-800-309-2500

*Chambers*
Tasteful bed linens, garden furniture, bath towels, accessories, and furniture
1-800-334-9790

*Crate & Barrel*
Great selection of furniture, rugs, kitchenware, and accessories
1-800-323-5461

*Gardener's Eden*
Decorative accessories for the home and garden, furniture for indoor/outdoor, and gardening supplies
1-800-429-7678

*Garnet Hill*
Creative bed linens, throws, rugs, and a small amount of adult and children's bedroom furniture stressing natural elements
1-800-622-6216

*Hold Everything*
Unique organizing and storage pieces, plus furniture for the home office
1-800-421-2264

*Ikea*
Affordable furniture and storage pieces with stylish designs
1-800-434-4532

*L.L. Bean*
Quality furnishings with real-life styling
1-800-441-5713

*Laura Ashley*
Tasteful and well-coordinated fabrics, custom and premade draperies, furniture, and accessories
1-800-463-8075

*Martha Stewart: The Catalog for Living*
A variety of tasteful products for the home, décor, cooking utensils, crafts, and gifts
1-800-950-7130

*Pottery Barn*
Great Selection of furniture, ready-made window treatments, and accessories
1-800-922-5507

*Rocky Mountain Hardware*
Architectural hardware handmade and cast with integrity
1-888-788-2013

*Rue de France*
A variety of lace curtains and shades
1-800-777-0998

*Smith and Hawken*
Quality indoor/outdoor furniture, garden accents
415-389-8300

*Smith and Noble*
Wood blinds, shades, and shutters
1-800-560-0027

*Williams Sonoma*
A cook's catalog with kitchen accessories, utensils, linens, dishes, and bonus recipes
1-800-541-1262

# Websites

**www.amazon.com**
Largest book seller on the Internet with plenty of home décor books

**www.anthropologie.com**
Fresh and interesting clothing and home accessories with a Bohemian edge

**www.bakerfurniture.com**
Traditional, bamboo, rattan, and wood furniture

**www.benjaminmoore.com**
A wide selection of indoor and outdoor paints and stains in many colors and finishes

**www.crateandbarrel.com**
Contemporary beds, linens, storage, and kitchenware

**www.ebay.com**
Largest auction house on the Internet with just about everything for sale

**www.ikea.com**
Affordable, stylish home furnishings and storage pieces

**www.marthastewart.com**
A variety of lifestyle information on decorating, cooking, décor, crafts, and kids

**www.pier1.com**
Furnishings, linens, lighting with an Asian flair

**www.rockymountainhardware.com**
Reproduction hardware with a tasteful selection

# Templates and Other Tools

To use your templates on graph paper, first measure your room on graph paper using one square for each square foot of floor space. Measure each length of wall and draw it on the graph paper/floor plan. Place a double line for windows and a blank area for door widths. (Mark the swing of the door.) Include any features that will affect furniture arrangement, such as sliding glass doors, fireplaces, stairways, and bay windows. Use the furniture templates on your floor plan. You may want to make a copy of the templates so you can cut them out. Measure your furniture and cut out the corresponding-size template. Place on your floor plan. Trace the template on Post-it notes if you want to reposition templates.

Be sure your arrangement allows for good traffic flow, placing furniture so there are pathways that are at least 2½ to 3 feet apart. Furniture acts as traffic guides arranged so a room can be easily passed through.

For more tips, read the section on "Planning Like a Pro" in Chapter 3.

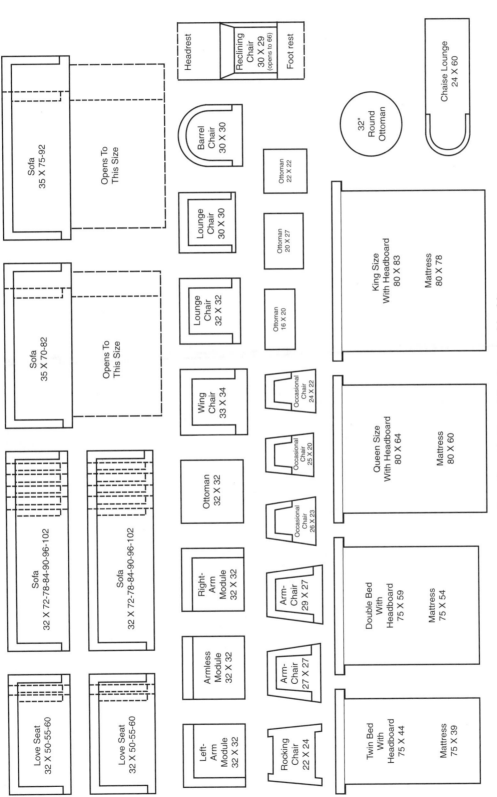

**Templates for upholstered furniture and bedding.**

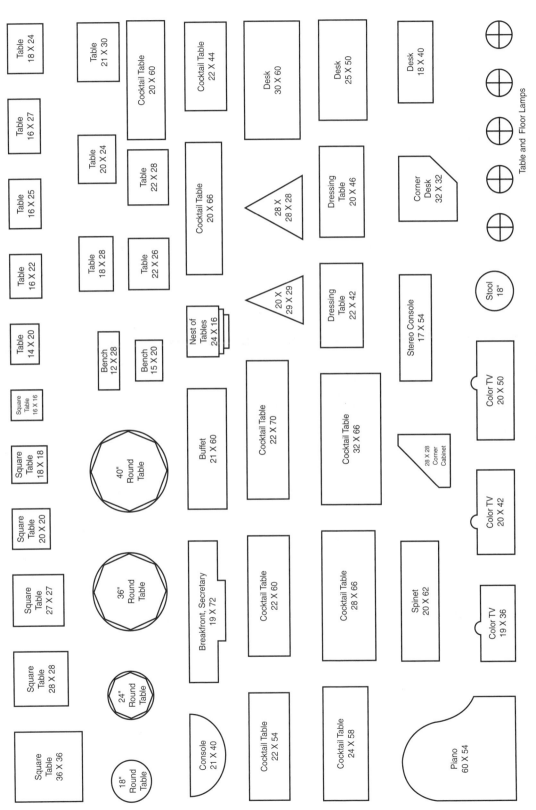

**Templates for occasional pieces.**

Table 18 X 24

Table 16 X 27

Table 16 X 25

Table 16 X 22

Table 14 X 20

Square Table 16 X 16

Square Table 18 X 18

Square Table 20 X 20

Square Table 27 X 27

Square Table 28 X 28

Square Table 36 X 36

Table 21 X 30

Table 20 X 24

Table 18 X 28

Bench 12 X 28

Bench 15 X 20

40" Round Table

36" Round Table

24" Round Table

18" Round Table

Console 21 X 40

Cocktail Table 20 X 60

Table 22 X 28

Table 22 X 26

Nest of Tables 24 X 16

Buffet 21 X 60

Breakfront, Secretary 19 X 72

Cocktail Table 22 X 44

Cocktail Table 20 X 66

Cocktail Table 22 X 70

Cocktail Table 22 X 60

Cocktail Table 22 X 54

Desk 30 X 60

28 X 28 28

20 X 29 29

Cocktail Table 32 X 66

Cocktail Table 28 X 66

Cocktail Table 24 X 58

Desk 25 X 50

Dressing Table 20 X 46

Dressing Table 22 X 42

Stereo Console 17 X 54

28 X 28 Corner Cabinet

Spinet 20 X 62

Piano 60 X 54

Desk 18 X 40

Corner Desk 32 X 32

Stool 18"

Color TV 20 X 50

Color TV 20 X 42

Color TV 19 X 36

Table and Floor Lamps

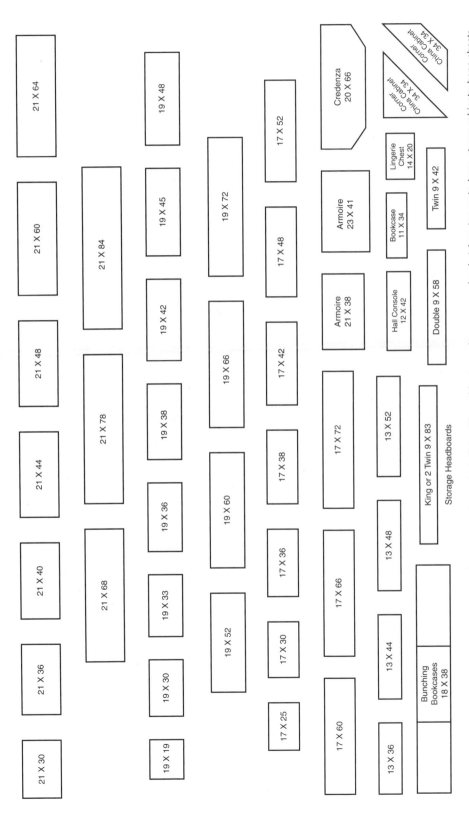

21 X 64

21 X 60

21 X 48

21 X 44

21 X 40

21 X 36

21 X 30

21 X 84

21 X 78

21 X 68

19 X 48

19 X 45

19 X 42

19 X 38

19 X 36

19 X 33

19 X 30

19 X 19

19 X 72

19 X 66

19 X 60

19 X 52

17 X 52

17 X 48

17 X 42

17 X 38

17 X 36

17 X 30

17 X 25

17 X 72

17 X 66

17 X 60

13 X 52

13 X 48

13 X 44

13 X 36

Corner
China Cabinet
34 X 34

Corner
China Cabinet
34 X 34

Credenza
20 X 66

Armoire
23 X 41

Armoire
21 X 38

Lingerie
Chest
14 X 20

Bookcase
11 X 34

Hall Console
12 X 42

Twin 9 X 42

Double 9 X 58

King or 2 Twin 9 X 83

Storage Headboards

Bunching
Bookcases
18 X 38

These templates can be used for charting chests, dressers, serving carts, buffets, china cabinets, credenzas, consoles, hutches, tea carts, bars, stereo cabinets, hope chests, window chests, secretaries, and many other pieces of furniture onto your floor plan.

**Templates for storage and special pieces.**

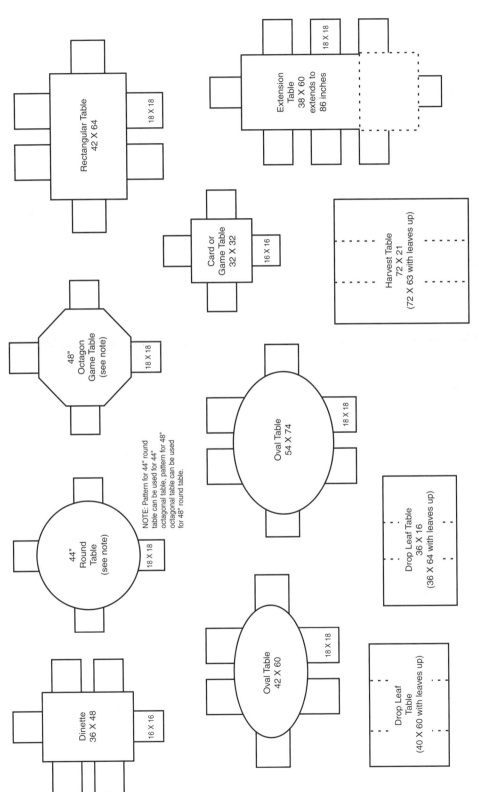

Rectangular Table
42 X 64
18 X 18

Extension
Table
38 X 60
extends to
86 inches
18 X 18

Card or
Game Table
32 X 32
16 X 16

Harvest Table
72 X 21
(72 X 63 with leaves up)

48"
Octagon
Game Table
(see note)
18 X 18

Oval Table
54 X 74
18 X 18

44"
Round
Table
(see note)
18 X 18

NOTE: Pattern for 44" round
table can be used for 44"
octagonal table, pattern for 48"
octagonal table can be used
for 48" round table.

Drop Leaf Table
36 X 16
(36 X 64 with leaves up)

Dinette
36 X 48
16 X 16

Oval Table
42 X 60
18 X 18

Drop Leaf
Table
(40 X 60 with leaves up)

**Templates for dining tables.**

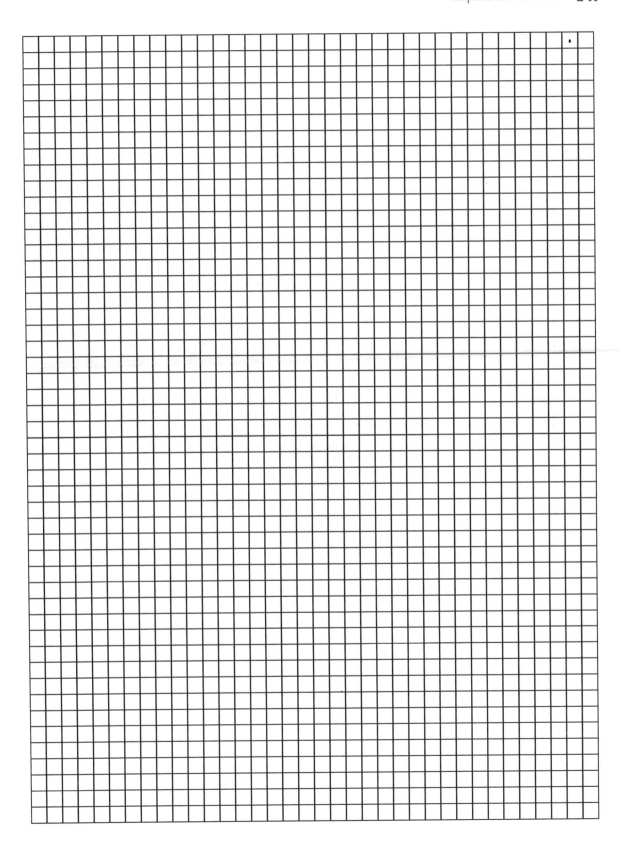

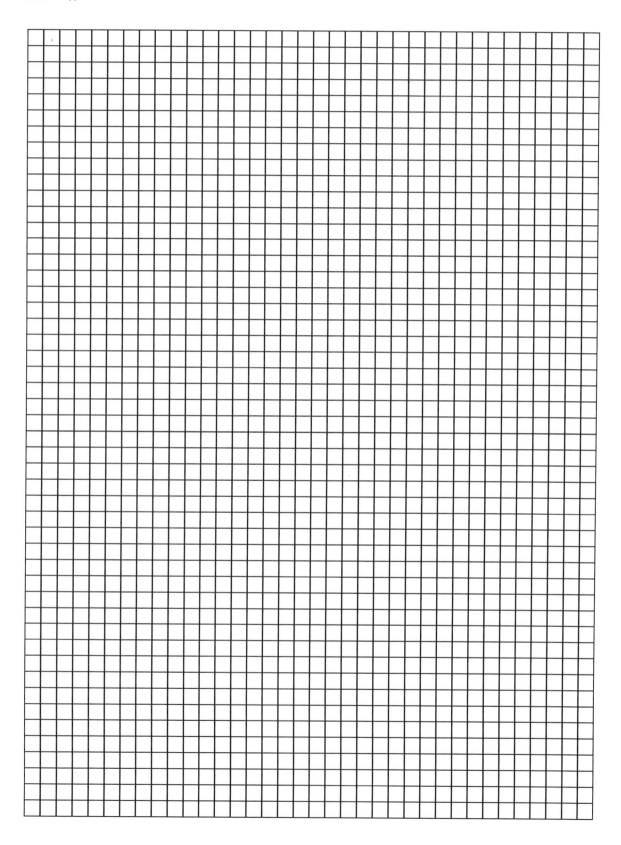

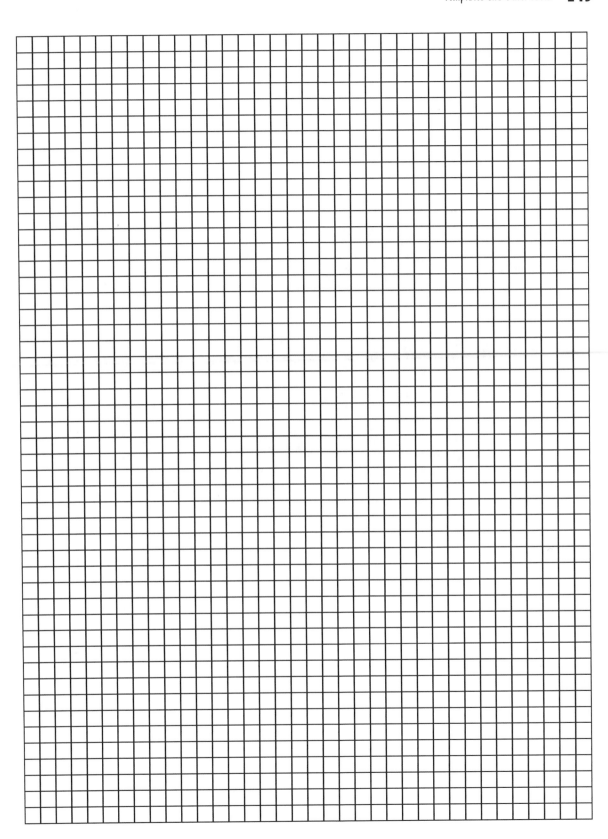

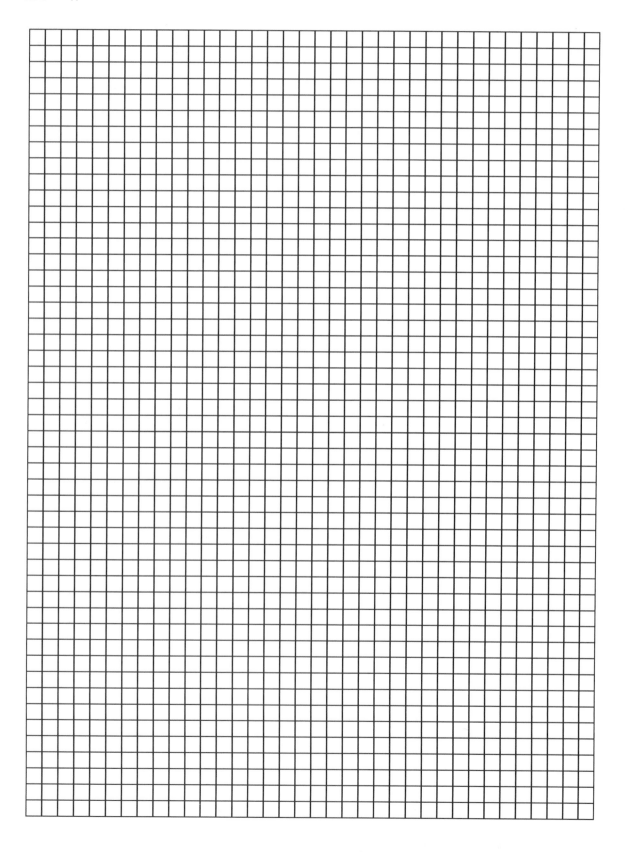

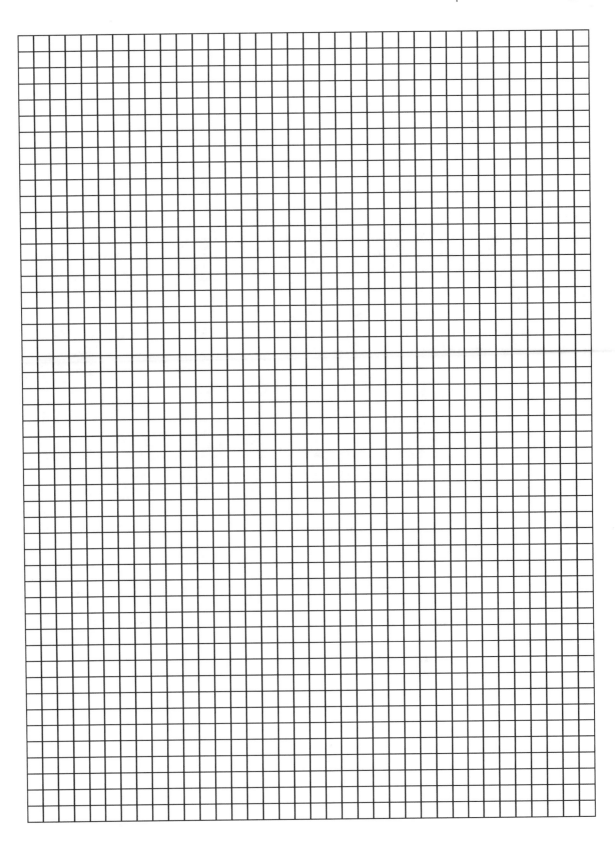

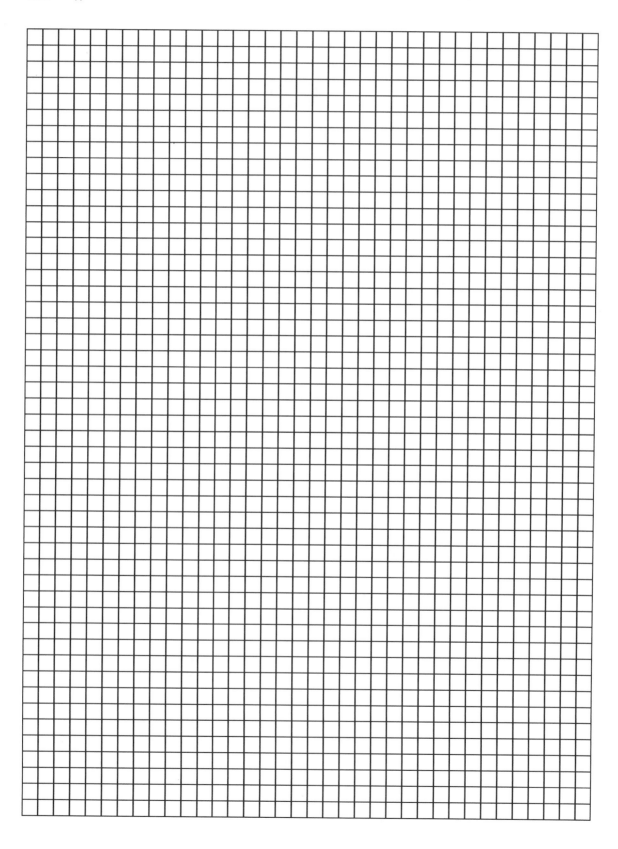

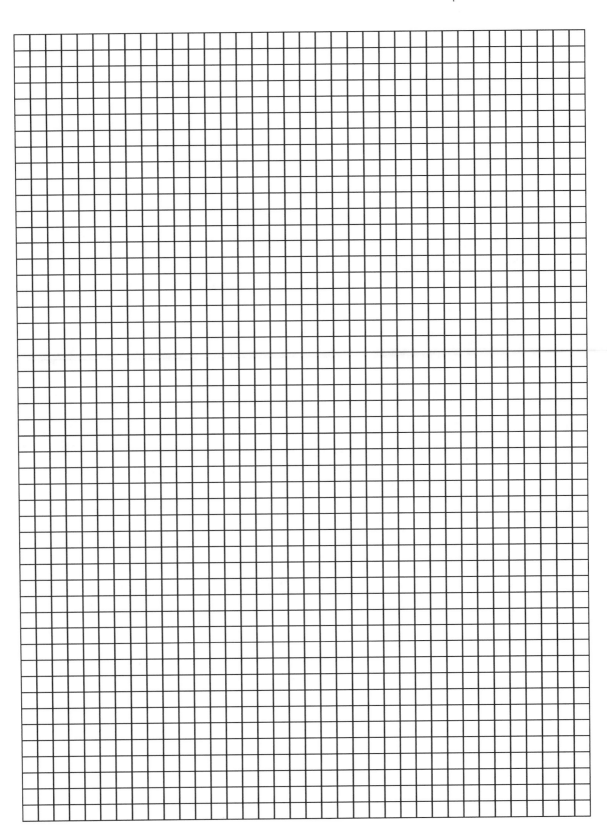

# Sketchbook

# Sketchbook

# Sketchbook

# Glossary

**armoire**   A French term for a large, free-standing wooden wardrobe used as storage for clothing and linen. Today an armoire can be a wonderful hiding place for high-tech multimedia equipment.

**Art Deco**   A style of architecture and furnishings popular in the 1920s and 1930s. It includes geometric, stylized, and streamlined motifs in glass, plastic, and chrome.

**Art Nouveau**   The forerunner of Art Deco, a style of decoration from 1890 to 1910 characterized by curves and flowing lines, and styles from nature.

**asymmetry**   A balance achieved by arranging equal visual weights that are not identical, such as a vase of flowers and a bowl of fruit placed on either side of a chest.

**Aubusson**   A classic French rug that is usually hand-woven in muted colors with a center design.

**baluster**   Any of the small posts that support the upper rail of a railing, as on a staircase balustrade (a railing held up by balusters).

**Bessarabian**   A flat-weave rug depicting geometrics and florals, usually of Russian or Turkish origin.

**beveled**   A sloping part or surface, as in the angled edge of plate glass.

**Bohemian**   In decorating, refers to a style that mixes many different, often offbeat elements into a mesmerizing scheme.

**breakfront**   Tall unit that usually has glass-enclosed shelves on top of a drawer cabinet, with a projecting center section.

**brocade**   A heavy-weight fabric, richly decorated with raised patterns that resemble embroidery. Brocade was historically made of silk but now is made of synthetics and cottons.

**burlap**   A loosely woven, coarse fabric of *jute* that is simple but very textural, used for shades, drapes, dust ruffles, and table skirts. Burlap is popular in today's interiors and is very inexpensive.

**canvas**   A heavy, tightly woven cloth of cotton or linen that is perfect for shades and outdoor cushions.

**chaise**   A long chair designed for reclining.

**chambray**   A lightweight cotton in a close weave that has a "frosted" appearance. Popular today is a blue *denim* that resembles light-weight denim. Good for light slipcovers, pillows, and draperies.

**chenille**   A fuzzy-surfaced cloth that is produced by clipped, twisted yarns; it is popular today for soft upholstery, throws, trims, and accessories.

**chinoiserie**   An ornate style of decoration, based on Chinese motifs, of furniture, textiles, ceramics, etc., especially popular in the eighteenth century.

**chintz**   A fine cotton in a glazed finish in solids and popular florals. Used primarily for light slipcovers, pillows, and draperies.

**china cabinet**   A cabinet designed for the display of china or glasses.

**Colonial**   Furnishings that are characteristic of styles of the first 13 British colonies, including Windsor and Chippendale styles.

**complementary colors**   Colors that are opposite each other on the color wheel.

**cornice**   A horizontal molding at the top of a wall, often used to cover drapery rods or accent a window top.

**corona**   A crown or something resembling a crown. In décor, a crownlike piece that is placed above a headboard that draperies can be attached to.

**Country**   A less formal interior that is characterized by warm, eclectic, and traditional styling, including simple rustic décor from regional styles and artifacts.

**curio cabinet**   A cabinet with glass doors and sides to display various types of collectibles.

**damask**   A reversible, flat fabric richly patterned by a combination of weaves. Once made of silk, it now is available in various fibers and often combined with homespun fabrics. A sturdy and lustrous fabric, damask is used primarily for upholstery and decorative accessories.

**demilune**   A half-moon-shaped table.

**denim**   A coarse, twilled, sturdy cotton cloth used for jeans but also as contemporary sturdy slipcovers, pillows, and other accessories.

**dhurrie**   Flat-weave rug hand-woven in India, usually of muted colors and numerous designs in wool or cotton.

**eclectic**   A form of interior design that is composed of various periods and styles that are harmonious.

**electrolier**   The correct term for an electrically fitted chandelier.

**enfilade**   A French word, *enfiler*, meaning to thread or string.

**English Country**   Attributed to country interiors of homes in England, this is a décor characterized by rooms filled with upholstery in faded florals with lots of accessories and artwork.

**ergonomics**   The study of the relationship between workers and their office surroundings and equipment.

**faille**   A plain, woven fabric that has fine ribs with good draping qualities and a luster.

**faux bois**   A false wood look that is brought to art level and used as tables, accessories, and mirror frames.

**fleur de lis**   A French term directly translated as "flower of the lily," it actually refers to three iris-type flowers bound by an encircling band. It was used as the coat of arms of the former royal family of France. The fleur-de-lis pattern is a popular motif in printed fabrics and wall-coverings today.

**flokati**   A rug with a thick, rough nap that originated as a hand-woven white wool rug in Greece.

**French Country**   A decorating style that embodies the use of provincial prints in deep reds, yellows, greens, blues, and terra cottas; gingham-checked or faded toile de Jouy fabric, and fabric-lined armoires, among other characteristics.

**gilding**    To overlay with a thin layer of gold on surfaces and furniture.

**gingham**    A lightweight cotton cloth with a checked pattern, usually of two colors, typically red or blue with white. Great in informal interiors and pleasantly unexpected in formal interiors. For curtains, cushions, and lightweight slipcovers.

**hand**    The drapability of a fabric.

**highboy**    Tall chest that appears to be in two sections.

**hutch**    A tall cupboard or sideboard that usually has open shelves on the top section and cabinets below.

**Japanning**    The art of covering furnishings with opaque varnishes, which may be decorated later with paint or gilding.

**jute**    A strong, glossy fiber used for making burlap sacks, rope, and mats.

**kilim**    Similar to a *dhurrie*, but colors are usually richer.

**lace**    Delicate, open-weave cloth made by hand or machine of cotton, linen, silk, or synthetics. Lace is often used for draperies, table covers, and pillows to create an informal, romantic atmosphere.

**Lucite**    Trademark for an acrylic resin or plastic that is cast or molded into transparent or translucent sheets, rods, and so on.

**matelasse**    A double-woven fabric with puckered surface effects. Used for draperies, upholstery, and slipcovers. Especially popular today in natural cotton.

**mis en place**    A French phrase that means everything is put in its proper space.

**modern**    Having to do with the latest styles and trends in design and decorating. Also a period of design where a variety of contemporary styles occurred after World War I.

**modular furniture**    Seating or storage units designed to fit many configurations.

**monochromatic**    A color scheme limited to one color in various tones such as red, burgundy, and pink.

**Murphy bed**    A bed named after its inventor, W. L. Murphy, that swings up or folds into a closet or cabinet when not in use.

**muslin**    A plain, inexpensive cotton that varies in weight. Unbleached muslin is natural with brown flecks, and bleached muslin is much whiter. Muslin makes good slipcovers and plain draperies for a relaxed interior.

**Neoclassical**    A decorating style with origins in ancient Egypt, Greece, and Rome that follows the classic rules of scale, balance, and proportion dictating every furniture line and decorative motif.

**node**    That part, or joint, of a stem from which a leaf starts to grow, as in bamboo.

**ottoman**    A low, cushioned footstool that sometimes has storage space inside.

**oriental rug**    A hand-knotted or hand-woven rug native to the Near East or Far East. Their patterns are usually named after their place of origin.

**pantry**    Derived from the Latin word *panis* meaning bread, a pantry is a small room or closet in or off the kitchen in which canned goods, silverware, dishes, and other supplies are stored.

**patina**    Any thin coating or color change resulting from age, as on old wood or silver.

**Postmodern**    A decorating style developed in response to industrial materials being used in homes creating sterile environments. A lot of colors were used in outrageous ways to inject humor into everyday objects. A mix of styles were emphasized from different periods, combining new finishes and new vision.

**primary colors** Red, blue, and yellow, from which all other colors are derived.

**radial** A circular balancing of parts around a center, often found in small, round items such as plates and bowls. Radial balance can also be asymmetrical, like the circular flow of a spiral staircase; or symmetrical, like a round dining table with chairs.

**rag rug** Flat-weave rug made with cotton or wool strips on a loom and created with a charming, handcrafted look.

**ragging** A textured effect produced by passing a crumpled rag over wet paint or glaze.

**Roman shade** A flat fabric shade that folds into neat horizontal pleats when raised.

**sailcloth** A material that is similar to *canvas*, but lighter in weight. It is great for draperies, cushions, slipcovers, and shower curtains.

**sari** Indian silk wrap that is worn as a dress. Often in bright colors with embroidery, patterns, or gold trims.

**secondary colors** Colors produced by mixing two primary colors such as red and yellow to form orange.

**sideboard** Long, low cabinet usually placed against a wall. It can have drawers and compartments or a combination of both.

**silk** A lustrous natural fiber that varies in appearance. Some silks are woven with their natural slubs, which enhance their appearance. Dyed silks are usually of bright, beautiful colors that are stunning for draperies and lightweight upholstery and slipcovers.

**sisal** A natural-fiber rug woven into different textural patterns that can be decoratively bordered, hand-painted, or dyed.

**shirring** A gathering made in cloth by drawing the material up on parallel rows of short, running stitches.

**soft goods** The fabrics, rugs, and textures—collectively known as soft goods—which add softness to the sharp lines of a room.

**spattering** A decorative paint effect produced by dipping a paint brush in paint and tapping it to "spatter" on a floor or walls.

**sponging** A paint effect achieved by dabbing on paint colors with a sponge.

**stencil** A thin sheet of paper, metal, or impermeable film that is perforated or cut through in such a way that when paint or ink is applied, the decorative pattern is transferred to a surface. Stencils are typically used on walls or floors.

**symmetry** A type of balance achieved by arranging furniture or objects on each side of a center or dominant point, such as two wing chairs placed on either side of a fireplace.

**tapestry** A heavy cloth (heavier than *brocade* or *damask*), woven by hand or machine, that shows pictorial scenes or floral patterns. Tapestry is typically used for wall hangings or as upholstery fabric and is made from cotton, wool, or cotton blends.

**tea-stained** Fabrics or materials are instantly "aged" with tea colors to take on an antique appearance.

**terrycloth** An absorbent cotton cloth made with a pile of uncut loops used in toweling. Often used for bathroom or vanity slipcovered seating and pillows.

**tertiary colors** Colors produced by mixing a primary color with an adjacent secondary color on the color wheel; for example, red + orange = orange-red, red + purple = red-purple.

**ticking** Heavy, closely woven fabric of cotton. Usually in a stripe such as blue and white, black and white, or brown and white. Great for upholstery, slipcovers, and decorative accessories.

**toile de Jouy**   Traditionally, an ivory cotton with scenic designs of pastoral life in red or navy. Originally made in Jouy, a town in France. Today toiles are made in vibrant background colors with varying contrasting colors.

**topiary**   Designating or of the art of trimming and training shrubs or trees into unusual, ornamental shapes.

**torchiere**   A floor lamp with a reflector bowl (inverted shade) for casting light upward so as to give indirect illumination.

**trompe l'oeil**   A French term for "fooling the eye," a paint technique that is two-dimensional but painted to look three-dimensional.

**valance**   A window covering made of wood or fabric that covers the top of a window.

**velvet**   A heavy-weight fabric with a soft pile made of silk, cotton, or rayon. Used for upholstery, slipcovers, and draperies. Velvets that look aged and faded are especially popular today.

**Venetian blind**   Slatted window shades named after the early Venetian traders who brought them to Europe centuries ago.

**verd antique**   Old French term referring to a green, mottled, and veined marble. Today it refers to finishes as well.

**Victorian**   A period of decoration that refers to the reign of Queen Victoria from 1837 to 1901, characterized by large-scale furniture, flowery carving, and ornate design.

**vintage**   Representative of or dating from a period long past.

**wainscoting**   An added material—usually wood panels or boards—that covers the lower part of the wall (typically about 3 feet up from the floor) and sets it apart from the finish of the upper wall. This is a traditional decorating technique that is many centuries old.

# Index

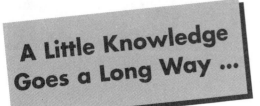
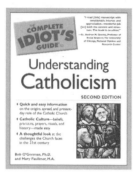
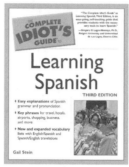
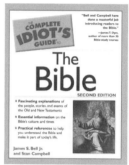

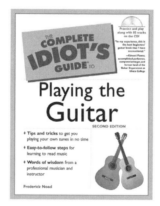